This is a book which if you are a SENCO, or are thinking of becoming one, ignite the passion you have for inclusion, and your belief in the right of e to be offered the highest quality education provision possible, whatever their promotes the professional agency of readers, encourages critical engagement, and provides the evidence and knowledge needed for valid and valuable discussion. Every chapter has been written by either practitioners or academics who have 'been there,' and as such there is a feeling of authenticity throughout, with each author sharing their own priorities and views. It is a book which highlights not only the uniqueness of being a SENCO, but also the resilience, knowledge, skills, and commitment that individuals need to fulfil this role. It is an empowering read.

Dr Sue Soan, Senior Lecturer in SENI, Canterbury Christ Church University

This book provides a unique collection of chapters authored by contributors with a wealth of experience in the field of special educational needs and disability as practitioners, teachers and academics. They bring an authenticity of practice to their texts that is both personal and engaging and will speak to readers interested in making thoughtful, effective provision for learners who face barriers to their learning of various kinds. While focusing on the leadership role of the SENCO in schools in England, the chapters offer the opportunity to engage in reflection on a range of key aspects of the SENCo role from a very thoughtful, well-informed position. This book will provide a very useful resource for those preparing to become SENCos as well as those more experienced in the field.

Professor Janice Wearmouth, University of Bedfordshire

A must-read for SENCOs who lead on inclusion, this book covers a range of timely topics with sensitivity to the experiences of children, young people, their families and the professionals who work with them.

Professor Lani Florian, Bell Chair of Education, University of Edinburgh

Leading on Inclusion

This comprehensive resource provides a range of perspectives on inclusion, giving Special Educational Needs Co-ordinators (SENCOs) the opportunity to consider the principles and practice that underpin their leadership role.

Offering a blend of academic and professional knowledge, each chapter explores different aspects of the role of the SENCO and supports areas that will be considered as part of the National Award for SENCOs. A variety of essential topics are covered, from the importance of SEND provision and multi-disciplinary practice, to the role of the SENCO and leadership.

Key features of this book include:

- Contributions by leaders of the National Award for Special Educational Needs Co-ordinators working with trainee SENCOs across the country
- A focus on encouraging SENCOs to think deeply about their own individual practice through engagement with cutting-edge research
- A flexible structure that can be read as a whole, or dipped in and out of as professional learning needs require

This book provides an opportunity for readers to engage with a multiplicity of voices and approaches, allowing them to critically explore their role as leaders of SEND provision in schools. It is an invaluable resource both for students and those already within the role of Special Educational Needs Co-ordinator.

Mhairi C. Beaton is a reader at the Carnegie School of Education at Leeds Beckett University, where she leads the MA in Inclusive Practice in Education. Her research focus lies at the interface of inclusion, teacher education and student voice.

Geraldene N. Codina is a senior lecturer at the University of Derby. She is the programme leader for the National Award for SENCOs, co-convenes the Derby City SENCO Forum and chairs the Derby Opportunity Area SEND Project Management Group. Prior to working in higher education, Geraldene was a SENCO.

Julie C. Wharton is the course leader for the National Award for Special Educational Needs (SEN) Coordination at the University of Winchester. Julie joined the university in 2014, having spent seven years working as a SEND Inspector in Southampton. Prior to this she was an Advanced Skills Teacher for SEN.

nasen is a professional membership association that supports all those who work with or care for children and young people with special and additional educational needs. Members include SENCOs, school leaders, governors/trustees, teachers, teaching assistants, support workers, other educationalists, students and families.

nasen supports its members through policy documents, peer-reviewed academic journals, its membership magazine nasen Connect, publications, professional development courses, regional networks and newsletters. Its website contains more current information such as responses to government consultations.

nasen's published documents are held in very high regard both in the UK and internationally.

For a full list of titles see: www.routledge.com/nasen-spotlight/book-series/FULNASEN

Other titles published in association with the National Association for Special Educational Needs (nasen):

Leading on Inclusion: The Role of the SENCO
Mhairi C. Beaton, Geraldene N. Codina and Julie C. Wharton
2021/pb: 978-0-367-42050-5

The Governance Handbook for SEND and Inclusion: Schools that Work for All Learners
Adam Boddison
2020/pb: 978-0-367-37003-9

The School Handbook for Dual and Multiple Exceptionality
Denise Yates and Adam Boddison
2020/pb: 978-0-367-36958-3

Creating Multi-sensory Environments: Practical Ideas for Teaching and Learning, revised edition
Christopher Davies
2020/pb: 978-0-415-57330-6

Dyslexia and Inclusion: Classroom Approaches for Assessment, Teaching and Learning
Gavin Reid
2019/pb: 978-1-138-48749-9

Using an Inclusive Approach to Reduce School Exclusion: A Practitioner's Handbook
Tristan Middleton and Lynda Kay
2019/pb: 978-1-138-31691-1

Supporting SLCN in Children with ASD in the Early Years: A Practical Resource for Professionals
Jennifer Warwick
2019/pb: 978-1-138-36950-4

How to be a Brilliant SENCO: Practical Strategies for Developing and Leading Inclusive Provision
Helen Curran
2019/pb: 978-1-138-48966-0

Leading on Inclusion

The Role of the SENCO

Mhairi C. Beaton, Geraldene N. Codina and Julie C. Wharton

Routledge
Taylor & Francis Group

LONDON AND NEW YORK

First published 2021
by Routledge
2 Park Square, Milton Park, Abingdon, Oxon OX14 4RN

and by Routledge
52 Vanderbilt Avenue, New York, NY 10017

Routledge is an imprint of the Taylor & Francis Group, an informa business

British Library Cataloguing-in-Publication Data
A catalogue record for this book is available from the British Library

Library of Congress Cataloging-in-Publication Data
Names: Beaton, Mhairi, editor. | Codina, Geraldene, editor. | Wharton, Julie, editor.
Title: Leading on inclusion : the role of the SENCO / [edited by] Mhairi Beaton, Geraldene Codina, Julie Wharton.
Description: Abingdon, Oxon ; New York, NY : Routledge, 2021. | Includes bibliographical references and index.
Identifiers: LCCN 2020042895 (print) | LCCN 2020042896 (ebook) | ISBN 9780367420499 (hardback) | ISBN 9780367420505 (paperback) | ISBN 9780367821463 (ebook)
Subjects: LCSH: Special education—Great Britain—Administration. | Special education teachers—Great Britain. | Inclusive education—Great Britain. | Educational leadership—Great Britain.
Classification: LCC LC3986.G7 L43 2021 (print) | LCC LC3986.G7 (ebook) | DDC 371.9/0460941—dc23
LC record available at https://lccn.loc.gov/2020042895
LC ebook record available at https://lccn.loc.gov/2020042896

ISBN: 978-0-367-42049-9 (hbk)
ISBN: 978-0-367-42050-5 (pbk)
ISBN: 978-0-367-82146-3 (ebk)

Typeset in Helvetica
by Apex CoVantage, LLC

In memory of Dr Bridget Egan (1946–2020), who inspired so many

Contents

Figures and tables

Figures

Tables

Contributors

Helen Ackers is a senior professional tutor and leads SEND continuing professional development (CPD) at Liverpool Hope University. She is the programme leader for the National Award for SENCOs and the PGCert SpLD (dyslexia). Prior to working in higher education (HE), Helen worked in settings from primary schools to further education colleges and was SENCO in several schools.

Louise Arnold is a senior lecturer at the University of East London, teaching across undergraduate and postgraduate programmes in early childhood and special education. She also co-convenes the inclusive education special interest group for the British Educational Research Association (BERA). Louise is undertaking doctoral studies on participation of children and young people in their Education, Health and Care Plan (EHCP).

Helen Curran is a senior lecturer at Bath Spa University. She is the award leader for the Masters in Inclusive Education and National Award for SENCO. Helen's research focuses on SEN policy and the SENCO role, leading on the annual National SENCO Workforce survey in conjunction with nasen. Previously Helen was a primary SENCO.

Becky Edwards is a senior lecturer at the University of Chichester. As a former early years teacher, portage worker and manager of a children's centre, Becky has a strong background in working with and supporting parents/carers of children with special educational needs. She is also the co-founder of the charity Parents and Carers Support Organisation (PASCO).

Tracy Edwards has undertaken a range of roles within special and mainstream education and has successful experience of leadership across a large teaching school alliance. Currently she is a freelance education consultant and researcher. She is also a PhD researcher at the University of Aberdeen and a part-time lecturer at Leeds Beckett University.

Heather Green is a senior lecturer at the University of Chichester. She is the programme leader for the National Award for SENCOs, and tutor on the Initial Teacher Training (ITT) and Special Needs and Disability studies programmes. Prior to working in HE, Heather was a SENCO, assistant headteacher and a Specialist Leader of Education (SLE) in SEND.

Janet Hoskin is a senior lecturer at the University of East London, where she teaches undergraduate and postgraduate programmes in special education as well as on the professional doctorate. Janet's recent research has explored the impact of new SEND legislation on the lives of disabled young people, their families and schools.

Lorna Hughes is a senior lecturer at Canterbury Christ Church University. She is the programme director for the National Award for SEN Coordination and Postgraduate Certificate in Dyslexia. Her PhD studies focus on the role of parents and schools in the co-production of statutory assessment plans for children.

Lynda Kay is a senior lecturer for Inclusive Education/SEN at the University of Gloucestershire and course leader for the NASENCO Award and MA Education courses. She is Vice-Chair of Directors of the Leading Learning for SEND Community Interest Company (LLSENDCiC). Before this, Lynda held roles including primary school teacher, SENCO, senior leader and advisory teacher for learners with communication and interaction needs.

Gianna Knowles is an associate professor in Educational Studies and Social Justice at London South Bank University. She has over 12 years' experience of working in primary schools in England, in London and the Midlands and has worked extensively in the area of SEN.

Brian Lamb, *OBE,* is visiting professor in Special Educational Needs and Disability at Derby University and an associate with the National Sensory Impairment Partnership. He chaired the Lamb Inquiry into Special Educational Needs and Parental Confidence (2008–10) for the UK

Department for Education and has worked closely with schools, local authorities and parent groups in supporting the implementation of the SEND reforms.

Tristan Middleton is a senior lecturer at the University of Gloucestershire and course leader for the NASENCO Award and MA Education suite. He is Chair of Directors of LLSENDCiC and Associate Editor of the *International Journal for Nurture in Education*. Prior to this, Tristan was a SENCO, nurture group teacher and assistant head teacher.

Lisa O'Connor is Inclusion Programme Leader at Edge Hill University with responsibility for the National Award for SEN Co-ordination, PG Cert SpLD (Dyslexia), PG Cert/PG Dip Education (Dyscalculia) and PG Cert Education (Inclusion and SEN). Prior to working in HE, Lisa was a primary teacher and SENCO.

Dennis Piper is a highly experienced teacher, SENCO, headteacher and published author. As a SEN consultant and SEMH specialist, Dennis works nationally and internationally. At Manchester Metropolitan University, he has designed and delivered a number of advanced courses, including undertaking a key role in developing the partnership-based NASENCo course.

Jonathan Rix is a professor of Participation and Learning Support at the Open University and the Inland Norway University of Applied Sciences. His research focuses on policies, practices and language that facilitate inclusion within the mainstream, capture diverse perspectives and develop thinking about the form and function of education.

Deborah Robinson is a professor of SEND and Inclusion in the Institute of Education at the University of Derby. She has worked as a primary teacher, SENDCo and deputy head in London and Nottingham. Her current research explores leadership and school improvement for SEND and inclusion.

Angela Scott is the regional lead for SEND for the Eastern Partnership UK (SEND) and is programme lead for the National Award for SEN Coordination, Advanced SENCO and SENCOs as Leaders Awards. She has steered the professional development programme for the introduction of SENCOs into Hong Kong schools.

Acknowledgements

The editors of this book would like to take this opportunity to say a heartfelt thank you to all who have made this text possible. When we got together in May 2019 to envisage the shape of the book, no one could imagine what lay ahead in 2020. Despite all the challenges of COVID-19, every contributor to this book remained committed to critically analysing an aspect of the SENCO role. Our numerous emails to authors have always been answered with such warmth and commitment; we are proud to say that through their hard work and despite the pandemic, this book is published within the planned timeframe. To every author who has contributed to this publication, we thank you and all those who have supported you (SENCOs, schools, parents, children/young people, colleagues, family, friends).

We also wish to thank the Leading Learning for Special Educational Needs and Disability Community Interest Company, comprising and led by the accredited providers of the National Award for SENCOs; this organisation's members set in motion the inspiration and direction for this text. In addition to which, our sincere thanks extend to Routledge for their continued support, advice and kind words of encouragement. Mhairi and Geraldene wish also to acknowledge and thank Julie C. Wharton for deploying her artistic skills in designing the front cover of this book.

Part I Why SEND is important

1   Introduction

*Mhairi C. Beaton, Geraldene N. Codina
and Julie C. Wharton*

The origins of this book lie at the heart of the editors' own practice. All three editors currently lead or have led university courses providing professional learning and accreditation for Special Educational Needs Co-ordinators (SENCOs) within the English policy system. As we worked with our students to develop their knowledge, expertise and practice, we became increasingly aware of a pressing need for a publication that focused on the leadership role of the SENCO. The editors felt there was an urgent need for a book that permitted SENCO students the opportunity to critically explore this key element of their role within schools as leaders of special educational needs and disabilities (SEND) provision. The editors felt strongly that the book should enable SENCOs to think deeply about their own individual practice through engagement with recent cutting-edge research. As such, this book is aimed primarily at SENCOs, both those already in post and those seeking accreditation through the Post Graduate Certificate SENCO courses. This book will also be of interest to a wider audience, including qualified and qualifying teachers, members of a school's senior management team, and those working in different policy contexts who are interested in the inclusion of 0–25-year-olds.

It is widely acknowledged that many elements of SEND provision and inclusive practice remain contested and indeed at times are viewed as controversial. What is not at issue is that teachers must provide effective educational provision for all children and young people in their care; the dilemma arises as to how to do this. For the educational practitioner faced with this task, the multiplicity of professional choices on offer can be daunting and the numerous elements of the role overwhelming. In response to this complexity, this edited book does not seek to provide simplistic answers or a single narrative, for it is argued the best inclusive practice is context specific, nuanced and co-constructed. Through a focus on the leadership role of the SENCO in English schools, this book provides an opportunity for the audience to engage with a multiplicity of voices and approaches, each voice introducing the reader to their own expertise in one key element of the SENCO role. Each contributor to the book has written their chapter from their own perspective on SEND; chapters have therefore an authenticity of practice, which is relevant and personal to each author's own priorities and standpoints. What is common across all chapters is the contributors' commitment to inclusion and SEND provision of the highest quality.

The editors therefore see this book as a catalyst for further discussion, relying on the commitment of readers to engage with the ideas expressed by each of the authors. We encourage those reading the chapters to engage critically with them to inform their professional knowledge, understanding, skills, abilities, values and attitudes in relation to the leadership role of SEND in their own individual context. This permits the avoidance of a paper-based reading exercise, instead promoting the professional agency of the reader to engage with academic research, which is translated into ways of working that enhance the participation of all young people. The focus on schools building their own authentic, relevant inclusive values, policies and practices is designed to support schools to achieve the expectations in the Education Inspection Framework (Ofsted, 2019) around inclusion:

> Leaders have a clear and ambitious vision for providing high-quality, inclusive education and training to all. This is realised through strong, shared values, policies and practice.
>
> (Ofsted, 2019:11)

The book is designed to be read either as a whole exploring each of the elements of leadership in SEND or for the reader to choose individual chapters as their professional learning need requires. For clarity, the book is divided into three themes.

In the first section, the reader is invited to consider why SEND provision is important – an opportunity to think about the values and attitudes that underpin the practice of leadership of SEND provision and why it is critical to education.

Jonathan Rix explores inclusive relationships that lie at the heart of effective SEND provision. Taking a reflective and deeply personal approach, Jonathan considers the complexity and uncertainty that the practitioner must embrace to create new opportunities for young people in educational settings.

Geraldene N. Codina and Julie C. Wharton look at the language of SEND from past to present. Drawing on the philosophy of Wittgenstein, they argue that language matters and is more than fashion or political correctness. Rather, language gains its meaning from the way in which it is used. Schools, leaders and professionals are invited to consider the language of SEND used in their setting, unpicking its meaning in relation to their own values, expectations, assumptions, responses and practice.

Deborah Robinson examines the SENCO's role in leading professional learning for inclusion for all staff. Critically examining the epistemological complexity of this task, the chapter discusses the benefits of a lesson study approach for teacher development.

Brian Lamb explores the efficacy of the SEND reforms five years after their introduction. Drawing on the latest available information, the chapter focusses on the options for change, ranging from alterations to policy and guidance, to undertaking a more substantial revision of the legislation. Concerning both SEN Support and Education, Health and Care Plan (EHCP) reforms, the chapter addresses enhanced support for SENCOs, improved accountability across the system and co-production (including within the Local Offer).

In the second section of this book, the focus is on the leadership role expected of SENCOs in their daily work practices: critically exploring the tasks that are expected to be undertaken by those in the role.

Lynda Kay and Tristan Middleton consider the policy of exclusion from school and its implications for children and young people with SEND. They outline an inclusive approach to reducing school exclusions that provides a strategy for SENCOs to consider.

Angela Scott problematises constructs of expected childhood development promoted in the early years by viewing milestone 'norms' through the lens of inclusive leadership and practice. Highlighting the importance of creating a leadership culture which genuinely celebrates the uniqueness of each child, Angela points to the importance of developing systems and structures that promote coherent communication.

Lisa O'Connor examines a variety of approaches to social, emotional and mental health (SEMH) and the SENCO's leadership role in the process of co-ordinating a whole-school approach to address learners' needs.

Dennis Piper outlines further thoughts of meeting the needs of children and young people with the SEMH. In his chapter, Dennis presents the PIPER Model (Personalised Interventions Promoting Emotional Resilience) as a way of supporting children and young people with SEMH in a mainstream setting.

Lorna Hughes considers the ways in which a leadership approach is vital in supporting children and young people with medical needs in school.

Angela Scott discusses the approaches to Person-Centred Planning (PCP) and how the SENCO as a leader might facilitate the participation of learners in this process.

Tracy Edwards and Mhairi C. Beaton consider SENCOs' role in leading assessment processes in their setting. Critically analysing current policy and practice in assessment, the chapter proposes new and innovative approaches that might enhance learning and teaching.

Louise Arnold and Janet Hoskins focus on the aspirational nature of the 2014 SEN and disability reforms and the extent to which EHCPs support children, young people and their families to achieve the outcomes to which they aspire. Theoretical perspectives and practical strategies for co-production of EHCPs with children and young people and their families are identified, explored and analysed.

Finally, in the last section, the focus shifts to the leadership role within multi-disciplinary practice that all SENCOs must adopt.

Helen Ackers draws on conversations she has had with SENCOs to identify some of the common challenges associated with establishing multi-professional teams. Key issues are analysed and strategies for establishing effective dialogue, trust and partnerships are explored.

Gianna Knowles starts from the premise that parents/carers know their children best, and although schools and parents/carers may have differences of opinion, it is essential that schools and families work in partnership to meet the needs of children and young people with SEND. Including a good practice case study, the chapter focusses on the voice of the child and family, the legal definition of a 'parent' and the importance, psychology and sociologies of family, all set within the legislative context of the Children and Families Act 2014.

Becky Edwards and Heather Green focus on SENCOs' professional response to the lived experiences of parents/carers of children with a label of SEND. Drawing on Chapter 2 in this book, Becky and Heather emphasise the importance of establishing a culture of genuine partnership with parents which seek to challenge tensions concerning power.

Julie C. Wharton thinks about the ways in which SENCOs find themselves working in an interagency way with social workers. This chapter considers the SENCO's role and responsibilities alongside those of the social worker.

Mhairi C. Beaton considers SENCOs' leadership role in encouraging the voices of young people with SEND to be heard. The chapter explores the benefits of listening to those voices within education and points to professional learning materials that will support practitioners' development of skills in this area.

Finally, *Helen Curran* considers the unique role adopted by the SENCO in educational settings. Acknowledging that many of the SENCOs' colleagues do not understand the role, the chapter examines both the contribution to education that SENCOs make and also the resilience required to fulfil the role.

Reference

Ofsted (2019) *The Education Inspection Framework*, Manchester: Ofsted.

2 Inclusive relationships

Creating the space for each other

Jonathan Rix

Do we need to start somewhere special?

In 2015, I was asked to speak at a seminar in Norway about special education and transformative learning. I was troubled. So, I went for a walk and thought about what I was struggling with; then I lay in bed and ruminated; onward across the weeks I found myself thinking about it when others were thinking of something else. I had a number of moments when I seemed to be getting to the root of my problem and then it slipped away. I tried to talk to people about it, but I soon realised that I was just going over old ground; I could hear I was boring them as well as myself, and then I had what seemed like a point of resolution, a transformative moment. It happened when I was driving my son to watch a game of cricket.

Cricket is a strange game. It comes in all different shapes and sizes. It can go on for five days, one day or two hours. You can lose it with the delivery of 10 balls or it can still be a draw after more than 2400 balls. Players stand in different places on the pitch depending upon how someone bowls a ball or hits it, and each place has its own name depending upon which way these batters and bowlers are facing. It is a game with a strange language of its own, a history and culture which beguiles the uninitiated. It is not something which can be explained in a few minutes (or a few hours). It has to be experienced and shared. But how do you begin playing it or watching it or talking about it?

It was this game to which I was taking my son. A young man, who in a world of schooling has always attracted one-to-one support (perhaps eager, perhaps not) and been too easily left to one side; who speaks in a flurry of sounds which leave one scrambling for meaning; who half-listens to explanations with a well-worn expectation of not understanding; who would always choose to engage in an activity for its sensory delights rather than seeking its meaning to others; and whose focus of attention is governed by his own priorities.

Why was I taking him? What was I intending him to gain from this? Would he understand cricket as I did? Or as I thought it ought to be understood? Was it something I wanted to share with him, as I had shared with my father? The possible questions seemed to multiply as I began to ask them.

Clearly, what I was seeking was transformative learning, but I would not be able to achieve this if I approached it in the way my father had taught me about cricket. My boy would not engage in the game in front of him as I had. His approach would be his own. It would be different to mine. My role was to help him make sense of the many small aspects of the whole.

And this was my moment of resolution.

What I was trying to achieve for my son was nothing special, though it was transformative.

Even though I had to do it on his terms, even though it required him to engage with an activity with its own cultural meanings, social practices and physical actions which were of little relevance to him and of which he had no predictable understanding. Even though . . .

Isn't this what all education is about?

Isn't it about finding ways to enable the uninitiated to engage? Surely, it is about transformation of understanding and identity and agency to enable participation, spread across many years.

The while of participation

From 2016 to 2019, I was part of a participatory research project, funded by the European Union, which ran across four European cities and involved disabled people, family and other supporters working with educators in six museums and with four technology partners. As part of this project we undertook a range of systematic literature reviews and developed a way of understanding participation called the *while* of participation (Rix *et al.*, 2019). The *while* involves the underpinning tensions around power, support and voice. The participatory nature of these underpinning tensions is evident in the learning, value and representation which emerge and are constructed through the practicalities of participation, its component parts. These component parts emerge and are constructed through:

- shifting language, roles and attitudes;
- a capacity to adapt practices and spaces that emerge from and enable relationships;
- a recognition of the need for being flexible, taking time and for people to enjoy themselves.

Figure 2.1 The underpinning tensions, outcomes and component parts of the while of participation (Rix *et al.*, 2019)

The underpinning tensions, outcomes and component parts can be seen as multiple interactions which create and are created by participation. These moments form around each other. They are a wave and a particle – a flow from many directions. They are also the layers through which we can understand activities. They are a means to explore the inclusive nature of our practices and people's experiences of them.

Participation is the experience that occurs in the moment, and it defines our experience of that moment; the experience that emerges from and creates the boundaries in which people find themselves. The *while* is both a physical and personal experience, socially created from the collective resources, understandings and interactions. In its widest sense, it is an ongoing process. If there is such a thing as a singular moment, it is more than a sum of preceding moments.

Participatory practice is therefore not about activity type but the manner in which all activity is undertaken.

And whilst all participation can be inclusive, often it is not.

The risk at the heart of participation and inclusive practice

Inclusion can be seen as an "assault on oppressive vestiges of the past as a way of contributing to alternative futures" (Slee and Allan, 2001:176). It involves adopting a pedagogy which is underpinned by a principle of transformability (Hart, 2010), perhaps using a curriculum based upon values and rights (Booth, 2011), and requiring changes in the 'behaviour' of adults (Ainscow and Sandill, 2010). It is often suggested that it needs to draw flexibly upon a class-community and cooperative learning structures (Naraian, 2011), and that it needs to be understood as an ongoing process (UNESCO IBE, 2008), active and without end (Flem and Keller, 2000), evolving and changing continually (Hausstätter, 2014). There is a strong message that people work towards reaching out to all learners, they continually strive for this goal, but do not arrive (Ainscow, 2000). It can be seen as mixed with exclusion in "a messy series of compromises, adjustments and individual preferences" (Corbett, 1997:55). It can simply be seen as a matter of how we define good education, with a beautiful risk at its heart (Biesta, 2010, 2015).

Underpinning most of the writing around inclusion is that the nature of human experience is fundamentally uncertain and that knowledge is emergent and situated. Much that is written recognises that understanding is always incomplete, and there is no single correct way to support the learning of any child. Hart (1996), in exploring Innovative Thinking, for example, recognises that our thinking and conclusions must be questioned.

Approaches associated with inclusion encourage us to begin with a model of doubt and uncertainty – perhaps accepting it or recognising it for what it is; perhaps seeking to confront it or thinking through it. We should arrive wanting to question any preconceptions about the situation and the context in which it has arisen. We should acknowledge a situation's uncertain relational nature and the interdependence of people within it. In seeking to explore or confront difficulties, challenges and opportunities, we should try to critically engage and reflect on the situation. This involves thinking in hypothetical ways, seeing the dilemmas which surround us or seeking pragmatic, proactive, reactive or radical pathways. We should recognise difficulties within a system as an experience for all involved. As Florian (2014) suggests, we can see an experience as individualised but it will be primarily socially situated.

To move beyond doubt, we need to find possibilities. These can only arise from the situation in which we are. This requires us to develop an understanding of the context, accepting its relational nature – both in terms of personal and cultural relationships. This is perhaps why Allan (2008) talks of the unpredictability of learning, the search for something undecidable taking place within an ethically rich drama. It is perhaps why she calls for teachers to create openings for inclusion.

To enable the creation of these openings, we benefit from the perspectives of others who have an insight into the experience. This develops a collective view of the experience, and it involves us in asking questions of the people and the systems. This is perhaps why approaches associated with inclusion call for collaborative models of teaching and learning, though this comes in many forms (Solis *et al.*, 2012). It is also perhaps why educators and learners need to move from being 'participators within' to 'contributors to' educational spaces (Veck, 2009).

Out of this collective focus, a possible way forward will emerge, one that is not defined in a fixed way, but has expectations and recognises the uncertainty of any solution and the need to continue questioning. Conclusions which we may come to will be recognised as momentary positions (Benjamin *et al.*, 2003). They will contribute perhaps to an understanding of the identity of people within the learning context as complex and shifting (McDermott and Varenne, 1995) or "more than one single other" (Dederich, 2015). These identities will be relational to the context and to others' perspectives. They will be momentary positions which themselves open up other possibilities. Things will not fit neatly. They will be positioned amongst opportunities and risks. Responses will need to be flexible within the possible disorder. We will be dealing with shifting identities with porous boundaries.

It is hopefully clear why at the heart of such an approach is a constant engagement with risk. 'Valid' participation is not situated in a singular or neatly defined space. It is based on continual negotiation, with participants needing to move to where others are. To do so requires a willingness to embrace the risk inherent in being open to the power of participants, in how one conceives of and delivers support, and in how we recognise the voices of all those within that learning context. It requires taking practical risks in challenging people in their language, roles and attitudes, requiring us to open up our practices and spaces to enable relationships that are flexible, enjoyable and generous with time. This is a risk not only to our identities and practices as professional educators, but also in that it seems to create conflict with the context of established 'mainstream' practices, which are seeking certainty.

Can we find support within the evidence base for building practice upon a model of uncertainty?

Teachers tend to claim that they lack the skills and knowledge about the nature of SEN groupings and how to work with them (Scruggs and Mastropieri, 1996; OFSTED, 2004; Ali *et al.*, 2006; Sharma *et al.*, 2008; Florian and Black-Hawkins, 2011; Delgado-Pinheiro and Omote,

2010). There is a temptation to seek an ordered, hierarchical, 'common-sense', evidence-based response which combines both the group-based and individualised processes. But by giving in to temptation, we create a continuum model of delivery (Mcleskey and Waldron, 2011), where improvements are small, are only evident in some students and are dependent upon consistent delivery of specified teaching programmes (e.g. Fuchs *et al.*, 2008; Torgesen, 2009).

There is no question that teachers benefit from good initial training, but the kinds of skills at the heart of both special and inclusive are primarily ones which practitioners can develop through experience and practice (Feng and Marcos, 2013). These skills are already situated in 'good teaching'.

Good teaching is widely regarded to be active, highly skilled and providing rich opportunities for students within a well-planned and organised setting. The complexity of teacher and learner interactions is also widely recognised, as is the importance of recognising individual values and experiences and framing learning opportunities in meaningful contexts which serve a purpose relevant to the intended learner (Brownell and Kiely, 2010). Forness (2001) reported on a review of meta-analyses looking at the evidence associated with 20 interventions. The review concluded that unequivocal improvement was associated with those practices which arose from general education, whereas practices involving related services tended to rest between effective and ineffective (with a potential 20-percentile improvement), and those associated with a specific deficit had minimal impact (with less than a 10-percentile advantage for students receiving these interventions).

In a review of effective pedagogies in mainstream classrooms for learners identified with Special Educational Needs, which I was involved in from 2003–2009 (Rix *et al.*, 2009), we recognised that studies of effective pedagogies were actually describing facets of 'good teaching' for all (Sheehy, 2013). It did not really matter which research paradigm they emerged from or whether they were traditionally practiced in relative isolation, the practices themselves relied upon everyday practices which teachers readily understand. Teachers needed to:

- recognise their responsibility for all pupils, having respect for them and for all learning, whilst seeing everyone as a learner and engaging with teachers who shared this model of learning;
- recognise social interaction as the means to develop knowledge as well as having clear learning goals, subject skills and knowledge;
- plan to scaffold both cognitive and social content, delineating group roles, and using pupils' own understandings as resources for learning;
- explore pupils' understandings, encouraging questioning, making links between areas of student knowledge whilst actively developing skills in a meaningful way, using a range of modes'
- understand the aims of the structured programme and subject, with a shared understanding of the characteristics, skills and knowledge associated with the subject to be taught.

The research which I have examined since this time has simply affirmed that everyday teacher skills are at the heart of effective, inclusive practice. For example:

- In 2010, the Irish *National Council for Special Education* commissioned an international literature review of best practice models associated with children identified with emotional disturbance/behavioural difficulties (Cooper and Jacobs, 2011). They found high empirical evidence to support only three approaches, all of which could be delivered collectively by teachers and across institutions with relatively little training (The Good Behaviour Game, Friends, Career Academies).
- Marschark *et al.* (2011) systematically reviewed evidence for effective practice in relation to deaf children. They identified everyday strategies and materials which scaffold learning, which were multimodal, focused upon the representation of concepts and the links between them, making them relevant and authentic.
- A systematic review into best practice for persons with autistic spectrum disorders (Parsons *et al.*, 2009) suggested some short-term evidence for behavioural approaches, but recommended early intervention focused on communicative behaviours, and multimodal, naturalistic, child-centred and child-led approaches. A follow-up review (Bond *et al.*, 2016) specifically focused upon the educational utility of these approaches, and concluded that many of the included interventions were ones which could be integrated into the school day by school

staff with some additional training (e.g. behavioural, narrative and technology-assisted interventions), and less required more extensive or accredited training (e.g. CTMs and multicomponent interventions).

The everyday approaches which emerge from categorical research also echo the empirical research into creative pedagogies (Cremin and Chappell, 2019). These focus upon generating and exploring ideas, encouraging autonomy and agency, playfulness and problem-solving, involving co-constructing, collaboration and teacher creativity. They rely upon an open ethos and high degree of acceptance of children's ideas, setting aside time for learners to explore resources and generate ideas. They recognise a need for direction, boundaries and support but advocate independence and choice, having high expectations of the children, whilst accepting and encouraging the emergence of agency. They seek authentic, real-world, practical, open-ended problems, that allow for imaginative scenarios and extended projects. At their heart is risk-taking, an embrace of experimentation and acceptance of failure. Teaching and learning are seen as coevolving and involve reflection and dialogue. The teacher's creativity is a background presence, a model for others and an identity that learners can relate to.

Opening up spaces for learning

Florian and Black-Hawkins (2011) undertook an in-depth study of 'teacher craft' in two Scottish schools, to explore approaches that included all learners. They wanted to move teachers on from thinking about what works for most and what is additional for some. They sought to shift the focus to creating rich learning opportunities for the whole community of learners. They talked about creating spaces where children are trusted to make good decisions about how, where, when and with whom they learn. Teachers discussed ideas about teaching and learning with colleagues both inside and outside the class. They created options for learning, consulting students about how they could be assisted, developing situations which supported people to work with a variety of others.

This socially situated approach reflected the work of Hart *et al.* (2010), who argued that educationalists need to focus on the context of the child's experience, setting aside the language of special educational needs and individualised 'outside' support. It echoed too the views of teachers engaged effectively with children identified with social and emotional behavioural difficulties (Goodman and Burton, 2010). They discussed building respectful relationships with students, with both parties seeking to negotiate rather than confront each other. They talked about the need to find out about people's backgrounds and interests, in order to develop collaborative working. They sought to give the student responsibilities within the learning situation, as well as encouraging them to manage their own behaviour.

At the centre of the approaches discussed is a commitment to work in open-ended ways, which can be responsive to needs and strengths as they emerge and as they are identified. Perhaps unsurprisingly, working in this manner is constrained (and undermined) by our current curriculum and assessment systems and their underlying ideological values. It seems very odd to me that open-ended learning is the kind which we encourage in pre-school and post-school but not within school. We want our very young people to play and we want people in their late teens to increasingly take on a research role; we want a flexible, collaborative and problem-resolving workforce; but within school we go in the other direction. Our requirement that people make the grade and learn specific information or skills restricts what they can achieve, what they can be taught and how that teaching can take place. This does not mean policy makers cannot construct processes to maintain standards, but it requires recognising that how we define what is to be learned constrains the processes of teaching.

A focus upon context also needs to become an everyday expectation in relation to wider processes of planning. We need to deliberately consider the wider context when we make decisions about the use of resources and the provision of support. Our documentation and funding mechanisms need to call for such a focus. They need to encourage local discussions about weaknesses and strengths, challenges and opportunities, possible ways forward and barriers to be overcome. Appropriate mechanisms can support a growing collective understanding of the challenges which we face. People can better discuss what they cannot do, as well as what they might be able to do and why. Creating an expectation and facilitating such discussions would aim to encourage a more flexible and responsive learning space but it would also facilitate agitation and planning for change.

Do we need to end up somewhere special?

So, what did this open-ended learning look like for my son and the game of cricket? At the time of writing, it is four years since we went to our first match. We have been to about four matches a year. He has spent about six days watching International Test cricket, a couple of days watching one-day matches and has been to eight Twenty-Twenty matches at Sussex's Hove ground. His greatest excitement is definitely the food, even though he was part of a group who formed the guard of honour at one home match and got to meet Jofra Archer (England's great new hope at the time).

Food has served many functions; not just as a break in the day, but also as a means to explore the rhythms of the match. For example, I could not say to him "An over is when the bowler has bowled six balls" and expect him to understand what I was talking about. I had to make him aware that something happened every few balls and that this thing was called an over. We did this with twiglets (another strange English obsession). At the end of the over we would have some more twiglets. "Wait until the next over," I said as he asked for more twiglets. "Look, a new man is bowling. He is bowling from the other end. It is a new over." A few more twiglets. And so on.

But being in the space with me (and often his mum) has woven a particular magic, too. He came to understand what a 4 is and what a 6 is, thanks to waving a big piece of card with a 4 and a 6 on it when he was witness to a remarkable 34 runs scored in 6 balls by David Willey. Other experiences in the space, such as music when someone is out, silly halftime games and badly dressed mascots, have also been really important. I never really cared about marching bands before now, but now I too look forward to them, particularly if they are playing the bagpipes. And this perhaps is one of my biggest surprises; not only has my son developed an identity as a cricket fan (who is already telling me to organise tickets for next year), but my identity has shifted, too. In supporting someone else I have learned new things about this game and my relationship with it.

I can tell you similar stories about my son learning to ride a bike, to swim and to ski. All of these learning experiences have involved seeking and building sensory and emotional connections, drawing upon his interests and following our leads, making time and being open to possibilities. They involved determination but very rarely did they involve pre-determined goals. And the learning has always been far more than a one-way process. I could talk about what we have learned from him in so many areas; for example, through his use of cameras and websites, his string collection, his love of music and films, and his entirely novel way of using WhatsApp to develop shared understandings and to enhance his reading and writing.

And all of these things have taken place outside of formal learning situations.

Within formal learning settings, this kind of approach has been far less in evidence.

The purpose of education seems to be subsumed by processes and structures, dominated by an overemphasis on what might be seen as component parts of that wider goal (e.g. behaviour, grades, subject knowledge, school identity). Many are disabled by what we offer and expect. Under everyday pressures, and drawing on a history of practice, schools focus upon mechanistic processes. They decide who can learn, what they can learn and how it will be taught. They see a lack of learning or desired behaviour as a reason to pass responsibility for a child to someone else or as a reason to fill their time with whatever comes to hand. Frequently, this response is supported through the teachers' training or their very partial understanding of theory. It is within this context that someone and their support becomes special.

But it need not be so. It is in the power of every teacher, every teaching assistant, every head teacher and all the rest of us who support learning to do something about it. Everything we do is situated within a dynamic multiplicity of relationships which are bounded only by convention and conceptualisation, without which they can be traced in endless directions. We create our participation *while* we undertake our activity. It is possible to find ways to open up our working – not simply for the last lesson on a Friday (if the kids behave), but whenever we are in a learning situation. We can approach these situations with a model of uncertainty, embracing doubt, creating the space for new relationships, new identities and unexpected expectations. We can use the skills that we already have to build on the knowledge, capacities, priorities and aspirations of the learners with whom we work. We can trust them to make decisions about how, where, when and with whom they learn. We can discuss ideas about teaching and learning with colleagues both inside and outside the class. We can create situations which support people to work with a variety of others. And by attempting to do these kinds of things, we will create moments, new opportunities which will lead us somewhere together.

It might even turn out to be an Olympic ski black run, but that is another story – without end.

Reflective questions

- Thinking back to the start of this chapter, where do you think special education needs to start? Is it somewhere special?
- Thinking back to the *while* of participation, why do you feel participation is often not inclusive?
- Thinking back to the model of uncertainty, how might you embrace more risk within your work?

References

Ainscow, M. (2000) Profile. In Clough, P. and Corbett, J. (Eds.), *Theories of Inclusive Education: A Students' Guide* (39–42). London: Paul Chapman.

Ainscow, M., and Sandill, A. (2010) Developing inclusive education systems: The role of organisational cultures and leadership. *International Journal of Inclusive Education*, 14(4), 401–416.

Ali, M. M., Mustapha, R., and Jelas, Z. M. (2006) An empirical study on teachers' perceptions towards inclusive education in Malaysia. *International Journal of Special Education*, 21(3), 36–44.

Allan, J. (2008) *Rethinking Inclusive Education: The Philosophers of Difference in Practice*. Dordrecht: Springer.

Benjamin, S., Nind, M., Hall, K., Collins, J., and Sheehy, K. (2003) Moments of inclusion and exclusion: Pupils negotiating classroom contexts. *British Journal of Sociology of Education*, 24(5), 547–558.

Biesta, G. J. (2010) *Good Education in an Age of Measurement: Ethics, Politics, Democracy*. London: Routledge.

Biesta, G. J. (2015) *Beautiful Risk of Education*. London: Routledge.

Bond, C., Symes, W., Hebron, J., Humphrey, N., Morewood, G., and Woods, K. (2016b) Educational interventions for children with ASD: A systematic literature review 2008–2013. *School Psychology International*, 37, 303–320.

Booth, T. (2011) The name of the rose: Inclusive values into action in teacher education. *Prospects*, 41(3), 303–318.

Brownell, M., and Kiely, M. (2010) Special education teacher quality and preparation. *Exceptional Children*, 76(3), 357–377.

Cooper, P. and Jacobs, B. (2011) *An International Review of the Literature of Evidence of Best Practice Models and Outcomes in the Education of Children with Emotional Disturbance/Behavioural Difficulties*. Trim: National Council for Special Education.

Corbett, J. (1997) Include/exclude. *International Journal of Inclusive Education*, 1(1), 55–64.

Cremin, T. and Chappell, K. (2019) Creative pedagogies: A systematic review. *Research Papers in Education* (Early Access).

Dederich, M. (2015) Heterogeneity, radical otherness and the discourse on inclusive education – A philosophical reflection. In Kiuppis, F. and Hausstätter, R. (Eds.), *Inclusive Education Twenty Years after Salamanca*. New York: Peter Lang.

Delgado-Pinheiro, E. and Omote, S. (2010) Conhecimentos de professores sobre perda auditiva e suas atitudes frente á inclusão (Teachers' knowledge about hearing loss and attitudes towards the inclusion). *Rev. CEFAC* [online], 12(4), 633–640.

Feng, L. and Marcos, S. (2013) What makes special-education teachers special? *Economics of Education Review*, 36, 122–134.

Flem, A. and Keller, C. (2000) Inclusion in Norway. *European Journal of Special Needs Education*, 15(2), 188–205.

Florian, L. (2014) Inclusive pedagogy: An alternative approach to difference and inclusion. In Kiuppis, F. and Hausstätter, R. (Eds.), *Inclusive Education Twenty Years after Salamanca*. New York: Peter Lang.

Florian, L. and Black-Hawkins, K. (2011) Exploring inclusive pedagogy. *British Educational Journal*, 37(5), 813–828.

Forness, S. (2001) Special education and related services: What have we learned from meta-analysis? *Exceptionality: A Special Education Journal*, 9(4), 185–197.

Fuchs, L., Fuchs, D., Craddock, C., Hollenbeck, K., Hamlett, C., and Schatschneider, C. (2008) Effects of small-group tutoring with and without validated classroom instruction on at-risk students' math problem solving. *Journal of Educational Psychology*, 100(3), 491–509.

Goodman, R. and Burton, D. (2010) The inclusion of students with BESD in mainstream schools: Teachers' experiences of and recommendations for creating a successful inclusive environment. *Emotional and Behavioural Difficulties*, 15(3), 223–237.

Hart, S. (1996) *Beyond Special Needs: Enhancing Children's Learning through Innovative Thinking*. London: Sage.

Hart, S. (2010) Learning without limits. In Rix, J., Nind, M., Sheehy, K., Simmons, K., Parry, J. and Kumrai, R. (Eds.), *Equality, Participation and Inclusion 2: Diverse Contexts*. Oxon: Routledge.

Hausstätter, R. (2014) In support of unfinished inclusion. *Scandinavian Journal of Educational Research*, 58(4), 424–434.

Marschark, M., Spencer, P. E., Adams, J. and Sapere, P. (2011) Evidence-based practice in educating deaf and hard-of-hearing children: Teaching to their cognitive strengths and needs. *European Journal of Special Needs Education*, 26(1), 3–16.

McDermott, R., and Varenne, H. (1995) Culture as disability. *Anthropology & Education Quarterly*, 26(3), 324–348.

McLesky, J., and Waldron, N. L. (2011) Educational programs for elementary students with learning disabilities: Can they be both effective and inclusive? *Learning Disabilities Research & Practice*, 26(1), 48–57.

Naraian, S. (2011) Seeking transparency: The production of an inclusive classroom community. *International Journal of Inclusive Education*, 15(9), 955–973.

OFSTED (2004) *Remodelling the School Workforce*. HMI 358. London: Office for Standards in Education.

Parsons, S., Guldberg, K., MacLeod, A., Jones, G., Prunty, A. and Balfe, T. (2009) International review of the literature of evidence of best practice provision in the education of persons with autistic spectrum disorders. NCSE Research Reports No. 2.

Rix, J., Carrizosa, H. G., Seale, J., Sheehy, K. and Hayhoe, S. (2019). The while of participation: A systematic review of participatory research involving people with sensory impairments and/or intellectual impairments. *Disability & Society*. https://doi.org/10.1080/09687599.2019.1669431

Rix, J., Hall, K., Nind, M., Sheehy, K. and Wearmouth, J. (2009) What pedagogical approaches can effectively include children with special educational needs in mainstream classrooms? – A Systematic literature review. *Support for Learning*, 24(2), 85–93.

Scruggs, T. and Mastropieri, M. (1996) Teacher perceptions of mainstreaming/inclusion, 1958–1995. *Exceptional Children*, 63(1), 59–74.

Sharma, U., Forlin, C. and Loreman, T. (2008) Impact of training on pre-service teachers' attitudes and concerns about inclusive education and sentiments about persons with disabilities. *Disability & Society*, 23(7), 773–785.

Sheehy, K. (2013) Educational psychology and inclusive education. In Holliman, A. (Ed.), *Educational Psychology: An International Perspective*. Oxon: Routledge.

Slee, R. and Allan, J. (2001) Excluding the Included: A reconsideration of inclusive education. *International Studies in Sociology of Education*, 11(2), 173–191.

Solis, M., Vaughn, S., Swanson, E., and Mcculley, L. (2012) Collaborative models of instruction. *Psychology in the Schools*, 49(5), 498–511.

Torgesen, J. K. (2009) The response to intervention instructional model. *Child Development Perspectives*, 3(1), 38–40.

UNESCO IBE (2008) *Inclusive Education: The Way of the Future*. Conclusions and recommendations of the 48th session for the International Conference on Education (ICE), Geneva, 25–28 November 2008.

Veck, W. (2009) From an exclusionary to an inclusive understanding of educational difficulties and educational space. *Oxford Review of Education*, 35(1), 41–56.

3 The language of SEND

Implications for the SENCO

Geraldene N. Codina and Julie C. Wharton

Introduction

The central tenet of this chapter is that language matters. Over the centuries as human beings have represented and categorised both themselves and others in different ways, so interpretations and the language of disability (physical and learning) shape-shifts, altering through time (Goodey, 2016). The language of disability and the societal and political values which underpin it are therefore not cross-historical; let two or three generations pass and the labels associated with disability alter. Sometimes such changes in language usage can seem little more than semantic fashion or a professional challenge to keep up-to-date with. The language of disability is, however, more than fashion and political correctness (Mallett and Slater, 2014), for words gain their meaning from the manner in which they are used (Wittgenstein, 2009). This chapter argues the language of special education shapes SENCOs' values, expectations, assumptions, responses and practice. Through an exploration of historical and current language usage, this chapter analyses the language of special education and the implications for the school community.

The language of disability: a historical analysis

The 1870 Forster's Education Act was the first piece of British legislation to establish a nation-wide compulsory system of education for all pupils aged five to thirteen. Following complaints from teachers about so-called 'uneducable' children (Arnold, 1964; Hurt, 1988), the Egerton Committee sought to assess how widespread the 'problem' was. The values and assumptions belying the label 'uneducable' speak to a construction of education which perceives some groups of children as unsuitable for learning. More disturbingly at the time, this narrative worked alongside social Darwinism and eugenics, which promoted the idea, as Sir Francis Galton put it, of getting 'rid' of the 'undesirables' whilst multiplying the 'desirables' (Kevles, 1995). Believing that education was of no benefit to the 'least able', proponents of social Darwinism espoused a view that intelligence was not gained through education, but must be 'bred in' (Thomas and Loxley 2007; Kevles, 1995). Such views were also expressed in the work of the prominent educator, philosopher and scholar Herbert Spencer, who coined the term 'survival of the fittest'. Taking a keen interest in intellect, Spencer (1911) laid out seven principles for education, including encouraging educators to start 'from the concrete and end in the abstract' (Spencer, 1911:60). Progressive in nature, Spencer's principles will be familiar to many working in education today; however, the wholly unpalatable part of Spencer's work concerned *for whom* this system of education was designed. Believing the weak, poor and unintelligent should develop the skills needed to face the oppressive odds or be discouraged from breeding (Egan, 2002), Spencer's interest in intellectual education extended only to the middle/upper classes. For this reason, in the 21st century Spencer's name rarely surfaces, appearing only sometimes in the footnote of a better-known text (Egan, 2002). The language of eugenic thinking ('desirables' and 'undesirables'; weak, poor and unintelligent) speaks to a value system of condemnation and measuring people's worth. Judgements of this nature created social boundaries for what was 'acceptable', leading to the development of policies and practices to deal with those deemed as 'undesirable' outsiders.

By the close of the 19th century, the combined effect of industrialisation and social Darwinism led to a strong campaign to urgently deal with the problems of 'mental deficiency'. Underlying this call was a belief that '"mental defectives" were not only the cause of most social evils but were also an economic burden' (Fido and Potts, 2003:38), taking more than they gave and causing problems for other more worthy souls. It is important not to idealise the pre-industrial era for disabled people; it is, however, worth remembering that increasing industrialist pressures made it less likely that a family could support a 'non-productive' member (Fido and Potts, 2003).

In 1913, the Mental Deficiency Act addressed the 'problem' of 'uneducable' children through the wide-scale institutionalisation of those judged to be impaired. Underpinned by eugenic ideology, the purpose of the Act was to prevent the 'degenerate' population from breeding with 'the healthy', thus avoiding contamination of 'the fit' with the 'ills' of the 'morally', 'physically' and 'mentally defective' (Armstrong, 2003). Under the 1913 Act, 'uneducable' children were deemed to be 'idiots', 'imbeciles', 'feeble-minded' or 'moral imbeciles' and as such sent away to single-sex institutions. The girls to whom the term feeble-minded was given were often viewed as sexually 'uncontrolled', 'incapable' of independent living and thus capable of managing themselves only under supervision (Goodman, 2005). The policy directed those in positions of power to limit and restrict the freedoms of the so-called degenerate, thereby removing their agency and control over their own lives. It is not well documented exactly how many children were institutionalised during this period (Armstrong, 2003), but what is known is that most came from families described as working-class (Humphries and Gordon, 1992). Other labels such as 'invalid' and 'illegitimate child' were also used during this period and, like the terminology of the 1913 Act, speak the language of hostility and dehumanisation. Such language constitutes a political, cultural and social act of othering and is thus inseparable from the action of sectioning the 'degenerate' away from the 'healthy'. Something of this hostility is illustrated in the seemingly innocent photo of Lucy Stone (Figure 3.1, left). Labelled in the 1920s as an 'invalid', Lucy had a hip deformity which caused one of her legs to be shorter than the other. The studio photographer thought her 'deformity' looked 'ugly' and so made Lucy adopt a pose which hid the 'unsightly leg'. Lucy described always disliking this photograph and the memory of the discomfort caused by her awkward posture, so she much preferred the photograph (Figure 3.1, right) which gives no hint of her physical impairment.

Figure 3.1 Photos of Lucy Stone, born in 1920

Other personal narratives from this period capture the moment when the families of disabled children were visited by government officials. Humphries and Gordon (1992) argue that most parents wanted to look after their disabled children themselves, and in this sense the narrative of parents fighting and disagreeing with the authorities for the rights of their children (Lamb, 2009) is not a new one. Elise Cooper describes how her father 'refused point blank' to let her go to an institution:

> [He] said I wouldn't learn anything there and that I was brighter than some of my brothers who went to the local school. It was only thanks to him sticking his heels in that I wasn't packed off there for good.
>
> (Humphries and Gordon, 1992:16)

For those who were institutionalised, the curriculum was very basic, activities such as basket weaving gave rise to the expression 's/he's a bit of a basket case', which is widely taken to mean someone who cannot communicate effectively or is mentally unstable and unable to cope emotionally (Jack, 2004). The low-level curriculum devoid of aspiration provides further evidence of the values underpinning a policy that saw disabled children's lives as 'worthless'.

The treatment of disabled children at this time is starkly illustrated in Mary Baker's account of her experiences in an institution. Like Lucy, Mary had a hip deformity, which resulted in her being sent to the Halliwick Home for Crippled Girls. On entering the institution Mary describes being taken to a bathroom to be stripped and scrubbed with carbolic soap, following which her hair was cut short above her ears. The next day she was given the number twenty-nine and no longer referred to as Mary; her flannel, hairbrush and clothes also bore this number. The removal of Mary's name is more than a simple act of swapping four letters for two numbers, but rather the power of referring to Mary as a number generates a denial of her human qualities and makes permissible the impermissible. During her time in the institution, Mary's own voice was regularly used to cover and conceal her dehumanisation from her relatives. Tasked each week with writing to her family, Mary's own words were edited and censored. Permitted only to say how congenial life was in the home, Mary described receiving letters from her father and grandmother 'saying they were so thrilled that I was happy, but my letters were all lies' (Humphries and Gordon, 1992:74). Silencing the authentic genuine voice of the child is also a feature of Evelyn King's experience. Born in 1945 with cerebral palsy, Evelyn was labelled as an 'imbecile', meaning she was deemed 'unfit for education' and thus sent to a hospital for the mentally handicapped. Evelyn describes not being allowed to speak with any of the boys who were also in the hospital, 'so I just kept my mouth shut' (Humphries and Gordon, 1992:102). The practice of censoring and silencing a child's voice speaks of the power words can have and the importance for those in authority to gain control of this power – power of this nature providing access to a person's liberty and freedom, choice and opportunity, hope and identity.

The rise of the eugenics movement was not confined to the UK, as distinct and identifiable from 1880 (Levine and Bashford, 2010) eugenic practices could be found in other parts of Europe, the United States (US) and Canada (Kevles, 1995). Regardless of location, the aim of eugenics was always to judge and evaluate which lives were of more value than others to a nation, state, race or future generation (Levine and Bashford, 2010). Eugenic practices varied from deciding which lives should be promoted or prevented to extinguishing life. In Canada and to a greater extent the US, this meant the forced sterilisation of the 'mentally retarded' or 'mentally ill' (Reilly, 1991; McLaren, 1990). At its most extreme under the Nazi regime, eugenics took on the shape of forced euthanasia and genocide. From 1939 onwards in Germany the so-called T4 euthanasia programme, named as such because the directing offices were located in Tiergartenstraße 4, forcefully took the lives of those described as 'useless eaters' or of having 'burdensome lives' (Rieser, 2007). The language used to describe this genocide was chosen deliberately to instil and illicit responsible compassion: 'the propaganda began to work as families wrote to Hitler asking for help to kill their poor disabled relatives out of an act of mercy' (Rieser, 2007:14). Such acts of 'compassion' were once again an illustration of the ways in which disabled people had their free will removed and given to the care of another more suitable and responsible agent.

By the end of the Second World War the eugenics movement had come under considerable scientific and political criticism (Levine and Bashford, 2010). From an educational perspective, the discourse of eugenic philosophy gave way to constructs of 'normalisation'. This change heralded a policy shift away from 'removing the disabled' towards a policy of 'treating' and 'fixing the broken'. Under the normalisation agenda, boundaries for defining what was normal were established and methods appropriate to treating persons 'suffering' from a 'disability of mind or body' applied (Education Act, 1944:8.2c). The language of 'suffering' and 'treatment' set an expectation for teachers, parents and children that disability should be construed and responded to as a 'tragedy' to be corrected by experts. Thus, once again underpinning disability with a defined value system and suppressing the voices of those who did not perceive disability through this lens. From 1944 the Minister of Education was responsible for the regulation of the so-called 'categories of handicap' for 'pupils requiring special educational treatment and make provision as to the special methods appropriate for the education of pupils in each category' (Education Act, 1944:33.1). By 1945, the eleven categories of handicap were defined as: blind, partially sighted, deaf, partially deaf, delicate, diabetic, educationally subnormal, epileptic, maladjusted, physically handicapped and those with speech defects (Warnock, 1978). The construction of categories for the 'educationally subnormal' and 'maladjusted' required the development of decontextualised assessments of both children's intelligence and behaviour, respectively. In addition to which, it was the Ministry of Education (1945) policy that all children labelled blind, deaf, physically handicapped, epileptic or aphasic must attend special schools. This policy decision was later criticised in the Enquiry into the Education of Handicapped Children and Young People (Warnock, 1978) for treating children with the same label as homogenous constituents of a group with the same educational needs and requirements.

Attitudes toward disability continued to change throughout the 1950s and 1960s. This is illustrated in the Plowden Report (1967:297), which describes nearly all its witnesses, including the National Union of Teachers, as in agreement with the principle that 'no handicapped child should be sent to a special school who can be satisfactorily educated in an ordinary school' (Plowden, 1967:29). The report goes on to say the 'handicapped' child who spends:

> his life in the society of normal people and often in competition with them must learn to accept his disabilities and his differences though he needs the assurance that he is not alone in them and that help is available. The unnecessary segregation of the handicapped is neither good for them nor for those with whom they must associate. They should be in the ordinary school whenever possible.
>
> (Plowden, 1967:297)

The distinction made in the Plowden Report (1967) between 'normal people' and those with a 'handicap' speaks to the normalisation agenda of the day. The reality of 'accepting' one's disability and the 'help' available often meant putting up with others' low expectations, prescribed 'treatments' and exclusion from activities deemed too demanding or unsuitable. The idea, however, that segregation serves neither 'group' marks a fundamental turn away from the language and values of eugenics agenda and points towards later constructions of inclusion. By 1973, the government of the day appointed a committee to review and make recommendations about the educational provision for 'handicapped' children (Warnock, 1978:1). With reference to the 'categories of handicap', the Report of the Committee of Enquiry into the Education of Handicapped Children and Young People (Warnock, 1978) recommended they were abolished, citing the following disadvantages:

- many children 'suffer' from more than one disability, making it difficult to place them in any one category;
- labels tend to stick, and children diagnosed as educationally sub-normal or maladjusted can be stigmatised unnecessarily for the whole of their school careers and beyond;
- categories suggest that every child with the same label requires the same kind of educational regime;
- if children do not readily fit into the statutory categories it can be hard for local education authorities to make appropriate provisions available.

(Warnock, 1978:3.23)

Although through the use of the word 'suffering' the report continues to align disability with pity and tragedy, it makes some fundamentally important points which shine a light on the discriminatory practice associated with the language of 'handicap'. Referring to the sharp contrast between the 'handicapped' and the 'non-handicapped', the report describes the importance of eliminating this distinction as far as possible (Warnock, 1978:3.25) and goes on to propose the categories of handicap be abolished in favour of the term *special educational needs*.

The language of special educational needs

The definition of *special educational need* presented in the report into the Education of Handicapped Children and Young People (Warnock, 1978) referred to the significance of additional provision, through environmental modification, additional resources, curricular adaptation and social and emotional support:

In very broad terms special educational need is likely to take the form of the need for one or more of the following:

(i)   *the provision of special means of access to the curriculum through special equipment, facilities or resources, modification of the physical environment or specialist teaching techniques;*
(ii) *the provision of a special or modified curriculum;*
(iii) *particular attention to the social structure and emotional climate in which education takes place.*

(Warnock, 1978:41)

This definition suggests that a child or young person's special educational needs require adaptations to be made, therefore rendering their needs as a societal rather than an individual problem (Oliver, 1996). The 1981 Education Act and the subsequent 1993 Education Act built on the idea that a child might need additional provisions, but there was also a suggestion that a child's 'difficulties' might be the result of a deficit, situating the need within the person. The following definition of *special educational needs* from the 1981 and 1993 Education Acts was included in the first *Code of Practice on the Identification and Assessment of Special Educational Needs (SEN)*:

Meaning of special educational needs . . .

(1) For the purposes of the Education Acts, a child has special educational needs if he has a learning difficulty which calls for special educational provision to be made for him.
(2) For the purposes of this Act, subject to subsection (3) below, a child has a "learning difficulty" if –

(a) he has a significantly greater difficulty in learning than the majority of children of his age;
(b) he has a disability which either prevents or hinders him from making use of educational facilities of a kind generally provided for children of his age in schools within the area of the local education authority.

(DfE, 1994:5)

This definition of SEN in the second *Special Educational Needs Code of Practice* (DfES, 2001) remained the same apart from the use of 'children' and 'them' instead of the gendered 'he' and 'him'. The most recent *Special Educational Needs and Disability Code of Practice: 0–25* (DfE and DoH, 2015) retains this definition with the clarification of the educational facilities being mainstream or Post-16 settings (DfE and DoH, 2015), hence also referring to 'he' and 'she' rather than children. Reference to the Local Education Authority was also removed from the current SEND Code of Practice (DfE and DoH, 2015).

Informed by the legislation in Part 3 of the Children and Families Act 2014, the Special Educational Needs Code of Practice (DfE and DoH, 2015) makes clear that professionals should categorise children and young people according to the legal definition of special educational needs. SENCOs need therefore to make judgements about the identification of children and are required to organise pupils into a binary system of SEN and non-SEN (DfE and DoH, 2015). It is argued this kind of sorting applies an essentialist approach to SEN, necessitating assessment of children and young people's difficulties which are deemed to be located within the individual (Slee, 1997). However, as Ekins (2015:93) explains:

Definitions and understandings of 'SEN' vary widely, nationally, internationally, but also within local areas, and even within schools, where individual staff members may have widely differing understandings and interpretations of the term.

SENCOs' judgements about who to place on the SEN register are reliant on their own values and/or the school's understanding of SEN, which is situated in a web of meanings spun through discussion and consensus. For example, SENCOs' understanding of 'significantly greater difficulty' will vary dependent upon the environment and network in which the child or young person is situated. As Graham (2015:131) outlines, the identification of SEN is 'a product of funding and placement eligibility and the assumptions of the adults who teach, refer, and assess children who experience difficulties in school and with learning'. The term *special educational needs* lays at the heart of this complex web of discourses, located in a network of overlapping ideas and concepts. In this way, the concept of SEN can be viewed as the centre point of a 'language game'

(Wittgenstein, 2009:8), the term *special educational needs* gaining meaning from the way it is enacted in each school. Illustrative of this game, Wittgenstein (2009:8) points to descriptions of the duck/rabbit 'picture-object' (Figure 3.2).

Figure 3.2 Picture-object illustration – drawing of a rabbit/duck (Kihlstrom, 2020)

A person's gestalt-shift of the picture-object enables seeing both a duck and a rabbit. Just as the line drawing of the duck and the rabbit has features in common but can be looked at in two different ways, so the label of SEN can also be viewed from multiple perspectives. Unlike the value-laden labels of the past, such as 'idiot' or 'maladjusted', which point to a deficit analysis of disability, the term SEN can be aligned with several differing viewpoints dependent on the values of the organisation and/or individual. In this way schools, SENCOs and teachers of the late 20th to early 21st centuries can be viewed as having more agency over how the label SEN is applied than their historical counterparts had regarding application of the labels of disability in their day. The language of special educational needs can be understood therefore as a frame schools can build for their values, through which their policies, procedures and practices are contextualised.

When the term *special educational needs* was put forward by the Warnock committee (1978), a key hope was to remove the stigma associated with being labelled. The removal of the categories of handicap in favour of the term SEN does not, however, automatically herald the removal of stigma. Rather like a spider at the centre of a web, the use of the word 'special' depends on the web of language games to which it is connected. Wittgenstein (2009:51) describes this connectedness as a returning to the 'rough ground':

> We have got onto slippery ice where there is no friction, and so, in a certain sense, the conditions are ideal; but also, just because of that, we are unable to walk. We want to walk: so we need friction. Back to the rough ground!
>
> (Wittgenstein, 2009:51)

Viewing the word 'special' outside of its web is like being on the ice with no friction: the conditions seem ideal, but the surrounding void means a move back to the rough ground is both inevitable and necessary. In this instance, the web of the rough ground points to several challenges with the word 'special': firstly, its association with the word 'needs' and secondly, with the nature of the rough ground. Starting with the former, when put together the words 'special' and 'need' imply deficits which frame people's understanding of SEN (Runswick-Cole and Hodge, 2009). As Corbett (1996:3) explains:

> What does the word 'special' mean? If we detach this word from its anchor in 'educational' we can see that 'special' does not mean especially good and valued unless we use a phrase like, 'you are a special person'. It is linked to 'needs' which implies dependency, inadequacy and unworthiness.

Corbett's (1996) analysis of the term *special educational needs* clearly brings to the fore the question of whether removing the categories of handicap was the significant change it was heralded to be. Secondly, the web of the 'rough ground' (Wittgenstein, 2009:51) can also be viewed as the connective threads which spin out from the words 'special educational needs'. The rough ground of SEN being context (Ekins, 2015; Graham, 2015) and also narratives about SEN being a difficulty, tragedy or affirmation of the individual situated within models of disability, such as the social, medical or interactive models. The medical model focuses on disability as a medical problem to be fixed (Oliver, 1996); the social model throws light on the removal of barriers to disability through environmental change (Oliver, 1996); and the interactive model shows disability as an interaction between a person's impairment and the environment in which they are situated (WHO, 2001). Whilst the move from categories of handicap to special educational needs was clearly welcome, the meaning behind this change is only established when SEN is situated in the rough ground.

Like the label of special educational needs, the language of the rough ground (the connectedness of SEN) also gains meaning from the way in which words are used (Wittgenstein, 2009). For example, although SENCOs all share the same job title and the essence of their role is the same, their values and consequently their practice may vary enormously. This idea is exemplified in Wittgenstein's photograph in Figure 3.3 (Mustich, 2005):

Figure 3.3 Composite picture of Ludwig Wittgenstein

This is not a photograph of a person who existed, but rather it is a composite of four photographs that explore the family resemblance of Wittgenstein and his three sisters (Mustich, 2005; University of Cambridge, 2011), as seen in Figure 3.4.

Figure 3.4 Photos of Ludwig Wittgenstein (bottom left) and his three sisters

So while all the members of Wittgenstein's family resemble each other in the composite photo-graph, there are differences in distinguishing each individual from the other. However, when over-laid it is possible to see a different depiction of a person, someone who is extant as an image but has never existed as a living person. Each person's eye has a similar shape, comprising the same component parts: a pupil, an iris and a sclera. Each eye is set in the context of each individual's face, from which an image can be seen and interpreted as a face. Similarly, different SENCOs have analogous roles, many of the component parts of their jobs being the same: the develop-ment of school policy and the co-ordination of additional support for children and young people (Peterson, 2010). The requirements of English legislation (Children and Families Act, 2014:67) and the statutory guidance provided by the Special Educational Needs and Disability Code of Practice: 0–25 (DfE and DoH, 2015) ensure that the 'family resemblances' of the SENCO role are maintained across settings. That said, whilst there are similar aspects to each SENCO's role, there will be differences in the day-to-day enactment of policy, its impact on the school culture and the provision made for children and young people. These differences are enactments of the meaning each SENCO attributes to the label SEN and the surrounding rough ground. The label of SEN that each SENCO applies is the same on the face of it; however, the meaning attributed may be very different (Ekins, 2015), speaking as much about a school as the children within it.

The concept of 'family resemblances' provides a holistic view and a way of seeing that allows for conflicting models of special education and disability to be explored. Take, for example, the debates around the models of special education and disability presented by Anastasiou and Kauffman (2010) versus Gallagher, Connor and Ferri (2014). These protagonists in the explora-tion of the medical and social models of special educational needs and disability are engaged in their own language games with some common ground.

The first threads of the social model in the United Kingdom were started in the discussions of the Union of the Physically Impaired Against Segregation (UPIAS) and The Disability Alliance in 1976:

> It is society which disables physically impaired people. Disability is something imposed on top of our impairments, by the way we are unnecessarily isolated and excluded from full participation in society.
>
> (UPIAS, 1976:3)

This reframing of the language used to conceptualise disability meant it was the environment and societal attitudes that 'dis-abled' an individual and that, in spite of an impairment, a person could now be 'en-abled' to overcome 'barriers to learning and participation' (Booth and Ainscow, 2016:23). A person no longer had to be ostensively labelled as 'disabled'. Oliver (1983) drew on the work of UPIAS (1976) to name this new way of conceptualising disability as 'the social model'. In this model an individual is 'disabled' by the context in which they find themselves.

Anastasiou and Kauffman (2013:443–444) contend that identified disabilities have 'legitimate factual reference and are approximations of scientific truth', whereas Gallagher, Connor and Ferri (2014:1134) advocate the social model asserting that:

> We can have our descriptions of people and their 'predicaments' if it means that we recog-nise human needs. In making these descriptions we need also to affirm that what we take as a predicament is fundamentally conditioned by culture and context.

Both arguments resemble each other in the acknowledgement the individual can be said to have a 'need', but Gallagher, Connor and Ferri's (2014) rough ground and web of meaning is reliant on the social context in which someone's needs are defined, whereas Anastasiou and Kauff-man's (2013) web of meaning relies on measuring, grading and ranking an individual without reference to the environmental context. Oliver (2004) developed the two models further by con-sidering how one might interact with the other. Outlining the criticisms of the social model, Oliver (2004) acknowledges there is a risk the impact of an impairment might be minimised by a rigid adherence to the social model but contends the social model is firmly embedded in the lived experiences of disabled activists in the 1970s. The World Health Organisation's (2001) definition, whereby a person's functioning and disability is conceptualised as an interaction between their health conditions and contextual factors, brings these two models together like Wittgenstein's (2009) family resemblances.

Wittgenstein's (2009) construct of language games, rough ground and family resemblance provides a lens through which to understand the duplicitous nature of special educational needs and shines a light on the range of ways SENCOs enact the role. Focusing specifically on the concept of a family resemblance, the medical model of SEN with its positivist identification of need may be balanced with the social model, whereby an individual's needs are defined by the context/environment in which they find themselves and not by an intrinsic set of attributes. As Pumphrey (2010:6) states, 'subjective judgements concerning the labelling and categorisation of individuals and groups represent an ever present potential educational danger: the oversimplification of complex concerns'. For this reason, it is important that a school works to develop a shared understanding of what the term *special education* means and how this interpretation is effectively captured in the school's values, expectations, assumptions, responses and practice.

Conclusion

In conclusion, the values underpinning schools' practice shape the meaning of their language and conversely their culture and policies. Pre-1978 the language used to refer to disability was value laden with dehumanising constructs and perceptions of problems, burden, deficit, tragedy and charity. The rough ground surrounding terminology such as 'imbecile' and 'maladjusted' lead to both segregation and stigmatisation. When the Warnock committee abolished the categories of handicap in favour of the term *special educational needs*, the rationale focused on challenges associated with labelling (Warnock, 1978:3.23). Since that time, the term *special educational needs* has been criticised for reinforcing constructs of inadequacy and unworthiness (Corbett, 1996).

As this chapter has shown, the language of disability (physical and learning) has shape-shifted, altering through time (Goodey, 2016), and it seems highly likely that future legislative changes will bring more changes to the language of SEN. For example, both Scottish and Welsh legislation has replaced the term SEN with additional support needs (ASN) and additional learning needs (ALN), respectively. By considering the language games (Wittgenstein, 2009) associated with the terminology used to describe SEN, there is an opportunity to impact thinking and attitudes towards children and young people in educational settings. Like the duck/rabbit picture-object, special educational needs can be viewed in a number of ways. The term does not sit in isolation but is located within the rough ground, connected to values, assumptions, responses and practice. These complexities can be challenging and highly problematic to a school, but unlike the value-laden labels of the past, they do create a need for school leaders to open up discussions around a shared understanding of SEN. As part of a school's development, discussions led by the SENCO and senior leadership team could consider the language games played in a setting and the associated rough ground. Subsequently, a school could agree on a common understanding of the terminology used within their cultures, policies and practices. As Wittgenstein's biographer, Monk (1990:65), wrote:

> We need to look at the problems afresh, as it were from a different angle . . . we do not need a new discovery, we do not need a new explanation and we do not need a new theory; what we need is a new perspective, a new metaphor, a new picture.

Acknowledgment

The photo of Lucy Stone has been provided by Julie Wharton. Lucy Stone was born in 1920, she is Julie Wharton's paternal grandmother. Labelled as an 'invalid' Lucy spent much of her childhood in Evelina Hospital in London.

Reflective questions

- Are there any SEND terminology, values and practices from the present day which in 50 years' time may come to be viewed as dehumanising, speaking the language of problems, deficits and tragedy?
- Focusing on two SENCOs with different language games (i.e. different value systems and assumptions about SEND and inclusion), identify the distinctions between the rough ground their practice operates within.
- What does an examination of the language used in SEN information reports, school policies and websites and SEND meetings (both formal and informal) reveal?

References

Anastasiou, D. and Kauffman, J. (2010) Disability as a cultural difference: Implications for special education. *Remedial and Special Education*, 33(3), 139–149.

Anastasiou, D. and Kauffman, J. (2013) The social model of disability: Dichotomy between impairment and disability. *The Journal of Medicine and Philosophy*, 38(4), 441–459.

Armstrong, D. (2003) *Experiences of Special Education: Re-evaluating Policy and Practice Through Life Stories*. London: Routledge.

Arnold. J. (1964) *Slow Learners at School, DES Pamphlet, No 46*. London: HMSO.

Booth, T. and Ainscow, M. (2016) *The Index for Inclusion: A Guide to School Development Led by Inclusive Values*. Bristol: Centre for Studies on Inclusive Education.

Bringham, L. (2000) Understanding segregation from the nineteenth to the twentieth century: Redrawing boundaries and the problems of 'pollution'. In Bringham, L., Atkinson, D., Jackson, M., Rolph, S. and Walmsley, J. (eds.), *Crossing Boundaries Change and Continuity in History of Learning Disability*. Kidderminster: BILD, 27–42.

Children and Families Act 2014, Part 3:67. London: Her Majesty's Stationery Office.

Corbett, J. (1996) *Badmouthing: The Language of Special Educational Needs*. London: Falmer Press.

Department for Education (1994) *Code of Practice on the Identification and Assessment of Special Educational Needs (SEN)*. London: DfE.

Department for Education and Department of Health (2015) *The Special Educational Needs and Disability Code of Practice: 0 to 25 Years*. London: DfE and DoH.

Department for Education and Skills (2001) *Special Educational Needs Code of Practice*. London: DfES.

Education Act 1944. London: His Majesty's Stationery Office.

Education Act 1981. London: Her Majesty's Stationery Office.

Education Act 1993. London: Her Majesty's Stationery Office.

Egan, K. (2002) *Getting it Wrong from the Beginning: Our Progressivist Inheritance from Herbert Spencer, John Dewey and Jean Piaget*. New Haven and London: Yale University Press.

Ekins, A. (2015) *The Changing Face of Special Educational Needs: Impact and Implications for SENCOs, Teachers and Their Schools*. London: Routledge.

Fido, R. and Potts, M. (2003) Using oral histories. In Atkinson, D., Jackson, M. and Walmsley, J. (eds.), *Forgotten Lives: Exploring the History of Learning Disability*. Kidderminster: BILD, 35–46.

Gallagher, D., Connor, D. and Ferri, B. (2014) Beyond the far too incessant schism: Special education and the social model of disability. *International Journal of Inclusive Education*, 18(11), 1120–1142.

Goodey, C. (2016) *Learning Disability and Inclusion Phobia: Past, Present and Future*. Abingdon: Routledge.

Goodman, J. (2005) Pedagogy and sex: Mary Dendy (1855–1933), feeble-minded girls and the Sandlebridge schools, 1902–33. *History of Education*, 34(2), 171–187.

Graham, L. (2015) A little learning is a dangerous thing: Factors influencing the increased identification of special educational needs from the perspective of education policy-makers and school practitioners. *International Journal of Disability, Development and Education*, 62(1), 116–132.

Humphries, S. and Gordon, P. (1992) *Out of Sight: Experience of Disability, 1900–50*. Tavistock: Northcote House.

Hurt, W. (1988) *Outside the Mainstream: A History of Special Education*, London: Batsford.

Jack, A. (2004) *Red Herrings and White Elephants: The Origins of the Phrases We Use Every Day*. London: Metro.

Kevles, D. (1995) *In the Name of Eugenics: Genetics and the Uses of Human Heredity*. New York: Harvard University Press.

Kihlstrom, J. (2020) *Joseph Jastrow and His Duck – Or Is It a Rabbit?* Available at: www.ocf.berkeley.edu/~jfkihlstrom/JastrowDuck.htm [Accessed 18.08.20].

Lamb, B. (2009) *Lamb Inquiry: Special Educational Needs and Parental Confidence*. Nottingham: Department for Children Schools and Families (DCFS).

Levine, P. and Bashford, A. (2010) Introduction: Eugenics and the modern world. In Bashford, A. and Levine, P. (eds.), *The Oxford Handbook of the History of Eugenics*. Oxford: Oxford University Press, 3–24.

Mallett, R., and Slater, J. (2014) Language. In Cameron, C. (ed.), *Disability Studies: A Student's Guide*. London: Sage, 91–94.

McLaren, A. (1990) *Our Own Master Race: Eugenics in Canada, 1885–1945*. Toronto: McClelland and Stewart.

Mental Deficiency Act 1913. London: His Majesty's Stationery Office.

Ministry of Education (1945) *The Nation's Schools: Their Plan and Purpose, Pamphlet No.1*. London: His Majesty's Stationery Office.

Monk, R. (1990) *Ludwig Wittgenstein: The Duty of Genius*. London: Jonathan Cape.

Mustich, E. (2005) *Which Leading 20th Century Philosopher Took this Photo?* Available at: www.salon.com/2011/07/08/wittgenstein_photographs/ [Accessed 19.06.20].

Oliver, M. (1983) *Social Work with Disabled People*. Basingstoke: Macmillan.

Oliver, M. (1996) *Understanding Disability: From Theory to Practice*. New York: St. Martin's Press.

Oliver, M. (2004) The social model in action: If I had a hammer. In Barnes, C. and Mercer, G. (eds.), *Implementing the Social Model of Disability: Theory and Research*. Leeds: The Disability Press, 18–31.

Peterson, L. (2010) A national perspective on the training of SENCOs. In Hallett, G. and Hallett, F. (eds.), *Transforming the Role of the SENCO: Achieving the National Award for SEN Co-ordination*. Maidenhead: McGraw-Hill/Open University Press, 12–23.

Plowden, B. (1967) *Children and Their Primary Schools: A Report of the Central Advisory Council for Education (England)*. Vol. 1. London: HMSO.

Pumphrey, P. (2010) United Kingdom special educational needs (SEN) 2010: Reflections and current concerns. *The Psychology of Education Review*, 34(2), 3–12.

Reilly, P. (1991) *The Surgical Solution: A History of Involuntary Sterilisation in the United States*. Baltimore: Johns Hopkins University Press.

Rieser, R. (2007) Lest we forget: The useless eaters in the Third Reich. *Inclusion Now Magazine*, 17(Summer), 14–15.

Runswick-Cole, K. and Hodge, N. (2009) Needs or rights? A challenge to the discourse of special education. *British Journal of Special Education*, 36(4), 198–203.

Slee, R. (1997) Imported or important theory? Sociological interrogations of disablement and special education. *British Journal of Sociology of Education*, 18(3), 407–419.

Spencer, H. (1911) *Essays on Education and Kindred Subjects*. London: Dent; New York: Dutton.

Thomas, G. and Loxley, A. (2007) *Deconstructing Special Education and Constructing Inclusion*. 2nd edn. Maidenhead: Open University Press.

Union of the Physically Impaired Against Segregation (1976) *Fundamental Principles of Disability*. London: The Disability Alliance.

University of Cambridge (2011) *Wittgenstein's Camera*. Available at: *www.cam.ac.uk/research/news/wittgenstein's-camera* [Accessed 08.11.15].

Warnock, M. (1978) *Special Educational Needs: Report of the Committee of Enquiry into the Education of Handicapped Children and Young People*. London: Her Majesty's Stationery Office.

Wittgenstein, L. (2009) *Philosophical Investigations: The German Text, with an English Translation by G. E. M. Anscombe, P. M. S. Hacker and Joachim Schulte*. London: Wiley-Blackwell.

World Health Organization (WHO) (2001) *International Classification of Functioning, Disability and Health (ICF)*. Available at: www.who.int/classifications/icf/en/ [Accessed 20.07.20].

4   The SENCO as a leader of professional learning for inclusive practice

Deborah Robinson

Introduction

This chapter explores the theory and practice of professional development for inclusive practice. The SENCO's remit to 'inspire inclusive practice' (Wharton, Codina, Middleton and Esposito, 2019:16) through leading teacher learning and continuing professional development (CPD) is theoretically framed, in this chapter, within *epistemologies of difference* and *ontologies of change*. This is to ensure that the challenges of this remit are treated with the depth they demand. The chapter defends *practice inquiry* for transformational teacher development towards inclusion. Using the example of lesson study, it explores practice inquiry as a form of CPD of value to SENCOs. A core argument in the chapter is that practice inquiry has the capacity to loosen unhelpful, obdurate paradigms of learning difficulty with positive consequences for practice. The purpose of the chapter is to provide a meaningful framework for SENCOs to theorise their CPD remit and how it might be implemented to make inclusion more enduringly manifest in the classroom.

'To know' and 'to be' for inclusive practice: ontological and epistemological approaches to difficulty in learning

In order to theorise about the role of the SENCO as a leader of professional learning for inclusive practice, it is important to begin with some clarification of terms. What is meant by the term ontology in the construct *ontologies of change* and what is meant by the term epistemology in the construct *epistemologies of differences*? Though these terms are abstract, they can be explained quite simply. Ontology means the study of existence. Ontological study focusses on what it means to exist and what is in the world. Ontology asks about the material of reality and how this material can be labelled and classified. To support further explanation, we will consider two broad ontological positions on the nature of reality, *constructionism* and *objectivism*. Constructionism models reality as fluid and temporary. Reality is co-constructed by social actors who reproduce knowledge in the form of 'regimes of truth' bonded to the political and cultural fetters of their time (Foucault, 1973). For example, this position on reality would demand that we observe the concepts 'disability' or 'autism' or even 'special educational needs' as temporary realities which emerge through service to dominant ideas or systems in society. Timini (2011:5) adopts a constructionist ontology to describe autism as

> a catch-all metaphor for a disparate range of behaviours that suggest a lack of the type of social and emotional competences thought to be necessary for societies dominated by neo-liberal, economic and political foundations.

Here, Timini is presenting autism, not as a stable or objective reality, but as an artefact of capitalism where individuals who do not present as the 'ideal' worker are separated out to be dealt with in a system that cannot integrate them. From this viewpoint, 'disability', 'autism' and 'special educational needs' are revealed as illusions of truth when they are viewed outside their contemporary milieu. In contrast, the ontological position of objectivism identifies realities (including social phenomena) as stable and absolute. Reality exists independently of social actors being independent of their influence. From the ontological position of objectivism, autism (or disability or SEND) have not been *brought into existence* to serve the purpose of dominant social actors but *discovered to exist* by an objective method, one that is scientific, rational and replicable. To add further illustration, we can imagine a conversation between a child and an adult. The child asks, 'Does autism exist?' and the adult adopts a constructionist ontology to respond, 'Well, the answer to your question is a bit complicated because even though we have the word 'autism' and we use it a lot, autism is different for everyone so your autism is very, very individual and special.' With the child's repetition of the question, the next response is, 'Well, it is an interesting question because some people say that the word autism won't be around forever because, in the future, being autistic won't be seen as something different that needs a special name, and there might come a time when people who are not autistic have a label instead because they don't fit as well as people who are autistic.' After the twentieth iteration of the question, 'But does autism exist?' the adult is exasperated to the point of responding, 'Yes, it does exist' to which the child says, 'Why?' and the adults says, 'Because it just *does*, okay?' At this point, perhaps out of having many other things to do, the adult adopts an objectivist position. Of course, it is unfair to present objectivist positions as the last resort or as the easy way out because much hard-won knowledge about learning difficulty has emerged from objectivism and positivist research. It is also fair to say that objectivist or interpretivist positions on autism can serve as false dualities when applied to the real world and its complexities. For example, some individuals signified by autism may need the additional educational and social care support that often depends on a diagnosis that is perceived as objective. Additionally, objective acknowledgement of impairment is experienced as affirming and helpful for some people. When it comes down to it, the real world is rife with political struggle, and objectivist approaches can deliver certainties in ways that can be used to claim recognition and influence. However, such certainties are equally likely to be unhelpful because they can confirm an illusion of generality, which in the case of autism may lead to assumptions being made about an individual learner that are neither true nor helpful. With all of this complexity recognised, what is epistemology and how does it relate to ontologies and the issue of inclusive practice?

Epistemology is the study of knowledge, what knowledge is, what it means to 'know,' how we know and how we can come to know more. For these reasons, epistemology is a matter of special relevance to a SENCO who is leading professional development for inclusion, because these processes are centred on knowledge. A *positivist epistemology* emerges from an ontologically objectivist position. This means that the aim is to investigate social phenomena so that generalisable truths can be discovered and put to use. Positivist studies adopt a scientific method to test hypotheses through control of variables. An example of this would be the diagnostic criteria for autism in, for example, the *Diagnostic Statistical Manual*, 5th edition (American Psychiatric Association, 2013). Through standardised testing and clinical observations, a set of agreed criteria are developed and then used to form a 'reliable' diagnosis of a condition that exists. However, a constructionist would argue that the diagnosis itself is a subjective interpretation of a presenting reality. For constructionist ontologies, knowledge is framed as perception and what we know is a consequence of our subjective experiences of the world. For this reason, constructionists investigate reality through using a broadly *interpretivist* approach, with an interest in how social actors construct their world and experience it. There is interest in the specific case over the general one. When applied to the design of inclusive pedagogy, a teacher situated in a constructivist ontology and an interpretivist epistemology may start by asking, 'How does Georgia see the world, how do I teach Georgia and how is this going to operate in this classroom and school at this time?' Whereas a teacher who adopts an objectivist ontology and a positivist epistemology to disability may begin with the general question, 'How do I teach a learner diagnosed with autism like Georgia and what does the evidence say about effective teaching of this group?' Both questions can yield useful ways forward, and to be clear, this chapter does not argue for the elimination of one and the retention of the other since such dualism might not be helpful (Lewis and Norwich, 2004). Rather, in what follows, it argues that a constructivist, interpretivist pedagogic paradigm, if foregrounded, is more likely to result in inclusive practice. It offers this argument because it is relevant to how a SENCO might approach professional learning for inclusion and the types of learning processes they might choose.

Epistemologies of difference and professional learning for inclusion

To support the claim that when a constructionist, interpretive paradigm is our starting position, inclusive practice is more likely, we turn to insights from research. Jordan, Schwartz and McGhie-Richmond (2009) present the findings of a large-scale, Canadian research and development project, 'Supporting Effective Teaching.' The authors use the idea of *epistemologies of difference* to explore teacher readiness for inclusive practice and how this readiness might be enhanced through teacher preparation and development programmes. The concept *epistemologies of difference* refers to the mental maps or schemata that teachers use to understand learning difficulty and their relationship to it as practitioners. To identify types of schemata among

32 elementary teachers, Jordan *et al.* (2009) used an epistemological scale called the *pathognomic-interventionist (P-I) scale* and applied this to their analysis of open-ended interviews where teachers narrated the stories of two students with SENDs that they had worked with. The interviews were transcribed and coded by multiple independent scorers to identify what epistemological positions on learning difficulty were being adopted – interventionist, pathognomic or somewhere in between. They combined this with third-party classroom observation schedules to understand the relationship between epistemologies of difference and actions in the classroom. They found that where teachers were operating a pathognomic paradigm, they were likely to construct learning difficulty as organic and individualised with an 'inside-the-learner' locus. This linked, schematically, to an assumption that difficulties in learning are caused by impairment and that impairment is absolute and fixed and hence, beyond the thrall of social actors (such as the teachers) or social systems (such as curricula). In this way, a *pathognomic epistemology for learning difficulty* is influenced by an objectivist, positivist paradigm. In practice, this translates to 'Georgia is having difficulty learning because of her autism' with autism perceived as unreachable and intransigent even in the face of pedagogic efforts to impact it. Jordan *et al.* (2009) found that teachers who operated a pathognomic epistemology had lower self-efficacy for working with pupils with special needs. Consequently, they were less likely to take responsibility for learners with SEND, frequently referring them for support outside the classroom or expecting parents to do the necessary catch-up work outside school. They were also less likely to collaborate with parents and other professionals. When looking at the link between a pathognomic paradigm and practice, this paradigm was related to a preference for transmission styles of teaching, more use of tests as the basis of assessment, less ownership for children and less interaction between the teacher and children with SENDs. Less effective use of lesson time and less engagement with learning among pupils were also more likely where teachers held a pathognomic perspective.

In contrast, where teachers enacted *interventionist epistemology of difference*, they assumed that impairment was fluid and that learning potential was transformable, translating in practice to 'Georgia is having difficulty in learning because of the teaching approach, the curriculum and her experience of the classroom'. Such schemata construct models of reality such that social actors (like teachers) and social systems (like classrooms, schools and curricula) influence learning abilities in ways that can *include impairment that then transcend it*. This logic then promotes formative assessment as an essential tool for inclusion (Florian and Beaton, 2018). Jordan *et al.* (2009) found that where teachers took an interventionist perspective, they were more likely to collaborate with others, more likely to use continuous formative assessment as a shaper for their planning, more likely to use constructivist teaching approaches, more likely to give their pupils responsibilities and more likely to spend time with children with SENDs engaging in deeper learning interactions. They also used lesson time more efficiently and had better learning outcomes. Characteristic was the tendency to take responsibility for all learners and to feel stronger self-efficacy for teaching learners with SENDs. The researchers concluded that an interventionist epistemology was associated with more effective teaching generally and with more effective inclusive teaching for SEND because of its fluidity and assumption of transformability. They propose that models of teacher learning should be targeted at promoting an interventionist epistemology of difference, noting that it is very challenging to shift teachers from pathognomic schemata for learning difficulty. This signals a key challenge for SENCOs given that their remit involves supporting the classroom teachers in taking responsibility for pedagogy and outcomes for SEND.

> The class or subject teacher should remain responsible for working with the child on a daily basis. Here the interventions involve group or one-to-one teaching away from the main class or subject teacher, they should still retain responsibility for the pupil.
>
> (DfE and DoH, 2015:101)

Our argument so far suggests that supporting the class teacher in being more inclusive is not simply a matter of developing practice but also demands some attention to attitude change. The idea that inclusive practice demands the kind of fluidity of thought and action present in an interventionist epistemology is promoted in wider research. This is explored in what follows.

Ontologies of change and professional learning for inclusion

Researchers have sought to understand why some schools are more inclusive than others, and the findings of such studies cast light on the place of professional learning in this dynamic. They can alert us to matters of ethos and change management that are of importance to the SENCO remit for leading learning. In what follows, we will abridge the findings of several important studies spanning 2001 to 2017 to find patterns of interest to the theme of professional learning for inclusion.

Corbett (2001) provides an important account of the 'inclusive school' in her study of Harbinger primary school in London. Her proposal of 'Connected Pedagogy' presents a model of teaching that is fluid, social-constructivist, participatory and informed by continuous collaborative learning by practitioners who are connected to each other and their community. Researchers from Canada (Villa and Thousand, 2005, 2017) and Sautner (2008) identify similar phenomena to include flexible models of support and grouping and a shared belief that all learners can learn, are of value and can make a contribution to the school community. This is supported by Black-Hawkins, Florian and Rouse (2007, 2017), who offer a *Framework for Participation* as a basis for understanding how change and professional development must be centred on the pursuit of maximal participation for all through unrelenting attention to who is in and who is out to ensure inclusion. All of the studies propose a fluid ontology for change and development in recognising that at the heart of the inclusive school is an endless cycle of learning catalysed by the challenge of teaching diverse students, a population that is infinitely diverse and infinitely transforming (Darling-Hammond, 2006). The essential place of relationships is also emphasised:

> Above all, relationships – among students, among staff and between staff and students are at the heart of understanding and developing inclusion in school. This is not to promote a naïve or sentimental approach but to acknowledge that teaching and learning take place within the context of human relationships.
>
> (Black-Hawkins *et al.*, 2007:3)

With this emphasis on human relationships, Black-Hawkins *et al.* (2017) settle on a constructionist ontology for change, one that frames reality as subjective and socially constructed through the interaction of social actors with social systems. This notion is also supported by Clark, Dyson and Millward (2020), who argue that the project of educating all students within a common framework is inevitably problematic and cannot be resolved through the discovery of general, transferable, 'off-the-shelf' solutions. Inclusive outcomes are the result of a constant dialectic where the needs of one group must be balanced (or traded) against the needs of another in a complex social and political space. In this sense then, any conception of a learning culture for inclusion demands acceptance of dilemma and imperfection. Where professional learning is set within a constructivist ontology to frame inclusive practice as a process rather than an end goal, teachers are more likely to embrace its challenges than to settle in the refuge of pathognomic paradigms (Robinson, 2015). With this understood, what forms of CPD may create the right conditions for fluid professional learning in pursuit of interpretivist, interventionist models epistemologies of learning difficulty? Consideration of this practical question for SENCOs and leaders of inclusion follows.

Practice inquiry as an opportunity for a pedagogic turn towards more fluid models of learning difficulty

Pantic and Florian (2015) ask us to recognise teachers as complex agents of change who operate in highly contextualised ways to imagine alternative practices or to maintain the status quo. In this way, teachers, 'cannot simply be regulated to do things differently' (Pantic and Florian, 2015:337). The challenge of transforming *epistemologies of difference* must be met with more collaborative, participatory, contextualised and practice-oriented forms of professional learning than those associated with performance management. Wharton *et al.* (2019) summarise a range of approaches that the SENCO can deploy when leading CPD to include coaching, mentoring, joint planning, co-teaching and lesson study. All of these involve working together in context to bring about transformations of practice. In what follows, we take the specific case of lesson study to explore how it can be implemented and why it is a good vehicle for loosening the grip of pathognomic epistemologies through attitude change within a constructivist ontology of change.

Firstly, it is important to note that an authentic version of lesson study does not focus on teaching competence and so does not serve as a tool for performance management. Lesson study, in its authentic form, focusses on the learning of specific pupils in specific contexts. Where there is support for this approach (both philosophically and operationally) by senior leaders, it has been found to strengthen three pathways to learning improvement: teachers' pedagogic knowledge, teachers' commitment to pedagogic improvement through a learning community and developments to the quality of learning resources (Dudley, 2014). Lesson study is a form of systematic inquiry that can unravel assumptions about pupils with SEND and their impairment label, which is an important vehicle for inclusive practice. Assumptions drawn from labels 'can lead to teaching that is poorly pitched' (Norwich and Jones, 2014:30) because of subliminal categorisation and too much dependence on pre-formed, impairment-specific pedagogic programmes. Most importantly, lesson study's evidence-based approach means that teachers see learners with SENDs with fresh eyes to develop more nuanced schemata about their needs and capabilities (Dudley, 2014) to challenge pathognomic epistemologies of difference.

To offer further insight into the opportunities that lesson study offers, it is important to review its methodology. Though there are many ways that it can unfold, key steps in the methodology, as it can be applied to SEND (and all learners), are as follows:

- A teaching team review the learning, participation and progress of one or more learners with SEND in a specific learning context (e.g. a subject area), identifying an area of practice that needs improvement in order to improve the learners' experience.
- After using this process to identify an area for improvement, the collaborating team seek expertise on the area from research literature, practitioner literature, experts local to them and experts within the school (perhaps other teachers who have completed a lesson study in a similar area).
- Having collated and reflected on this area, the teaching team plan a lesson collaboratively, to improve the learning experience and progress of the pupil/group of pupils. The plan includes an account of what the pupil(s) will do or achieve at different stages of the lesson. For example, it might be that a pupil will 'initiate a learning interaction with another pupil' or that the pupil will 'model the concept of friction through mark making' at a specific stage of the lesson (e.g. in the plenary, in an independent activity).
- One member of the collaborating team will teach the lesson, while the others observe, recording their observations systematically on a pre-agreed format that tracks the pupil(s)' responses at each stage of the planned lesson. The recordings focus on what the pupil does/does not do and what the pupil learns/does not learn at various stages of the learning experience. The aim is to observe whether the pupil does experience the positive gains intended in the planning (e.g. to progress, social inclusion, depth of learning).
- As soon as possible after the lesson, the team pool their multiple perspectives to understand the flow of learning and teaching such that they can form hypotheses about effective inclusive practices for the focus pupil(s) in this context. This is repeated over a short sequence of two or three lessons, with different configurations of teacher/observer to include co-teaching. The teaching team commit to the pedagogic transformations for inclusion that have emerged as most promising for the specific pupil(s). Ideally, these hypotheses also take account of the pupil(s)' own reflections on the learning sequence.

An essential feature of this approach is that it is collaborative. It also supports teachers in using contextualised approaches to assessment of the pupil(s)' strengths and weaknesses such that they might override assumption. As a process, lesson study brings in different perspectives to enable biases or absolute conceptions to be challenged. This also contributes to a deeper, more nuanced view of a learner such that 'a teacher can discern learning needs more accurately' (Norwich and Jones, 2014) and in ways that transcend deterministic views of impairment. The approach has also supported more risk-taking and imagination because teachers feel less threatened within its collegial, collaborative milieu (Godfrey, Seleznyov, Anders, Wollaston and Barrera-Pedemonte, 2018). For these reasons, lesson study offers an opportunity for deep professional learning and can be a scaffold for developing interventionist epistemologies of difference because it challenges fixed ideas about learning difficulty and reveals the way social actors and systems influence the pupils' experience of school.

However, an approach like lesson study has several challenges since it relies on the support of senior leaders, not least because it demands changes to staff workloads and timetables. The challenge for SENCOs here is not underestimated because deep professional learning for inclusion demands a shift from the workshop or inset approach to understanding SENDs (e.g. development days about autism or dyslexia) to one of situated learning synchronous with the core business of the school during a school day. However, where teacher learning is seen as parallel core business, the SENCO will be able to design and implement forms of professional learning that are more likely to bring about lasting change for inclusion.

Conclusion

This chapter has explored *epistemologies of difference* and *ontologies of change* as mediators in professional development for inclusion. Its purpose was to offer a theoretical framework for understanding the principles and purposes of professional learning for inclusion. Within this framework, the deconstruction of a pathognomic epistemology of learning difference was presented as a key target for the CPD that SENCOs may enact within their remit. The chapter has offered a nuanced model for teacher development for inclusion by emphasising the fluidity of pedagogy and the fluidity of impairment. It is a call for CPD rooted in practice but formed through intellectual engagement with the philosophy of difference and philosophy of change. It calls for less dependence on generalisable certainties and more focus on what is specific and unique, and in so doing, models teachers as expert enquirers who can find solutions to the challenges of inclusion in their own hands, hearts and minds. The challenge for leaders of inclusion is to build the ethos and strategies for CPD that allow them to do so.

Reflective questions

- How might SENCOs work with other senior leaders to create opportunities for collaborative professional learning?
- How could the impact of increased collaborative professional learning be evaluated?
- How can SENCOs, as leaders of learning, work in collaborative professional learning activities with others within and beyond school?

References

American Psychiatric Association (2013) *Diagnostic and Statistical Manual of Mental Disorders* (5th ed.). Washington, DC: Author.

Black-Hawkins, K., Florian, L. and Rouse, M. (2007) *Achievement and Inclusion in Schools*. London: Routledge.

Black-Hawkins, K., Florian, L. and Rouse, M. (2017) *Achievement and Inclusion in Schools* (2nd ed.). London: Routledge.

Clark, C., Dyson, A. and Millward, A. (2020) *Towards Inclusive Schools* (2nd ed.). London: Routledge.

Corbett, J. (2001) *Supporting Inclusive Education: A Connected Pedagogy*. London: Routledge Falmer.

Darling-Hammond, L. (2006) Constructing 21st century teacher education. *Journal of Techer Education*, 57(3), 300–314.

Department for Education and Department of Health (2015) *The Special Educational Needs and Disability Code of Practice, 0–25 Years*. London: DfE and DoH.

Dudley, P. (2014) The general rationale and underlying principles of lesson study. In Norwich, B. and Jones, J. (eds.), *Lesson Study: Making a Difference to Teaching Pupils with Learning Difficulties*. London: Bloomsbury, 15–33.

Florian, L. and Beaton, M. C. (2018) Inclusive pedagogy in action: Getting it right for every child. *International Journal of Inclusive Education*, 22(8), 870–884.

Foucault, M. (1973) *Birth of the Clinic*. London: Bloomsbury.

Godfrey, D., Seleznyov, S., Anders, J., Wollaston, N. and Barrera-Pedemonte, F. (2018) A developmental evaluation approach to lesson study: Exploring the impact of lesson study in London schools. *Professional Development in Education*, 45(2), 325–340.

Jordan, A., Schwartz, E. and McGhie-Richmond, D. (2009) Preparing teachers for inclusive classrooms. *Teaching and Teacher Education*, 25(3), 535–542.

Lewis, A. and Norwich, B. (2004) *Special Teaching for Special Children? Pedagogies for Inclusion*. London: David Fulton.

Norwich, B. and Jones, J. (2014) *Lesson Study: Making a Difference to Teaching Pupils with Learning Difficulties*. London: Bloomsbury.

Pantic, N. and Florian, L. (2015) Developing teachers as agents of inclusion and social justice. *Education Inquiry*, 6(3), 333–335.

Robinson, D. (2015) The difficulty with inclusive pedagogy in teacher education: Some more thought on the way forward. *Teaching and Teacher Education*, 61, 164–178.

Sautner, S. (2008) Inclusive safe and caring schools: Connecting factors. *Developmental Disabilities Bulletin*, 36(1–2), 135–167.

Timini, S. (2011) *The Myth of Autism*. London: McMillan.

Villa, R. and Thousand, V. (eds.) (2005) *Creating an Inclusive School*. Alexandria, VA: Association for Supervision and Curriculum Development.

Villa, R. and Thousand, J. (2017) *Leading an Inclusive School: Access and Success for All*. Alexandria, VA: Association for Supervision and Curriculum Development.

Wharton, J. Codina, G. Middleton, T. and Esposito, R. (2019) *SENCO Induction Pack: Supporting the Start of Your Journey*. London: Department of Education. Available at: https://nasen.org.uk [Accessed 16.04.20].

5   The future of SEND Legislation in England

What next?

Brian Lamb

The Children's and Families Act 2014 sought to address perceived deficiencies in the Warnock framework for Special Educational Needs and Disability (SEND).[1] Reviews from statutory agencies (Ofsted, 2020; NAO, 2019; LGSCO, 2019), the House of Commons Education Select Committee (HCESC, 2019) and Public Accounts Committee (HCPAC, 2020), teacher organisations (NAHT, 2018; NASWUT, 2018), and parental and advocacy groups (National Autistic Society *et al.*, 2017) have all questioned how far the legislation is meeting its objectives, while recognising that elements of the reforms have been positive (Adams *et al.*, 2017; NAO, 2019).[2] As a result the Department for Education (DfE) has instigated a review of the reforms for the incoming government (DfE and Williamson, 2019). The review has also been caught up in the response to COVID-19 (DfE, 2020a). Options for change range from alterations to policy and guidance to undertaking a more substantial revision of the legislation (Lamb, 2019). Central to the implementation of the reforms is how far change can be achieved by ensuring that culture and practice aligns with the reforms aspirations, or is additional legislation, regulation and guidance required?

The reforms – EHCPs

The main structural change of the 2014 reforms replaced Statements of SEN with Education, Health and Care Plans (EHCPs) to secure a more personalised, outcome-focused and integrated assessment of need followed by more joined-up provision. EHCPs continue to be triggered by an educational need with a requirement to consider health and social care provision through a joint assessment of need. However, the right to appeal to the First Tier Tribunal – SEND jurisdiction, which enforces the legal entitlements contained in the EHCP, was not extended to health and social care provision. This has led to criticisms that the underlying legal structure of the Warnock framework was not altered to support the changes sought by the new multi-agency assessment regime (Norwich, 2014; Norwich and Eaton, 2015).

Since moving from Statements of SEND to EHCPs, the number of statutory assessments has increased by 64%, from 237,111 statements in 2014 to 390,109 children and young people with EHCPs as of January 2020 (DfE, 2020b). While, for the school population, the percentage of pupils with an EHCP has risen to 3.3% (294,800) of the total pupil population from 3.1% (271,200) in 2019 and 2.9% in 2018, after remaining constant at 2.8% from 2007 to 2017 (DfE, 2020c, 2019b). The expansion of the number of EHCPs has been driven by the extension of entitlement from 16 to 25 years of age and the growing complexity of need. However, there is now significant growth across all age groups (DfE, 2020b, c). Demand is also being driven by a need to secure funding for additional provision in schools, a lack of confidence in the SEN Support offer outside of a statutory framework and a less inclusive school system (HCESC, 2019, par 35; Ofsted, 2020; Parish *et al.*, 2018). The expansion in numbers has not been matched by sufficient funding for LAs, and this is threatening the sustainability of the SEND framework (NAO, 2019; Parish *et al.*, 2018).

The aim of integrated commissioning and service provision between education, health and social care through EHCPs has not been routinely achieved (Ofsted, 2017, 2018; Palikara *et al.*, 2019a), as educational provision is still the main focus of the plans (Boesley and Crane, 2018). There has also been a lack of consistency and quality of the plans, with significant regional variation in the number issued (HCESC, 2019; NAO, 2019; LGO, 2019) and a lack of the resources necessary to implement them successfully (Robinson *et al.*, 2018). The plans have been criticised for a lack of focus on outcomes, being weak on informing educational interventions and not including the views of children and young people (CYP) (Palikara *et al.*, 2019b; HCESC, 2019). SEND professionals' reactions have also been mixed, with 63% of participants in one survey agreeing that EHCPs convey a better picture of the needs of CYP than those conveyed by statements of SEND but 32.14% disagreeing (Palikara *et al.*, 2019a). The additional paperwork and bureaucracy involved in the process is also taking resources from delivering direct support (HCESC, 2019, par 140; Palikara *et al.*, 2019a; Castro *et al.*, 2019a). Tribunal cases have grown by 136% from 3,126 in 2015 to 7,385 in 2019, which questions how far the system has become less adversarial, even if the overall proportion of Tribunal cases is low at 1.8% of all appealable decisions related to EHCPs (MoJ, 2020).

SENCOs played a key part in supporting the transition from statements to EHCPs, though this has absorbed capacity which might otherwise have been deployed on early intervention and developing the SEN Support offer (NASWUT, 2018; HCESC, 2019, par 40, 130). While the transfer process is now complete, the growth in EHCPs will continue to put pressure on SEN-COs, with 59% of SENCOs stating that they did not have enough time to ensure that pupils with EHCPs accessed the provision that they require (Curran *et al.*, 2018, 2019). Further, less than one in five teachers (19%) who responded to the DfE Schools Snapshot Survey agreed that mainstream schools in England can effectively support the learning of children with EHCPs (IFF Research, 2020). Nevertheless, the greater level of co-production and outcome-focused assessment has been broadly supported by parents, with two-thirds saying they were happy with the overall process of EHCPs and around the same proportion confident about the outcomes of the plan being achieved (Adams *et al.*, 2017). Ofsted[3] has also found many good examples of practice, and the principles of the reforms continue to be supported (HCESC, 2019).

Potential changes for EHCPs

The DfE has a number of options to address the challenges in implementing EHCPs. Working within the current framework, the DfE could introduce a national template for EHCPs through the Code of Practice (CoP) in order to address the lack of consistency, help transfers of EHCPs between LAs, ensure legal clarity and reduce the level of bureaucracy (HCESC, 2019, par 43). This would also support the growing trend to use online standardised assessment services, or a national service could be established. The standardisation of the process could be achieved without changing person-centred planning (PCP) and co-production, which has been valued by parents and CYP and is supported by SENCOs (Adams *et al.*, 2017; Boesley and Crane, 2018). Nationally agreed additional guidance on training, legal requirements and skills to produce EHCPs would also help embed PCP in a more consistent way. Another suggestion is to establish clearer bandings of need within EHCPs at the national level to speed up the process and ensure early support, although such uniformity might endanger the gains made through personalisation. Streamlining the EHCP process would allow more time to improve the SEN Support offer with the aim of reducing reliance on statutory assessment in the longer term.

The SEND definition could be standardised across government departments and agencies to support more consistent identification and support. The International Classification of Functioning Disability and Health for Children and Youth could be used as a tool to inform the production of plans and introduce standard levels of information (Castro and Palikara, 2016). This approach could also be integrated into training programmes and help in defining more educationally based interventions and outcomes for EHCPs (Castro *et al.*, 2019a). Changing the definition of SEND, as opposed to clarifying it, might have a significant impact on identification and eligibility for services. Changing the definition does not necessarily alter the needs to be addressed and would be contentious if it resulted in a tightening of eligibility criteria.

While there is a clear legislative requirement to jointly prepare and commission EHCPs, this has not been routinely achieved in many local areas or the legal requirements enforced (Ofsted, 2017; HCESC, 2019). Ofsted and the Care Quality Commission, which inspects health and social care provision, have been reluctant to enforce joint commissioning as part of the area reviews (HCESC, 2019). One option is to strengthen the guidance on the current joint planning duties, encouraging a more interventionist approach in requiring LAs and health to take action following a failure to meet their duties. The House of Commons Education Select Committee (HCESC, 2019, par 73) has recommended establishing a national outcomes framework for the inspections to bring consistency, and the inspection regime could also be put on a bi-annual cycle. Inspections could also focus more on thematic issues to ensure an in-depth analysis in a similar way to how social care inspections operate. Further, if the Tribunal pilot on a single route of redress (DfE, 2018) confirms bringing health and social care cases within the Tribunals remit, albeit on a different legal basis, then this could drive more joint assessment and commissioning, which would support SENCOs in ensuring multi-agency assessments.

The expansion in special school placements (DfE, 2020c) has a disproportionate impact on LA budgets and contributes to the financial instability of the SEND system (NAO, 2019; Parish *et al.*, 2018). Placement in independent residential provision is inevitably more expensive and may not always be appropriate (Lenehan, 2017). LAs' inability to commission new maintained special schools means they are dependent on increasing the capacity of existing provision and independent school placements. LAs could be given more flexibility to expand their own main-stream provisions (HCESC, 2019, par 58), or simplify the process of establishing new special schools, but this would also need additional funding given LAs' current funding shortfall on the high-needs budget which funds EHCPs (Parish *et al.*, 2018). LAs could also be incentivised and supported to develop more high-quality local provision in mainstream and maintained special schools through the funding formula and better commissioning, thus improving capacity locally and reserving EHCPs for more specialist placements.

The growth in EHCPs questions the reliance on the statutory framework to secure support and parental confidence. The pressure on EHCPs may even out as the cohort of young people up to 25 years of age will have reached its peak by 2020 (Parish *et al.*, 2018), and the transfer process from statements to EHCPs is complete. However, the rise in EHCPs across all age groups suggests this pressure may not reduce without changes to provision (DfE, 2020a). There are also indications that the annual review process for EHCPs is not being effectively carried out due to the pressure of additional EHCPs (HCESC, 2019, par 169). If the drivers for additional EHCPs are not addressed, additional funding will only be a stopgap in a spiral of upward pressure on resources and capacity (Parish *et al.*, 2018; HCESC, 2019). While the government has been willing to partly fund the increases in demand, the National Audit Office (NAO, 2019) has concluded that the rise in EHCPs is 'unsustainable', and it is questionable how far the Treasury will be willing to extend funding without looking at more radical changes in the SEND framework to address costs.

There are a number of legislative options to address problems with the statutory assessment system, which would all represent very significant changes to the current arrangements and may make them less likely alternatives in the short term. All of these options were previously explored in the debates leading to the 2014 reforms and since then. Depending on the option, they could enhance, alter or restrict eligibility for statutory assessment (Lamb, 2019; HCESC, 2019):

Table 5.1 Potential legislative changes to statutory assessment

Proposal	Rationale	Issues
Restrict statutory protection to mainstream provision	Provision should already meet needs in special schools while mainstream provision is less secure and therefore needs more protection.	Creates dual assessment system and does not obviously reduce pressure on EHCPs unless there is additional investment at SEN Support.
Restrict statutory protection to specialist placements	Focus on the most complex CYP who need special school. SEN Support can address less complex needs if the system invests earlier.	Assumes that mainstream currently provides adequate support without additional assessment and provision.
Split assessment from provision to ensure more objective assessment	Create a new national or regional assessment agency(s) to ensure consistent assessment.	Raises questions about how plans would be aligned to resources and local accountability.
Restrict statutory assessment to those who need Education, Health and Social Care Provision	Focus on those who have the most complex needs and reduce bureaucracy in obtaining support for those just needing education provision.	Would result in a significant reduction in new EHCPs and would need additional investment at SEN Support to ensure provision was still available.
Change post-19 assessment to Employment, Health and Social Care Plan or restrict provision post-19 to very exceptional provision	Links more to life chances, independent living and employment. It was not the original intention to extend education provision routinely to post-19 years.	Reducing provision post-19 without additional educational support risks young people's futures.

With around 21% of the school SEND population now dependent on EHCPs (DfE, 2020c), parents of CYP with EHCPs represent a powerful constituency who will not want to see current or future rights to statutory provision eroded. Many parents also aspire to secure EHCPs, with initial requests increasing 14% in 2019 from 2018 to 82,300 (DfE, 2020b). It would be difficult for the DfE to progress any options which reduced access to statutory protection without first securing greater confidence in SEN Support provision or putting in place other routes to access specialist provision. Improving non-statutory provision and access to specialist support outside of EHCPs is most likely to secure a reduction in those seeking EHCPs without risking a crisis of parental confidence in the system overall. It has been proposed that one means of consulting on contentious issues around SEND entitlements would be to develop a citizen's jury approach (Norwich, 2019), which might be used to consult on more long-term changes.

Personal budgets for education support were an innovation of the 2014 Act for those with EHCPs, though they are well established in social care provision. The aim was to support more individualised provision and give control to parents who wanted it. There were 20,300 personal budgets in place for EHCPs in 2019, an increase from 15,700 in 2018. This represents 5.2% of all EHCPs and therefore remains at the moment an underutilised part of the new framework (DfE, 2020b). While personal budgets have been able to offer a greater element of personal choice, it has not been easy for the educational component to be integrated into educational provision, and there have been complaints from parents that it has been difficult to disaggregate provision through the personal budget from general provision in school settings (HCESC, 2019). Only 1,362 personal budgets were directly related to payment of education provision in 2019 though this was a 41% increase from the previous year's low base (DfE, 2020b). A further development could be for parents to be allowed a personal budget instead of a school placement so as to secure their own support. Supporting both the parents and the school in managing the complex process around personal budgets can help personalise support but also adds complexity to the SENCO role.

SEN Support – quality of the offer

The numbers of children identified with SEND had dropped significantly from a peak of 21.1% of all pupils in 2010 to 14.9% in 2019 but has risen to 15.5% in 2020 (DfE, 2020c). However, the number of CYP identified with SEND in a school cohort over time varies between 39–44% (Thompson, 2018; Hutchinson, 2017) illustrating that the potential demands on SENCOs for support and advice is higher than the national headline figure might suggest. Following from the reforms there have been concerns that CYP at SEN Support have not benefited sufficiently from the CoP (Ofsted, 2017, par30; NAO, 2019; HCESC, 2019) and that "those who do not quite meet the threshold for an EHC plan have poor outcomes" (Ofsted, 2020:13).

The abolition of School Action and School Action Plus in favour of a single category of SEN Support aimed to break the link between poor progression and confounding this with identification of SEND (DfE, 2011; Ofsted, 2010; Lamb, 2009). However, merging these categories and removing the national guidance on the format of non-statutory plans makes it more difficult for schools to demonstrate how needs are being addressed to parents, with 57% of parent career forums saying that they are not confident that schools provide good SEND support which enables children to achieve good outcomes (Contact et al., 2017). Moreover, 74% of SENCOs stated that they do not have enough time to ensure that pupils identified as requiring SEN Support are able to access the provision that they need (Curran et al., 2018). The lack of confidence in the SEN Support offer means that parents continue to see EHCPs as the 'golden ticket' to secure provision even when it might not be required (Ofsted, 2017). If parents routinely seek EHCPs as the means of securing support, this will undermine the schools' offer for all children at SEN Support (Parish et al., 2018).

The introduction of SEN Support has also been undermined by a lack of resources in schools, where per-pupil funding has decreased by 8% in real terms since 2010 (Belfield et al., 2018). This has led to additional pressure on resources for children with SEND, where school heads have indicated they have fewer resources (NAHT, 2018), though the government has promised to enhance per-pupil funding going forward. The funding of schools' SEND provision relies on the SEN notional budget, which is not ring-fenced and is allocated on a formula that does not always reflect actual needs in schools, especially in schools that attract more children with SEND, which has increased incentives for schools to push for top-up funding (HCSEC, 2019; Parish et al., 2018).

Potential changes to SEN Support

Enhanced support for SENCOs

There is a lack of specific guidance in the CoP on the content and structure of the graduated response or what is expected in terms of recording assessments and progress. The DfE could develop more specific guidance, working with schools, on what the content of a graduated plan should be, which could be used before statutory assessment. There are models which could be explored where LAs working with schools have used the opportunity to apply the principles of person-centred planning to pre-statutory plans (Essex County Council, 2017). Providing guidance would help support SENCOs in developing consistent practice, recording outcomes and demonstrating to parents the planning and provision being delivered to support children. This might help increase confidence in the pre-statutory offer and reduce demand for EHCPs, although the non-legally binding status of such plans would need to be clear. If this was combined with more delegation of resources to schools via increasing the SEN 'notional budget' or another mechanism, then this would support the provision of more support identified in an enhanced non-statutory plan before triggering an EHCP.

The currency of support is often still expressed in terms of teaching assistant (TA) hours, which underpins large aspects of the SEND system for both EHCPs and SEN Support. Primary schools (Webster *et al.*, 2015) and secondary schools view the use of TAs as a "key strategic approach to including and meeting the educational needs of pupils with high-level SEND", with expenditure on TAs estimated to be around £5 billion overall (Webster and Blatchford, 2017:11). There have been significant concerns about the effectiveness of TAs in supporting children with and without EHCPs in delivering better outcomes. The number of TAs has been increasing in primary but reducing in secondary schools as a proportion of total pupil numbers from 2013 to 2019 (NAO, 2019). Nevertheless, TAs are deployed as a key support for teachers and in helping SENCOs deliver support on SEND (Curran *et al.*, 2018). Future guidance on the use of the SEN 'notional budget' should encompass a focus on the role, training and deployment of TAs as part of moving from a culture of counting TA hours to developing SEND pedagogy (Webster and Blatchford, 2017). Minimum qualifications could be specified for TAs supporting children with SEND, and EHCPs would have to require specific interventions, not general one-to-one support from TAs. SENCOs could then take a more strategic role in reviewing practice and ensuring effective deployment and development of resources including TAs.

The 2014 reforms confirmed the strategic role of SENCOs in developing school SEND policy as well as supporting the classroom teacher (DfE and DoH, 2015, Ch. 6). However, there are mixed views about how far the SENCOs' role is integrated into schools' practice, with 92% of teachers in one survey reporting that they know when to engage the SENCO or access other forms of support in relation to pupils receiving SEN Support (IFF Research, 2020). Only 27% of SENCOs felt their role was understood by colleagues, with 46% overall stating it was understood by senior school leaders while in secondary settings this figure decreased to 26% (Curran *et al.*, 2018). This discrepancy in perceptions suggests that the successful implementation of the reforms in schools depends on the SENCOs' role being further reinforced in the CoP and supported better by senior leadership in schools. SENCOs' time needs to be protected, made full time (HCESC, 2019) and there should be a statutory requirement for them to be part of the senior leadership team.

As DfE policy has been "to foster a largely autonomous, self-improving schools' system" (DfE, 2019a), the capability and will of schools to develop the skills and SEND expertise they need is crucial to the success of the reforms. There is evidence of gaps in the skills of frontline staff, especially in low-incidence needs such as sensory impairment (Wall *et al.*, 2019). There has been additional support to develop training to schools from the DfE through funding Whole School SEND. However, this funding is limited compared to investment in additional support for EHCPs (Lamb, 2019). Without a national framework of evidence-based training, career development pathways at different levels of expertise and common practice around delivery of assessment and support, current variation in practice will continue (Palikara *et al.*, 2019a, b; Castro *et al.*, 2019a, b). The review of the mandatory qualifications for SENCOs and sensory impairments by the DfE suggests an intention to try to align qualifications which are required by the legislation. However, there are continued concerns that the current system overloads SENCOs with administrative tasks and undervalues their strategic role, which needs to be addressed in any reforms (Curran *et al.*, 2019). Further, there needs to be an overall qualification and training framework to guide schools and LAs' support services in developing skills and capacity across teachers, specialist and ancillary roles for SEND to ensure coherent practice and support against an established national framework of expectations.

Improved accountability across the system

LAs' limited powers to intervene with schools leaves a significant gap in accountably at the level of SEN Support (Parish *et al.*, 2018; HCESC, 2019). Of the available legislative tools, the SEN Information Report is the main accountability mechanism through which the SENCO and governors develop SEND policy and account for the deployment of the schools' 'notional' SEN budget. The DfE could require an account of what is 'ordinarily available' in schools, as some LAs have already done (CDC, 2016) as part of enhanced reporting requirements in the SEN Information Report, which could be reflected in the CoP. LAs would then be able to interrogate how effectively the budget is deployed to secure a good schools offer in the absence of any moves to ring-fence the 'notional' SEN budget. The offer would have to be taken into account in considering if an EHCP should be provided.

The effective deployment of SEND resources by SENCOs is hampered by the SEN notional budget being bundled within schools' general expenditure and a lack of oversight or control of the budget which is not ring-fenced (HCESC, 2019, par 142). This can also be exacerbated if the SENCO is not part of the senior leadership team. Enhanced accountability could be aligned by adjusting the SEN notional budget to a higher threshold than the current £6,000 per child per year (DfE, 2019b). This could lessen the incentive for schools to seek EHCPs, as LAs that invest more in their mainstream offer have fewer statutory plans and Tribunal cases (Lewis *et al.*, 2010; Marsh, 2017). The DfE is examining the use of the SEN notional budget, which may lead to further guidance on effective practice and interventions, as well as reviewing the overall funding framework.

The Equality Act 2010 framework, with its focus on anticipatory duties, could create a different culture of provision that is not based solely on individual assessment and provision planning, but also on removing barriers to learning for all children with SEND. The auxiliary aids and services requirement, which gives legal rights to aids and educational services for children with a disability, offers an alternative route to securing legal protection for SEN provision without recourse to an EHCP. As the Equality Act 2010 duties are linked to the SEN Information Report, this provides a potentially powerful additional tool for SENCOs to drive overall provision planning and school culture. A more strategic approach could be especially powerful if linked directly with provision planning in the Local Offer (Lamb, 2013). There would need to be a significant enhancement of the role of the Equality Commission and proactive enforcement supported by the government, but more awareness of the legal protections coupled with active enforcement could help secure parental confidence in the non-statutory offer. Ofsted/Care Quality Commission (CQC) area reviews could support these changes with a greater focus on the Equality Act duties.

The remit of the Local Government and Social Care Ombudsman could be extended to cover schools, as a successful pilot was undertaken in 2009 but was not implemented (HCESC, 2019 par30). This might provide a simpler process with more immediate redress than the Tribunal process for addressing some issues but has wider implications. One of the key remedies available to the Ombudsman is to award financial compensation but this could further hamper schools' ability to respond to SEND needs. SENCOs would have an important role in managing the schools' response to any investigation.

There is not enough clarity about how outcomes are being measured by the DfE (NAO, 2019) and concerns about the level of progression, attainment and outcomes between SEND and non-SEND children, especially for those at SEN Support (Ofsted, 2020; NAO, 2019, 1.17 to 1.22; HCESC, 2019). Clearer assessment of outcomes against a nationally agreed framework reflected in EHCPs, which are then monitored by Ofsted, could also help with consistency and assessing how the aims of the legislation are being realised. This would also give clarity to SENCOs and schools about what they should be aiming for. However, high-stakes accountability measures, such as Progress 8, which are skewed towards academic performance, are creating disincentives for schools to retain CYP with SEND and driving exclusions (Parish *et al.*, 2018; NAO, 2019). Reform of the Progress 8 measures to weight the improvements of lower attainment groups more fairly is crucial to address this issue. The new Ofsted (2019) schools inspection framework is helpful in focusing on SEND in a more holistic way and could help to alter the culture of inclusion at the school level. It would help if Ofsted also explicitly limited outstanding judgements on schools that did not also have good SEND provision to help secure a culture change in schools' focus and practice.

Co-production

Legislating to support parents' and CYPs' engagement in strategic and individual planning was a genuinely innovative aspect of the reforms. Enhanced strategic engagement aimed to change the culture of provision to be more aspirational and ensure that provision was more appropriate (Lamb, 2019). Outcomes could also be improved through good home-school working, which improved progression and attainment (Lendrum et al., 2015). There have been concerns that parental expectations have increased because of the reforms and fuelled additional demand (Parish et al., 2018). However, the significant increase in participation and influence of Parent Carer Forums has improved practice and helped ensure that more appropriate services are available and resources are used more efficiently.[4]

Within schools there is a discrepancy between teacher confidence and what parents experience, with 32% of parents feeling that schools are not putting in place the right level of support for their child or engaging them in their child's education (Panayiotou et al., 2018). There is little training on what methodologies and standards would constitute good practice for the workforce on parental engagement, with only 28% of school leaders having a plan for how to engage parents (Axford et al., 2019). Moreover, a recent analysis of SENCO assignments for the NASENCO qualification found that working with parents did not feature as a major theme (Esposito and Carroll, 2019). There are good models of co-production at the school level which are being adopted nationally; for example, those presented in the Rotherham Charter and the use of approaches like the structured conversation, which demonstrates the effectiveness of parental engagement as part of a broader programme (Lendrum et al., 2015). More emphasis on training teachers, SENCOs and other professionals in methodologies around parental engagement needs to be considered alongside other training needs for SENCOs and teachers. Adopting standards around an agreed national model of engagement, such as the four cornerstones developed by Rotherham (2020), would help provide a framework in schools and LAs.

The Local Offer's role in engaging parents in strategic planning is central to changing the culture of provision as the reforms intended (Lamb, 2013). The strategic function of the Local Offer has been underutilised in many LAs, and engagement with Parent Carer Forums is still mixed (Lamb, 2018),[5] while there have also been questions about the adequacy of the information for parents and CYP in the Offer (HCESC, 2019).[6] The Ofsted/CQC area reviews regularly take account of the quality of the Local Offer, but more could be done in a revised CoP to clarify the need for strategic co-production, which should be reflected in a new inspection framework. The revised code could include a requirement to produce an annual strategic plan as part of the published Local Offer. It is difficult for the Local Offer to directly influence schools outside of co-operative working, and SENCOs can be crucial in this area through ensuring that the links between LA and school are maintained and enhanced, acting as a catalyst for local co-ordination of services at the school level which are then reflected in the Local Offer.

Conclusion

Enhancing the SEN Support offer to ensure more parents and CYP feel provision is secure and better outcomes are being achieved will be central to ensuring the reforms are successful. For those with EHCPs, there must be confidence in the process of assessment and decision-making and that the plans are more integrated across education, health and social care. The changes sought in the 2014 reforms are about altering the culture of the system to be more inclusive, aspirational and outcomes focused for CYP with SEND. Legislation and guidance is crucial in setting the overall framework of rights and expectations, but changed values and behaviour need to be embedded across the system to secure the reforms' aspirations. SENCOs are at the fulcrum of ensuring these changes can be achieved in schools and so the support SENCOs receive, their status in the system and the capacity to fulfil their role will remain fundamental to the successful implementation of the reforms. How swiftly culture and behaviour can be changed in line with legislation's aspirations will determine whether there needs to be further piecemeal reform of the Warnock framework or a more wholesale change (Lamb, 2019).

Reflective questions

- Are EHCPs working in the way the reforms intended? If not, which of the possible reforms should be implemented and why would this help?
- What steps could be taken to ensure that confidence in the SEN Support category was enhanced and why would they work?
- What are the strengths and weaknesses of the current reforms and what single change would have the most impact on improving their implementation?
- How could the SENCOs' role be enhanced within the current framework?
- Are the problems with the current framework better addressed by more legislation and guidance or a greater focus on the culture of provision and the values informing the legislation?

Notes

1   SEND is used throughout for consistency including where using DfE figures, which generally refer to SEN. Only when referring to specific elements of the framework, such as the 'SEN support' category, is SEN used.
2   As evidenced in the Local Area SEND Inspection reports published by Ofsted. Local Area Inspection reports are available at: https://reports.ofsted.gov.uk/search?q=&location=&lat=&lon=&radius=&level_1_types=4&level_2_types%5B%5D=18
3   As evidenced in the Local Area SEND Inspection reports published by Ofsted.
4   As evidenced in the Local Area SEND Inspection reports published by Ofsted.
5   As evidenced in the Local Area SEND Inspection reports published by Ofsted.
6   As evidenced in the Local Area SEND Inspection reports published by Ofsted.

References

Adams, L., Tindle, A., Basran, S., Dobie, S., Thomson, D., Robinson, D. and Shepherd, C. (2017) *Experiences of Education, Health and Care Plans: A Survey of Parents and Young People*. Research Report. London: DfE.

Axford, N., Berry, V., Lloyd, J., Moore, D., Rogers, M., Hurst, A., Blockley, K., Durkin, H. and Minton, J. (2019) *How Can Schools Support Parents' Engagement in their Children's Learning? Evidence from Research and Practice*. Education Endowment Foundation.

Belfield, C., Farquharson, C. and Sibieta, L. (2018) *2018 Annual Report on Education Spending in England*. London: Institute for Fiscal Studies.

Boesley, L. and Crane, L. (2018) 'Forget the health and care and just call them education plans': SENCOs' perspectives on Education, Health and Care plans. *Journal of Research in Special Educational Needs*, 18(1), 36–47.

Castro, S. and Palikara, O. (2016) Mind the gap: The new special educational needs and disability legislation in England. *Frontiers in Education*. Available at: www.frontiersin.org/articles/10.3389/feduc.2016.00004/full [Accessed 27.7.20].

Castro, S., Palikara, O. and Grande, C. (2019a) Status quo and inequalities of the statutory provision for young children in England, 40 years on from Warnock. *Frontiers in Education*. Available at: www.frontiersin.org/articles/10.3389/feduc.2019.00076/full [Accessed 27.7.20].

Castro, S., Grande, C. and Palikara, O. (2019b) Evaluating the quality of outcomes defined for children with Education Health and Care plans in England: A local picture with global implications. *Research in Developmental Disabilities*, 86, 41–52.

Children and Families Act 2014. London: Her Majesty's Stationery Office.

Contact, National Network of Parent Carer Forums, Department for Education (2017) *Tenth Special Educational Needs and Disability Survey for Parent Carer Forums*. Available at: https://contact.org.uk/media/1175220/tenth_send_reforms_survey_summary_report.pdf [Accessed 24.07.20].

Council for Disabled Children and Department for Education (2016) *The Local Offer. Provision the Local Authority Expects to be Made Available by Schools, Early Years and Post-16 Providers*. Available at: https://councilfordisabledchildren.org.uk/sites/default/files/field/attachemnt/Local%20Offer_Online.pdf [Accessed 24.07.20].

Curran, H., Moloney, H., Heavey, A. and Boddison, A. (2018) *It's About Time: The Impact of SENCO Workload on the Professional and the School*. Available at: www.bathspa.ac.uk/media/bathspaacuk/education-/research/senco-workload/SENCOWorkloadReport-FINAL2018.pdf [Accessed 24.07.20].

Curran, H., Moloney, H., Heavey, A. and Boddison, A. (2019) *The Time is Now: Addressing Missed Opportunities for Special Educational Needs Support and Coordination in our Schools*. Available at: www.bathspa.ac.uk/media/bathspaacuk/education-/research/senco-workload/National-SENCO-Workload-Survey-Report-Jan-2020.pdf [Accessed 24.07.20].

Department for Education (2011) *Support and Aspiration: A New Approach to Special Educational Needs and Disability. A Consultation*. London: DfE.

Department for Education (2018) *SEND Tribunal: Single Route of Redress National Trial. Guidance for Local Authorities, Health Commissioners, Parents and Young People*. London: DfE.

Department for Education (2019a) *Government Response to Education Committee Report on School and College Funding*. Available at: www.parliament.uk/documents/commons-committees/Education/Correspondence/19-20/Government-Response-to-committee-tenth-report-of-Session-2017%E2%80%9319-a-ten-year-plan-for-school-and-college-funding-CP-190.pdf [Accessed 24.07.20].

Department for Education (2019b) *Provision for Children and Young People with Special Educational Needs and Disabilities, and for Those Who Need Alternative Provision: How the Financial Arrangements Work. Call for Evidence*. London: DfE.

Department for Education (2020a) *Education, Health and Care Needs Assessments and Plans: Guidance on Temporary Legislative Changes Relating to Coronavirus (COVID-19)*. Available at: https://www.gov.uk/government/publications/changes-to-the-law-on-education-health-and-care-needs-assessments-and-plans-due-to-coronavirus [Accessed 24.07.20].

Department for Education (2020b) *Education Health and Care Plans. England 2020*. Available at: https://explore-education-statistics.service.gov.uk/find-statistics/education-health-and-care-plans#sectionBlocks-dataBlock-2d21278c-1329–4ffb-9e2e-37aa077eb07b-charts [Accessed 24.07.20].

Department for Education (2020c) *Special Educational Needs in England. Academic Year 2019/20*. Available at: https://explore-education-statistics.service.gov.uk/find-statistics/special-educational-needs-in-england [Accessed 24.07.20].

Department for Education and Department of Health (2015) *The Special Educational Needs and Disability Code of Practice: 0 to 25 Years*. London: DfE and DoH.

Department for Education and Williamson, G. (2019) *News Story: Major Review into Support for Children with Special Educational Needs*. Available at: https://www.gov.uk/government/news/major-review-into-support-for-children-with-special-educational-needs [Accessed 14.12.20].

Equality Act 2010. London: Her Majesty's Stationery Office.

Esposito, R. and Carroll, C. (2019) Special educational needs coordinators' practice in England 40 years on from the Warnock report. *Frontiers in Education*. Available at: www.frontiersin.org/articles/10.3389/feduc.2019.00075/full [Accessed 28.07.20].

Essex County Council. (2017) *One Planning*. Available at: http://www.essexlocaloffer.org.uk/file/one-planning-guide/ [Accessed 22.01.2021].

House of Commons Committee of Public Accounts (2020) *Support for Children with Special Educational Needs and Disabilities. First Report of Session 2019–21*. Available at: https://publications.parliament.uk/pa/cm5801/cmselect/cmpubacc/85/85.pdf [Accessed 28.07.20].

House of Commons Education Select Committee (HCESC) (2019) *Special Educational Needs and Disabilities. First Report of Session 2019*. Available at: https://publications.parliament.uk/pa/cm201919/cmselect/cmeduc/20/20.pdf [Accessed 28.07.20].

Hutchinson, J. (2017) *How Many Children Have SEND?* London: Education Policy Institute.

IFF Research (2020) *The School Snapshot Survey: Summer 2019. 3. Support for Pupils*. Research Report. London: DfE.

Lamb, B. (2009) *Lamb Inquiry: Special Educational Needs and Parental Confidence*. London: DCSF.

Lamb, B. (2013) Chapter 6. Accountability the local offer and SEND reform: A cultural revolution? *Journal of Research in Special Educational Needs*, 15(1), 70–75.

Lamb, B. (2018) The SEND reforms and parental confidence: Are the reforms achieving greater parental confidence in the SEND system? In SEN Policy Research Forum. An early review of the new SEN/disability policy and legislation. *Journal of Research in Special Educational Needs*, 18(3), 160–169.

Lamb, B. (2019) Statutory Assessment for special educational needs and the Warnock report: The First 40 Years. *Frontiers in Education*. Available at: www.frontiersin.org/articles/10.3389/feduc.2019.00051/full [Accessed 28.07.20].

Lendrum, A., Barlow, A. and Humphrey, N. (2015) Developing positive school–home relationships through structured conversations with parents of learners with special educational needs and disabilities (SEND). *Journal of Research in Special Educational Needs*, 15(2), 87–96.

Lenehan, C. and Geraghty, M. (2017) *Good Intentions, Good Enough? A Review of the Experiences and Outcomes of Children and Young People in Residential Special Schools and Colleges*. London: DfE.

Lewis, J., Mooney, A., Brady, L., Gill, C., Henshall, A., Willmott, N., Owen, C., Evans, K. and Statham, J. (2010) *Special Educational Needs and Disability: Understanding Local Variation in Prevalence, Service Provision and Support*. London: DCSF.

Local Government and Social Care Ombudsman. (2019) *Not Going to Plan? Education Health and Care Plans Two Years On*. Coventry: Local Government and Social Care Ombudsman.

Marsh, A. (2017) Funding variations for pupils with special educational needs and disability in England, 2014. *Educational Management Administration and Leadership*, 45(2), 356–376.

Ministry of Justice (2020) *SEND Tribunal Tables: Statistics on the Appeal Rate to the SEND Tribunal January–March 2020*. Available at: www.gov.uk/government/statistics/tribunal-statistics-quarterly-january-to-march-2020 [Accessed 28.07.20].

NAHT (2018) *Empty Promises: The Crisis in Supporting Children with SEND*. Haywards Heath: NAHT.

NASWUT. (2018) *Special Educational Needs (SEN), Additional Learning Needs (ALN) and Additional Support Needs (ASN)*.

National Autistic Society and All Party Parliamentary Group on Autism (2017) *Autism and Education in England 2017. A Report by the All party Parliamentary Group on Autism and How the Education System in England Works for Children and Young People on the Autism Spectrum*. Available at: https://www.autism-alliance.org.uk/wp-content/uploads/2018/04/APPGA-autism-and-education-report.pdf [Accessed 14.12.20].

National Audit Office (2019) *Support for Pupils with Special Educational Needs and Disabilities in England*. London: NAO.

Norwich, B. (2014) Changing policy and legislation and its effects on inclusive and special education: A perspective from England. *British Journal of Special Educational*, 41(4), 403–425.

Norwich, B. (2019) From the Warnock report (1978) to an education framework commission: A novel contemporary approach to educational policy making for pupils with special educational needs/disabilities. *Frontiers in Education*. Available at: www.frontiersin.org/articles/10.3389/feduc.2019.00072/full [Accessed 28.07.20]

Norwich, B. and Eaton, A. (2015) The new special educational needs (SEN) legislation in England and implications for services for children and young people with social, emotional and behavioural difficulties. *Emotional and Behavioural Difficulties*, 20(2), 117–132.

Ofsted (2010) *The Special Educational Needs and Disability Review: A Statement is Not Enough*. Manchester: Ofsted.

Ofsted (2019) *School Inspection Handbook*. Manchester: Ofsted.

Ofsted (2020) *Annual Report of Her Majesty's Chief Inspector of Education, Children's Services and Skills 2018/19*. London: Ofsted.

Ofsted and Care Quality Commission (2017) *Local Area SEND Inspections: One Year On*. Manchester: Ofsted.

Palikara, O., Castro, S., Gaona, G. and Eirinaki, V. (2019a) Professionals' views on the new policy for special educational needs in England: Ideology versus implementation. *European Journal of Special Educational Need Education*, 34(1), 83–97.

Palikara, O., Castro, S., Gaona, G. and Eirinaki, V. (2019b) Capturing the voices of children in the Education Health and Care Plans: Are we there yet? *Frontiers in Education*. Available at: www.frontiersin.org/articles/10.3389/feduc.2018.00024/full [Accessed 28.07.20].

Panayiotou, S., Andersson, D., Matthews, P., Coleman, N. (2018) Omnibus Survey of Pupils and their Parents/Carers. *Research report wave 3*. DfE. January 2018.

Parish, N., Bryant, B. and Swords, B. (2018) *Have We Reached a 'Tipping Point'? Trends in Spending for Children and Young People with SEND in England*. Isos Partnership. Available at: https://static1.squarespace.com/static/5ce55a5ad4c5c500016855ee/t/5d1cdad6b27e2700017ea7c9/1562172125505/LGA+HN+report+corrected+20.12.18.pdf [Accessed 28.07.20].

Robinson, D., Moore, N. and Hooley, T. (2018) Ensuring an independent future for young people with special educational needs and disabilities (SEND): A critical examination of the impact of education, health and care plans in England. *British Journal of Guidance and Counselling*, 46(4), 479–491.

Rotherham (2020) *Rotherham Charter*. Available at: https://rotherhamcharter.co.uk/ [Accessed 12.12.20].

Thompson, D. (2018) Education Data Lab. More pupils have special educational needs than you might think. Available online at:; https://ffteducationdatalab.org.uk/2018/11/more-pupils-have-special-educational-needs-than-you-might-think/.

Wall, K., Van Herwegen, J., Shaw, J., Russell, A. and Roberts, A. (2019) *A Study of the Drivers, Demand and Supply for Special Educational Needs and/or Disabilities (SEND)-Related Continuing Professional Development (CPD) for School Staff*. London: DfE.

Webster, R. and Blatchford, P. (2017) *The Special Educational Needs in Secondary Education (SENSE) Study Final Report. A Study of the Teaching and Support Experienced by Pupils with Statements and Education Health and Care Plans in Mainstream and Special Schools*. Nuffield Foundation. Available at: www.nuffieldfoundation.org/sites/default/files/files/SENSE%20FINAL%20REPORT.pdf [Accessed 28.07.20].

Webster, R., Russell, A., and Blatchford, P. (2015) *Maximising the Impact of Teaching Assistants*. London: Routledge.

Part II The leadership role of the SENCO

6 Inclusion and school exclusion

Key issues for SENCOs in England

Lynda Kay and Tristan Middleton

Defining exclusion

The sanction of exclusion has been subject to much attention across varied arenas. It is a sanction that is frequently associated with disruptive or challenging behaviour (Kane, 2011; Munn, Lloyd and Cullen, 2000; Pomeroy, 2000). Exclusion may be employed as a fixed-period exclusion, in which a specific length of time for which the pupil is excluded is identified, or a permanent exclusion from the school's roll. Fixed-period exclusions may also exclude children and young people for a period of the day, such as for lunchtimes, over a particular period of time. The Department for Education (DfE) provides statutory guidance for schools in which the phrase 'barred from school' is utilised to describe exclusion (DfE, 2017:56). This conveys the notion of an enforced banishment (Kane, 2011; Cooper *et al.*, 2000), that is echoed within Hodkinson's (2012:678) construct of exclusion as a 'forced absence of children from their classrooms' during which they are not perceived to be the responsibility of the teacher. The authors define exclusion as a sanction which may be employed by schools, within the remit of school leaders and governors. Exclusion means that learners are banished from attending school or from learning or social activities with their peers within the school environment (Middleton and Kay, 2020:3).

Exclusion may also be implemented by schools as an informal or internal event. Informal exclusion is enacted by schools when they request that a pupil leave the school or not come in to school for a period of time and do not follow formal exclusion procedures. Such actions are clearly identified in statutory guidance as an unlawful exclusion:

> 'Informal' or 'unofficial' exclusions, such as sending a pupil home 'to cool off', are unlawful, regardless of whether they occur with the agreement of parents or carers. Any exclusion of a pupil, even for short periods of time, must be formally recorded.
>
> (DfE, 2017:10)

Internal exclusion is a

> short to medium-term strategy, used in response to learner challenges to schools' behaviour or discipline policies. It is an approach which moves the child or young person away from learning alongside their peers to a situation where they are constrained to a specific room or area for extended periods as a consequence of their actions.
>
> (Middleton and Kay, 2020:X)

One manifestation of this strategy is seclusion units or rooms, especially in secondary schools. There is little statutory guidance for internal exclusion or seclusion rooms.

Current context in England

Underlying the attention accorded to exclusion are some statistics from the DfE, which present a stark picture in which the most vulnerable pupils comprise the largest proportion of children and young people who have been excluded from school. Table 6.1 shows two examples of this: the comparison of pupils with and without special educational needs (SEN) and the high proportion of pupils with social, emotional and mental health (SEMH) needs who are excluded (Middleton and Kay, 2020).

Table 6.1 Exclusions examined in relation to pupils with SEN (adapted from DfE (2019:5)

Proportion	Permanent	Fixed-period
SEN pupils as a percentage of all exclusions	45%	43%
Percentage of pupils with SEN Support who are excluded	0.34%	15.1%
Percentage of pupils with ECHP who are excluded	0.16%	15.95%
Percentage of pupils with NO SEN who are excluded	0.06%	3.36%
Percentage of pupils with SEMH SEN who are excluded	1.02%	46.26%

Analysis of this data suggests that children and young people who start from a disadvantaged position, in relation to other peers in their cohort at school, are at risk of further challenges to their academic and social learning. This is owing to the interruptions to their education as a result of the exclusion. These interruptions elicit barriers to relationships with adults and peers within their school and augment risk factors affecting self-belief, self-esteem, resilience and mental health (Middleton and Kay, 2020).

It is difficult to gain an accurate picture of the scale of informal exclusions. The Children's Commissioner (2017) used the National Foundation for Educational Research (NFER) Teacher Voice survey of over 1000 teachers to explore the situation and identified that thousands of children have been affected. With regard to children with SEN, the Children's Commissioner identified that

> 2.7 per cent of schools have sent children with statements of SEN home when their carer or teaching assistant is unavailable; if these were evenly spread across the country, it would represent 650 schools, or an average of more than four in every local authority
>
> (Children's Commissioner, 2017:25)

This compounds the picture already provided by the statistics regarding formal exclusion from the DfE.

Education policy is subject to frequent change, and the development of policy is influenced by a range of interacting factors such as culture, political beliefs, societal views and the economic climate. The enactment of inclusion and exclusion within schools is influenced by the wider policy context and the broader environment in which schools operate (Brodie, 2001).

Government policy since the 1990s has been underpinned by a desire to reduce the role of the state within education and institute market forces within the education sector, which is predicated upon schools and settings being constructed as businesses (Ball, 2013). The application of market forces within the education sector is often described as quasi-market owing to the fact that state schools provide education free of charge and are not-for-profit organisations (Hayden, 1997). Supporters of the quasi-market focus upon education policy emphasise the positive impact this has upon effectiveness, independence and efficiency of schools (Ball, 2006, 2013). Our professional experience has witnessed circumstances in which schools have understated their inclusive practice in order to ensure that students with the potential to achieve good attainments are attracted to the school and deter those with SEN or who present with challenging behaviour. This aligns with the analysis from Ball (2013) regarding the influence market forces have upon schools' values.

In contrast to the reduction of state control through the introduction of market forces, the National Curriculum, first introduced by the 1988 Education Act and subject to several revisions since that time, bestows greater central control. Alongside the National Curriculum and other curricular guidance, formal assessment measures have been implemented (for example, Standardised Assessments Tests, SATs). Over time, the focus upon factors that can be measured and evaluated has widened and augmented within policy (Ball, 2013). The identification of metrics that are used to set targets and inform accountability judgements has engendered processes for appraisal of the performance of schools and individual practitioners at all levels of seniority. This philosophy has been encapsulated by Ball (2013:57) as 'a culture or system of "terror"'.

The emphasis upon attainment within evaluation of school, practitioner and pupil performance has been argued to elicit a focus upon deficit models of diverse needs (within learner deficits), as opposed to exploring how adjustments in their approaches or to the learning environment could be implemented (Glazzard, 2011; Hall *et al.*, 2004). Furthermore, the value placed on social relationships within policy becomes considerably reduced as increased value is accorded to measurable attainments (Ball, 2006). Ball (2006) notes that a performative culture encourages decision-making about investment to focus upon those areas which will lead to improved outcomes against the metrics used to evaluate school effectiveness. This, he suggests, means that the likelihood of SEN being considered for significant investment is reduced owing to the likely poor or limited return. One example of this has been provided by a report from *Schools Week* in which the CEO of Greenwood Academy Trust argued that schools that have low exclusion rates may be negatively rewarded owing to the impact upon their statistics for formal assessment results, which form a key part of external accountability metrics; this appears to be a negative reward for a determination to avoid excluding or off-rolling children (Schools Week, 2019). This is compounded by the potential for expected attainments for age-related expectations for all children and young people to effectively marginalise learners with SEN owing to the specified attainments being inappropriate for some learners with SEN (O'Brien, 2016). As SENCOs and other professionals, we need to challenge these notions – all children and young people should have our investment and best practice.

Government policy that has focused upon school improvement has formed part of a wider dialogue about issues related to social exclusion. This has been part of a recognition that exclusion is not just about the individual but is a matter of concern for wider society, thus necessitating political intercession and changes to systems. The beliefs held by policy makers regarding underlying causations of challenging behaviour informs the development of policies within schools and nationally. These causations are usually attributed to internal or external factors (Munn *et al.*, 2000). Examples of external factors include school and wider societal issues. Munn *et al.* (2000) postulate that policy and legislation expose the tensions between the focus upon the individual (need for intervention, therapeutic approaches or punitive sanctions) and the focus upon systems (national and school-based).

Government policy and regulations address a multitude of components which influence pedagogical decision-making; these include the curriculum, standards, inclusion, behaviour and exclusion. These contrasting elements elicit tensions for schools and 'within this pressure, there is a dichotomy in the discourse around exclusion between the notions of it being weak and positive practice' (Middleton and Kay, 2020:25).

Exclusion regulations and SEN

The DfE statutory guidance for exclusion reminds schools that they 'must not discriminate against, harass or victimise pupils because of . . . disability. . . . For disabled children, this includes a duty to make reasonable adjustment to policies and practices and the provision of auxiliary aids' (DfE, 2017:9, section 9). The regulations state that these responsibilities (set out within the *Equality Act 2010*) must be adhered to within decision-making related to exclusion. In addition, headteachers are required to comply with the *Special Educational Needs and Disability (SEND) Code of Practice* and advised that it is 'unlawful to exclude a pupil simply because they have additional needs or a disability that the school feels it is unable to meet' (DfE and DoH, 2015:9, section 13). Furthermore, the regulations set out the expectation that exploration to identify factors that underlie disruptive behaviours should include investigation of whether SEN or disability is part of this behaviour. Multi-professional investigation offers a holistic approach to identifying the causal factors of presenting behaviour. Rhetoric surrounding the latest iteration of the *SEND Code of Practice* (DfE and DoH, 2015), underpinned by the Children and Families Act 2014, suggested a move to a more inclusive approach and improved multi-professional collaboration. The reality on the ground, however, is that fundamental differences in ways of working, systems and perspectives towards assessment and support between agencies continue to represent a barrier to the work of the SENCO (Norwich and Eaton, 2015).

The regulations acknowledge that some groups of pupils are subject to 'disproportionately high rates of exclusion' and state that the sanction of permanent exclusion should be avoided for pupils with Education, Health and Care Plans (DfE, 2017:11, section 23). Schools are advised to work in partnership with parents in their work to support the behaviour of learners with SEN. Additionally, at times where a learner with an Education, Health and Care Plan is at risk of exclusion, schools are required to work collaboratively with others to explore and plan the provision for the learner, which may include an alternative setting. Schools are asked to consider arranging an early annual review (or interim review) meeting (DfE, 2017:11, section 25).

The context of the SENCO and school exclusion

The high correlation between recorded school exclusion and learners identified with SEN has been made clear earlier in this chapter. These links mean that the SENCO is often a key practitioner in the lead-up to exclusion. As a leader on inclusion, the SENCO will frequently be in the position of overseeing plans and provision, which are put in place at a school level with the aim of preventing exclusion and with supporting a return to school following fixed-term exclusion.

The definition of inclusion is widely contested, and the debate is subject to sensitive political implications. As such, the role taken by the SENCO and the plans made for learners who are at risk of exclusion are varied and open to debate. This can place the SENCO in a difficult or vulnerable position within their school setting.

Media attention has highlighted the view that a number of schools may be using exclusionary practices in order to reduce the negative impact on published whole-school outcomes which are communicated through records of attainment in national tests. These practices include:

- internal exclusion, through the use of isolation booths and rooms, as a way of removing particular learners from the classroom setting to enable 'teachers to teach and learners to learn';
- the use of strict behaviour regimes with swift routes towards school exclusion;
- off-rolling, which Ofsted (2019) has identified as a growing concern;
- various degrees of unwelcoming and unaccommodating responses to admissions requests from parents of learners with SEN.

The SENCO has a duty to ensure that 'pupils with SEN receive appropriate support and high quality teaching' (DfE and DoH, 2015: Section 6.89), and this responsibility can often be found at odds with the exclusionary practices identified earlier.

The skills and understanding of the SENCO place them in a unique position in schools. More often than not, practitioners become a SENCO as a result of an interest or affinity with learners who are marginalised or disadvantaged. Through career professional development and, more specifically, having completed the National Award for SEN Co-ordination, they are empowered to see special educational needs through a lens of inclusion, recognising that difference is not a byword for inability or limitation. Instead, they can recognise the attributes and benefits of diversity, and they have the knowledge of theory and practices to be able to identify practice which enables learners to access their educational potential. This perspective means that, at one level, the SENCO is in a position to be an advocate for the needs of learners with SEN, often taking a different perspective from that of other school leaders, by forefronting holistic needs and the possibility of alternative practices.

Furthermore, the SENCO's holistic perspective means that they are often the practitioner who spends a significant amount of time working with the parents and carers of learners with SEN. This is an element of practice which was strengthened by the *SEND Code of Practice* (DfE and DoH, 2015). Work with parents and carers often provides the SENCO with new and refreshed perspectives on learners' needs and possible provision and further adds to their position of advocacy.

Through implementing practices, such as person-centred planning for meetings (Corrigan, 2014), the SENCO can be seen as advocating for the voice of the learner and facilitating self-advocacy (Garner and Sandow, 2018).

The SENCO, as a leader overseeing the enactment of the principles of the *SEND Code of Practice* (DfE and DoH, 2015), is in a position to have a positive systemic impact on the exclusion of learners, through the implementation of approaches in their setting, including interventions, staffing and the development of ethos and vision. Such approaches are often instrumental in providing opportunities for learners to successfully remain in mainstream educational settings. Whilst it can be tempting to provide best practice approaches, recommending specific practice, the authors believe that appropriateness and relevance of specific ways of working can only be determined on a local, or contextual, basis. As such, what is needed is a SENCO who is equipped to make choices about approaches, through an understanding of what is available to them and what the outcomes might be, within the parameters of their conception of inclusion. This could be described as a high level of inclusive practice literacy or intervention literacy.

Definitions of inclusion

The SENCO, as a leader of inclusion, needs a solid understanding of the concept of inclusive education in order to lead the development of ethos and vision. This section will explain the authors' conceptualisation of inclusive practice.

Literature has moved forwards from the principles of the Salamanca Agreement (UNESCO, 1994), understanding that inclusive education cannot primarily be defined by the learners' placement, but that inclusive education embraces a number of factors (Mitchell, 2015). The authors identify the following as a theoretical framework through which to conceptualise inclusive education (Figure 6.1).

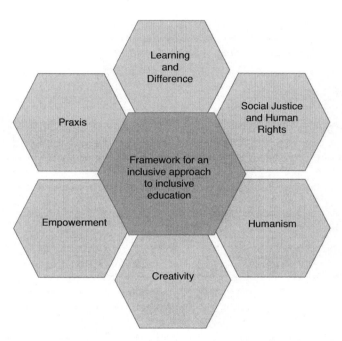

Figure 6.1 Framework for an inclusive approach to inclusive education (Middleton and Kay, 2020:68)

This framework is grounded within a particular conceptualisation of the purpose of education (Ekins, 2017), which moves away from a didactic approach focusing on the teaching of specific knowledge and skills and therefore measuring success in terms of norms related to these areas (Armstrong, Armstrong and Spandagou, 2010), towards a view of education as one based on principles of equity (Lumby and Coleman, 2016). The six dimensions are concisely elaborated upon as follows.

Learning and difference

Learning is fundamentally based within difference, through its concerns of exploring different approaches, positions and perspectives and moving us from one state of being to another, meaning we are different following a learning event. The benefits of difference, or diversity, within communities of learning is key to conceptualising inclusive education. Furthermore, as identified by astrophysicist Dame Bell Burnell, diversity is an asset in learning situations: 'The more diverse a group is, the more robust, the more flexible, and the more successful it is' (Bell Burnell, 2018).

Social justice and human rights

This dimension is based on the belief that there are core human rights and that a focus upon social justice will ensure these rights are reached. Article 22 of the Declaration of Human Rights

(United Nations, 1948) identifies that education is a human right and that this will promote peaceful and tolerant communities.

Humanism

The dimension of humanism is one which values relationships among humans with the belief that humans are fundamentally ethical beings who are concerned with others and are motivated to act with care for others rather than engage in competitive individualism (Slee, 2014:11).

Creativity

Creativity is the concept which is the antithesis of the dogmatic, normative approach to education. It is the belief that diversity and variation in outcomes is the most valuable goal of education, which seeks to create new learning and development.

Empowerment

Empowerment, or the development of individuals' voices and opportunities for decision-making, is both a route towards and an outcome of, inclusive education. In order to ensure that diversity is valued and provided for, the voices of diverse learners need to be heard and acted upon. As this happens, and learning opportunities for different learners are enhanced, those learners will become further equipped to develop their voices and access to decision-making opportunities.

Praxis

Praxis is a term which describes the use of evidence-informed practice, which is employed in order to reduce marginalisation and improve the participation and engagement of all.

This model of dimensions is designed to help the practitioner to explore inclusive education practice from the basis of a secure understanding. The SENCO can then effectively engage in the process of developing their school to support and benefit all learners (Kurth *et al.*, 2018:472). This approach to changing the educational systems and structures to fit with the needs of all learners in the community is a useful perspective from which to understand inclusive education and to reduce exclusion for diverse learners. Through this understanding, SENCOs will be empowered to reduce formal and informal exclusions as well as exclusion by default, where learners remain in school but are marginalised by practice, which aims to integrate (Barton, 2003) rather than develop.

Leading SEN: supporting colleagues with using inclusive approach to reduce school exclusion

Translating or mediating the concept of inclusion into practice engages schools in capacity building (Norwich, 2013), which is a crucial part of the strategic leadership of SEN and inclusion. The authors contend that inclusive practice is about finding spaces that are 'occupied by (relatively) inclusive values and approaches' (Dyson, Gallannaugh and Millward, 2003:238) and working collaboratively with colleagues to engage in reflective thinking and dialogue to support the development of inclusive practice. These spaces are not intended to refer to the literal physical interpretation, but rather time and an ethos of a safe space to engage in critical reflection and discussion which challenges everyone's thinking and looks to explore creative approaches to resolve issues in practice (Middleton and Kay, 2020). These spaces, and the ideas and resolutions facilitated through them, offer opportunity and hope for finding inclusive approaches to meeting diverse needs and thus reducing exclusion (Middleton and Kay, 2020). Ekins (2015) advocates for the importance of leaders engaging their teams with a critical analysis of, and reflection upon, the principles and values which are the foundations for their current practice.

This may appear challenging within the large number of demands upon schools and the work to develop practice. However, we contend that this serves the important purposes of:

- creating an ethos that has a positive embracement of diversity;
- developing a shared vision owned by all the school community regarding inclusion;
- keeping the ethos active.

This work needs to be a collaborative endeavour; it is not something that can be imposed from the top down (Alila, Maatta and Uusiautti, 2016). Leading and shaping a shared understanding of inclusion and inclusive practice for the school or setting will be supported positively through dialogical relationships (Watson *et al.*, 2012). The notion of safe spaces embodies one in which deep listening, honesty and courteous dialogue is adopted and respected by everyone within the community (Middleton and Kay, 2020). Booth and Ainscow's (2002) broad principles for inclusion as follows offer a supportive tool for analysing current practice:

- Reduce barriers to inclusion
- Increase participation and access to learning
- Support diversity

The dimensions of the framework for an approach to inclusive education offer a useful lens to support reflect dialogues about practice. We have developed a framework for inclusive practice which contains questions to support reflective thinking targeted to inclusive practice (Middleton and Kay, 2020). This is not intended as an audit tool. Here we present some questions which can support with reflecting upon leadership of SEN and pedagogy. The questions can be used for self-reflection and as group or staff meeting discussions. SENCOs act as advocates for children with SEN and disabilities, most especially at times of challenge, such as when behaviour places a child at risk of exclusion. Exploring practice in this way through the use of critical reflective spaces, SENCOs can work with school staff to develop (or make different choices) for pedagogical practice.

Conclusion

This chapter has presented the case that exclusion is an issue that needs to be of particular concern for the school SENCO and that the practice of exclusion is one aspect of a system which contributes to the marginalisation of particular learners who come under the remit of the SENCO. We have argued that a secure understanding of inclusive practice provides a firm basis from which to tackle exclusionary practices and that the SENCO, as a leader of inclusion, needs to create spaces in which practitioners can explore and negotiate their contextual understanding of inclusive practice for their own settings.

Reflective questions

We suggest that as SENCOs are reading through these chapters, they may find the following questions about their own practice useful:

- What is the current situation in your setting in relation to formal and informal exclusion?
- How does your school data in relation to excluded pupils or those at risk of exclusion compare with the national data?
- How do you think the wider policy context influences inclusion and exclusion in your own school or setting?
- What investigations are undertaken currently in your setting when a concern about disruptive behaviour is raised?
- Do you know the external agencies you can reach out to for support in your local area?

Furthermore, a selection of a framework of questions (extracted from Middleton and Kay (2020)) has been presented to support SENCOs to use dialogue to create the spaces to explore inclusive

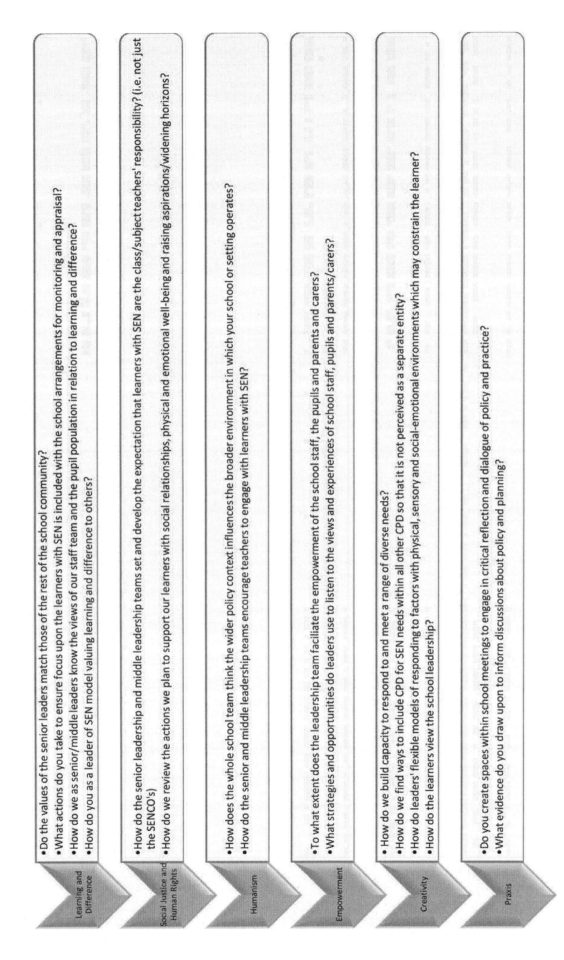

Learning and Difference
- Do the values of the senior leaders match those of the rest of the school community?
- What actions do you take to ensure focus upon the learners with SEN is included with the school arrangements for monitoring and appraisal?
- How do we as senior/middle leaders know the views of our staff team and the pupil population in relation to learning and difference?
- How do you as a leader of SEN model valuing learning and difference to others?

Social Justice and Human Rights
- How do the senior leadership and middle leadership teams set and develop the expectation that learners with SEN are the class/subject teachers' responsibility? (i.e. not just the SENCO's)
- How do we review the actions we plan to support our learners with social relationships, physical and emotional well-being and raising aspirations/widening horizons?

Humanism
- How does the whole school team think the wider policy context influences the broader environment in which your school or setting operates?
- How do the senior and middle leadership teams encourage teachers to engage with learners with SEN?

Empowerment
- To what extent does the leadership team faciliate the empowerment of the school staff, the pupils and parents and carers?
- What strategies and opportunities do leaders use to listen to the views and experiences of school staff, pupils and parents/carers?

Creativity
- How do we build capacity to respond to and meet a range of diverse needs?
- How do we find ways to include CPD for SEN needs within all other CPD so that it is not perceived as a separate entity?
- How do leaders' flexible models of responding to factors with physical, sensory and social-emotional environments which may constrain the learner?
- How do the learners view the school leadership?

Praxis
- Do you create spaces within school meetings to engage in critical reflection and dialogue of policy and practice?
- What evidence do you draw upon to inform discussions about policy and planning?

Figure 6.2 Framework for reflection (adapted from Middleton and Kay, 2020:X)

practice and support their work to reduce exclusion and promote beneficial practices and outcomes for learners identified with SEN.

References

Alila, S., Maatta, K. and Uusiautti, S. (2016) 'How does supervision support inclusive teacherhood?'. *International Electronic Journal of Elementary Education*, 8(3), 351–362.

Armstrong, A. C., Armstrong, D. and Spandagou, I. (2010) *Inclusive Education: International Policy & Practice*. London: Sage.

Ball, S. J. (2006) *Education Policy and Social Class: The Selected Works of Stephen J. Ball*. Abingdon: Routledge.

Ball, S. J. (2013) *The Education Debate*. Second Edition. Bristol: The Policy Press.

Barton, L. (2003) *Inclusive Education and Teacher Education: A Basis of Hope or a Discourse of Delusion?* Inaugural Professorial Lecture delivered at the Institute of Education, University of London, 3rd July 2003.

Bell Burnell, J. (2018) Radio 4 'Today Programme', 6th September 2018.

Booth, T. and Ainscow, M. and Centre for Studies on Inclusive Education (2002) *Index for Inclusion: Developing Learning and Participation in Schools*. Bristol: CSIE.

Brodie, I. (2001) *Children's Homes and School Exclusion*. London: Jessica Kingsley Publishers.

Children and Families Act 2014, Chapter 6. London: Her Majesty's Stationery Office.

Children's Commissioner (2017) *"Always Someone Else's Problem" Office of the Children's Commissioner's Report on Illegal Exclusions*. Available at: www.childrenscommissioner.gov.uk/wp-content/uploads/2017/07/Always_Someone_Elses_Problem.pdf [Accessed 16th July 2018].

Cooper, P., Drummond, M. J., Hart, S., Lovey, J. and McLaughlin, C. (2000) *Positive Alternatives to Exclusion*. London: RoutledgeFarmer.

Corrigan, E. (2014) 'Person centred planning "in action": Exploring the use of person centred planning in supporting young people's transition and re-integration to mainstream education'. *British Journal of Special Education*, 41(3), 268–288.

Department for Education (2017) *Exclusion from Maintained Schools, Academies and Pupil Referral Units in England: Statutory Guidance for Those with Legal Responsibilities in Relation to Exclusion*. Available at: www.gov.uk/government/uploads/system/uploads/attachment_data/file/641418/20170831_Exclusion_Stat_guidance_Web_version.pdf [Accessed 18th December 2017].

Department for Education (2019) *Permanent and Fixed Period Exclusions in England: 2017 to 2018*. Available at: www.gov.uk/government/statistics/permanent-and-fixed-period-exclusions-in-england-2017-to-2018 [Accessed 18th August 2019].

DFE and DoH (2015) *Special Educational Needs Code of Practice: Statutory Guidance for Organisations Who Work with and Support Children and Young People with Special Educational Needs and Disabilities*. London: DFE and DoH.

Dyson, A., Gallannaugh, F. and Millward, A. (2003) 'Making space in the standards agenda: Developing inclusive practices in schools'. *European Educational Research Journal*, 2(2), 228–244.

Ekins, A. (2015) *The Changing Face of Special Educational Needs: Impact and Implications for SENCOs, Teachers and their Schools*. Abingdon: Routledge.

Ekins, A. (2017) *Reconsidering Inclusion: Sustaining and Building Inclusion Practices in Schools*. London: Routledge.

Garner, P. and Sandow, S. (2018) *Advocacy, Self-advocacy and Special Needs*. Vol. 25. Abingdon, Oxon: Routledge.

Glazzard, J. (2011) 'Perceptions of the barriers to effective inclusion in primary school: Voices of teachers and teaching assistants'. *International Journal of Research in Special Educational Needs*, 26(2), 56–63.

Hall, K., Collins, J. Benjamin, S., Nind, M. and Sheehy, K. (2004) 'SATurated models of pupildom: Assessment and inclusion/exclusion'. *British Educational Research Journal*, 30(6), 801–817.

Hayden, C. (1997) *Children Excluded from Primary School: Debates, Evidence, Responses*. Buckingham: Open University Press.

Hodkinson, A. (2012) '"All present and correct?" Exclusionary Inclusion within the English education system'. *Disability and Society*, 27(5), 675–688.

Kane, J. (2011) *Social Class, Gender and Exclusion from School*. London: Routledge.

Kurth, J. A., Miller, A. L., Toews, S. G., Thompson, J. R., Cortés M., Dahal, M. H., de Escallón, I. E., Hunt, P. F., Porter, G., Richler, D., Fonseca, I., Singh, R., Šiška, J., Villamero, R. J. and Wangare, F. (2018) 'Inclusive education: Perspectives on implementation and practice from international experts'. *Intellectual and Developmental Disabilities*, 56(6), 471–485.

Lumby, J. and Coleman, M. (2016) *Leading for Equality: Making Schools Fairer*. Los Angeles: Sage.

Middleton, T. and Kay, L. (2020) *Using an Inclusive Approach to Reduce School Exclusion: A Practitioner's Handbook*. Abingdon, Oxon: Routledge.

Mitchell, D. (2015) 'Inclusive education is a multi-faceted concept'. *Center for Educational Policy Studies Journal*, 5(1), 9–30.

Munn, P., Lloyd, G. and Cullen, M. A. (2000) *Alternatives to Exclusion from School*. London: Paul Chapman Publishing.

Norwich, B. (2013) *Addressing Tensions and Dilemmas in Inclusive Education: Living with Uncertainty*. London: Routledge.

Norwich, B. and Eaton, A. (2015) 'The new special educational needs (SEN) legislation in England and implications for services for children and young people with social, emotional and behavioural difficulties'. *Emotional and Behavioural Difficulties*, 20(2), 117–132.

O'Brien, J. (2016) *Don't Send Him in Tomorrow: Shining a Light on the Marginalised, Disenfranchised and Forgotten Children of Today's Schools*. Carmarthen: Independent Thinking Press.

Ofsted (2019) 'Off-rolling: An update on recent analysis'. *Ofsted Blog*, 6th September 2019. Available at: https://educationinspection.blog.gov.uk/2019/09/06/off-rolling-an-update-on-recent-analysis/ [Accessed 12th November 2019].

Pomeroy, E. (2000) *Experiencing Exclusion*. Stoke on Trent: Trentham Books.

Schools week (2019) 'My Trust pays the price for being inclusive'. *Schools Week*, 15th November 2019. Available at: https://schoolsweek.co.uk/ceo-my-trust-pays-the-price-for-being-inclusive/ [Accessed 18th November 2019].

Slee, R. (2014) 'Discourses of inclusion and exclusion: Drawing wider margins'. *Power and Education*, 6(1), 7–17.

UNESCO (1994) *The Salamanca Statement and Framework for Action on Special Needs Education: Adopted by the World Conference on Special Needs Education; Access and Quality*. Salamanca, Spain, 7–10th June 1994: UNESCO.

United Nations (1948) *Universal Declaration of Human Rights*. Available at: www.un.org/en/universal-declaration-human-rights/ [Accessed 23rd August 2018].

Watson, D., Emery, C. and Bayliss, P. with Boushel, M. and McInnes, K. (2012) *Children's Social and Emotional Wellbeing in Schools*. Bristol: The Policy Press.

7   Inclusion in the early years

Angela Scott

Introduction

Early years' settings are populated with children who are on a journey from one key developmental milestone to the next, the 'norms' of which are characterised by a naturally occurring degree of flexibility. There is much discussion to be had about the theory through which children's development is framed and how this can be applied within an arena that is uniquely placed to be wholly inclusive. This chapter's purpose is to look at a range of theories underpinning an early years' pedagogy of inclusivity and to ask questions about the skills and styles of leadership needed to hone early years' environments into the very best they can be for all children.

Underpinning theory

A journey back to some of the roots of educational theory gives a useful theoretical starting point to the underpinnings of developmental milestones. Piaget (1957) created a structure from which education has not strayed too far. This four-stage model of cognitive development first defined in 1936 uses descriptive language for a child's journey within the categories of:

- Sensorimotor (birth to age 2)
- Preoperational (from age 2 to age 7)
- Concrete operational (from age 7 to age 11)
- Formal operational (from 11+ to adolescence)

(Piaget, 1957)

The categories need to be contextualised within the Piagetian concepts. These are 'cohesive, repeatable action sequences possessing component actions that are tightly interconnected and governed by a core meaning' (Piaget, 1957:7); in other words, how the brain structures knowledge based on past experiences (Pankin, 2013). Here there is a collaboration of internal and external factors. The internal workings of the brain are potentially wired and set on a trajectory as part of its genetic and neurobiological functioning, and the cultural, contextual, environmental factors aid and abet the knowledge gains. Where one begins and one ends is a continuing cause for debate amongst researchers of many different disciplines, and leading on inclusion in the early years must take on board these multifaceted strands to hone the way they impact on children's experiences.

When considering this historical framework within which children's cognitive development is frequently framed, a word of warning: Piaget's construct was predicated on the notion that children go through the stages in a similar order, determined by biological maturation and interaction with the environment. McLeod (2018:1) suggests that 'although no stage can be missed out, there are individual differences in the rate at which children progress through stages, and some individuals may never attain later stages'. This results in two important reflections for early years' practitioners. Firstly, if children are on the same developmental trajectory, then the structures and scaffolding around them must be focused wholly on helping them to pass successfully through each stage come what may. Secondly, if they do not, might this indicate failure on the part of the setting or the child, thus posing significant challenges for establishing an inclusive early years' environment?

Starting with object permanence as a focus for debate: this Piagetian concept sits within the sensorimotor stage and is a descriptor for babies aged 4–7 months. Put simply, it means that the baby will demonstrate an understanding that when an object disappears, it is not gone forever. Object permanence is a core test within the paediatrician and psychology toolkit (Green *et al.*, 2015) that is often used within multidisciplinary team child development centres as part of a process to define delay or difference.

There is a presumption that the developmental attribute of object permanence should be securely in place prior to a child's first birthday. The Early Learning Goal (ELG) for speaking supports this notion by stating that children must be able to connect ideas or events (DfE, 2019:28), implying that they must first have hold of a concept in order to make connections. A paper by Lawson and Dombroski (2017) raises the question about object permanence in relation to children with autism:

> A poor understanding of object permanence may be contributing to insistence upon sameness of routine due to non-comprehension of the continued existence of the object, person, time and event. It is not simply its removal that is cause for discomfort, it may be the belief it is never returning.
>
> (Lawson and Dombrowski, 2017:1)

This brings into sharp focus the Piagetian concept that no stage can be missed out. If in fact children have pieces of the puzzle missing or dormant in some way and educators fail to recognise this, then education becomes a slave to the next-step imperatives within the theories of child development and fails to recognise the unique nature of that child. Of course, much of this recognition is hooked into the ability to look under the surface at the things that are not obvious, and good inclusive leadership requires a high level of sleuthing. How much easier it is to recognise the child who cannot attain developmental milestones of a physical nature because they are in a wheelchair than to identify the missing attribute of object permanence, which may be causing extreme anxiety and consequent negative behaviours but is unseen and thus unrecognised.

Another example is that of egocentrism, a concept described within Piaget's preconceptual phase (age 4–7). The three mountains egocentrism test (Piaget and Inhelder, 1967) requires a child to place themselves at a table, on the opposite side of which is a doll. On the table are three mountains of varying heights. The child is asked to draw what the mountains would look like from the doll's point of view. According to Piaget, children have to reach a particular cognitive developmental phase before they are able to do this effectively. In contrast, Donaldson (2006) argues that young children have the ability to 'decentre', suggesting it is a 'failure of communication' (Donaldson, 2006:44) about the three mountains task and not the cognitive ability to carry it out that presents difficulty for the child. Whatever the causal factor may be, a classic difficulty described by many adults with autism is the ability to view life through different lenses and thus plan and manage consequences. For many this leads to difficulties in the area of social interaction (Hendrickx, 2015; Blackburn cited in Prizant and Fields-Meyer, 2016). The ELG requirement for children to describe 'their own and other's behaviour and its consequences' (DfE, 2019:29) may well provide particular challenges for children with autism or other similar profiles. Clear-sighted knowledgeable leadership in the early years must therefore create an environment in which the uniqueness of the child's neurological functioning, and importantly their styles of communication, are recognised and celebrated. This may be at odds with the strict developmental pathways' agenda, but it is the very child-led environment on which early years' pedagogy can be built. Leaders must guide staff in developing the social structures and communication scaffolds that can effectively embrace those children who are not developmentally ready to exercise set skills or for whom acquisition or understanding of some skills will be a lifelong journey.

It is important to note that leading on inclusion in the early years is not about categorising or labelling children using a deficit model (Trussler and Robinson, 2015). Rather, it is about gathering a wealth of information about a child from multiple sources and through varying means creating enabling environments (Allen and Whalley, 2010). This must be done speedily, thoroughly and without delay. The Special Educational Needs Code of Practice (SEND COP) (DfE and DoH, 2015:5.36) is clear that 'all those who work with young children should be alert to emerging difficulties and respond early'. Inclusion in the early years must be cognisant of multiple factors, and it is beholden on leaders to be knowledgeable and well researched so they can guide the thinking of others away from a stereotypical developmental milestones approach into the world of child-centredness.

A focus on inclusion

The subject of inclusion within early years goes back as far as the wider inclusion agenda itself and incorporates a plethora of challenging discussions. The thinking which helped shape the journey of inclusion leads educators to a key recommendation from the Warnock report (1978): the imperative to recognise and understand children's needs rather than a focus on categorisation or diagnosis. It could be said that some 40 years on, the categorisation and diagnosis phenomena has returned with a vengeance, and the world of inclusive education – even that within the early years – is peppered with medicalised terminology as a means by which to describe children and young people's 'difference'. See Chapter 3 of this book for further discussion on the topic of Warnock and terminology.

The history of early years' education is particularly interesting, and through its focus on child-centred approaches can be understood as having a natural synergy with the inclusive agenda. Elkind (2016:1) frames it first as 'the care and instruction of young children outside of the home . . .' but suggests it has since become a 'downward extension of schooling'. A number of well-recognised names can be associated with how early years' education has taken shape over the years; for example, John Locke, Friedrich Froebel, Maria Montessori and Jean Piaget, who together gave us the genesis of philosophical thinking about child development. However, their thinking does not point the pedagogy of the early years in one direction.

Currently early years' ideas and ideals are centred on a core belief 'that early childhood curriculum and practice must be adapted to the maturing needs, abilities and interests of the child' (Elkind, 2016:1). The basic principle here is that education starts with and centres around the child rather than the key driver being that of the curriculum. This, however, presumes a range of ideals, firstly that all children will follow a sufficiently well-defined developmental pathway that allows for community cohesion within every early years' environment, and secondly that children from a range of cultures, contexts and with birthdays placed 11 months apart in any given cohort will coalesce to form a vibrant, thriving, learning-rich early years' community. To avoid learning and social chaos, educators seem compelled therefore to provide a structure in the form of a curriculum to help frame the child's early years' experience. If, however, that curriculum does not sit in tandem with the child's natural development but as the driving force of the early years' agenda, retaining the golden thread of child-centredness with all its natural attributes of inclusivity becomes more difficult. If the learning pathway is but preparation for what lies ahead, then educators might be pushing child-centredness, and along with it inclusivity, in the early years into second position. Setting this point in its historical context, structuring early years' education based on the theories of Locke (1824) and Piaget (1957) predisposes it towards preparation for the academic and social world ahead, thus putting a fundamental strain on the ideals of early years' theorists who promote a child-centred journey (Froebel and Hailman, 1887; Montessori, 2007). These very structures and curricula frameworks could be said to mitigate against the naturally inclusive child-led world of the early years. If a child cannot 'conform' to the group dynamics of playing in the sand, or singing a song, or listening at storytime, then they are at risk of being excluded from the very place in which 'the greatest development is achieved' (Montessori, 2007:7).

The concept of developmental milestones and the inevitable monitoring thereof is considered to be a worldwide practice. That said, a dichotomy exists: in some parts of the world, parents attempt to delay the physical development of their babies due to fears about everyday hazards such as open fires. Research into Kenyan early years' developmental programmes by Ng'asike (2014) revealed a disconnect between Western pedagogical practices and important local value systems and cultural roots. Thus, different practices may inculcate different 'developmental norms' within various cultures and contexts. This leads to the question about whether a child's experiences within the early years' sector can and should always be based on a one-size-fits-all stance, outlined within an agreed framework and measured through Piagetian structures. Alternatively, the culture, context and the essential child-centred philosophies mean that achieving inclusivity for each child should take into account a more variable set of factors. If, for example, early years' environments could be designed with more fluid social norms, then the child who does not play collaboratively would be less noticeable. If there were flexible and inclusive measures in place to track the progress of children's communication skills, then the child whose communication route is nonverbal would be embraced naturally and equally.

Luna-Scott's 2015 paper on the future of learning and pedagogies for the 21st century poses radical ideas which could re-shape our schools and the notion of the early years' sector being, as Elkind (2016:1) described, the 'downward extension of schooling'. Drawing on Hampson *et al.* (2011, cited in Luna Scott, 2015), Luna-Scott suggests learning must be relevant at the big-picture macro level and must be fuelled by individuals' ability to approach problems, 'grasp ideas at their own pace and respond differently to multiple forms of feedback' (Hampson *et al.*, 2011 cited in Luna Scott, 2015:3). Luna Scott (2015) envisages that mindful of the continuing evolution of digital tools for learning, teachers will need to change from 'content conveyors to content curators' (Luna Scott, 2015:14). As children access learning through different mediums, teachers could thus become free to create more innovative learning environments.

The current context

The SEND Code of Practice (DfE and DoH, 2015:5.36–5.46) early years 'assess, plan, do, review' cycle contains some important principles which provide a clear structure for positive action. Putting the child at the heart of the process requires great skills of interpretive observation and a sound questioning approach supported by a mindset that avoids trying to fit children into a category. Too often educators hear 'has he got ADHD?', 'might it be autism?', 'could it be attachment?'. The work of Kirby (2014) challenges educators to view the door to diagnosis as potentially contributing to an unhelpfully narrow way of describing the child's need in contrast to the increasingly researched world of co-occurrence in which the complexity of the brain gives us a multidimensional child-centred modus operandi of diversity. Importantly, a label does not define the child. The underlying concept of child-centred inclusivity propels educators to consider the absolute uniqueness of the individual. The day after a diagnosis has been made, the child has not changed, and as such they still require the inclusive child-centred approach based on a sound assess, plan, do, review cycle (DfE and DoH, 2015), in which their views and experiences help shape the actions that are taken. Even a child with a clearly defined need, for example Down syndrome, has a unique character, their own set of interests and skills and an emerging personality that is waiting to be understood (see Chapter 2 of this book for further discussion on this topic). The SEND Code of Practice (DfE and DoH, 2015) concept of early years' assess, plan, do, review has at its heart a focus on problem-solving aimed at identifying the right match of provision to need to secure good progress and achieve agreed outcomes. The cycle is defined as one in which there is ongoing analysis of the impact of actions taken, supported by the views of the child and strong collaboration with parents. This is where clear insightful guidance from the SENCO comes into sharp focus. Good practice must be based on an understanding that the responsibility for day-to-day provision for each child lies with the teacher/early years' practitioner working in tandem with the SENCO, whose role is that of advice and support.

An area of work which requires particularly dynamic leadership is that of gaining the 'views of the child' (DfE and DoH, 2015:5.40), which in the early years' arena requires particular care. Those involved need to ensure that person-centred activities are worthwhile, positive and developmental for the child and that tokenism is avoided at all costs. A child's views can be gained through sound reflective observation using a collaborative interpretive approach (Boehm and Weinberg, 1997; Brodie, 2013). This involves use of visual tools, gesture and/or signing, journals, photographs and videos, all of which must be supported by guided discussion and, most importantly, an enabling environment for play. For more on pupil voice, see Chapters 11 and 12 of this book.

Leadership in this area requires a theoretical understanding of the two different constructs of pupil voice and person-centred approaches. It also requires practical and meaningful communication with parents with a view to gaining greater understanding whilst promoting a child's independent learning and social behaviours. This requires a strong knowledge of early child development as well as a deep awareness of the research into the impact of summer birthdays. There is emerging evidence in the work of Sharp *et al.* (2009), Long (2015), Sykes *et al.* (2016) and Gorard and Siddiqui (2017) that for some children who are young-for-year the risk of them being mistakenly identified as SEN can be greater than the norm. This can mean that rather than a well-rounded, play-based environment being prioritised, a 'what is wrong?' mentality begins to drive processes and provision, which may be fundamentally misplaced. The SEND Code of Practice (DfE and DoH, 2015:1.25) offers some clarity for leaders in this area: identification of SEN must be 'informed by the insights of parents and those of children and young people themselves' supported by monitoring and review of the progress and development of children throughout the early years and tested against the knowledge that a 'delay in learning in the early years, may or may not indicate a child has SEN' (DfE and DoH, 2015:1.26 and 5.28). Strong leadership of SEND in the early years must then be cognisant of multiple factors, the coordination and analysis of which provides appropriate approaches for each child within a genuinely inclusive environment.

Family engagement

Inclusive early years' leaders must have regard to the importance of effective communication with parents and/or carers. Research suggests that parental engagement in children's learning as opposed to parental engagement in the processes of education is likely to contribute in a positive and meaningful way to achieve outcomes for children at every stage (Harris and Goodall, 2007). Hattie's work suggests that 'parent engagement is more significant in learner success than structural issues' (Hattie, 2009 cited in Lucas, 2010:3). Much research (Desforges and Aboucher, 2003; Harris and Goodall, 2007; Allen and Cowdrey, 2012; Wilson and Gross, 2018) explores the subject of parental engagement from the perspective of the educational professional – be it early years' worker, teacher or specialist. Perhaps a useful way to frame such thinking is to look at it first from the perspective of the parent.

The entry into parenting and its subsequent journey has significant life-changing implications. The early years' stage is one of promise and adventure but one which is framed by a public discourse: with questions about birthweight, sleep patterns, early milestones of crawling, walking and talking and the inevitable interrogation about how the family are surviving. It is no wonder that parents feel a weight upon their shoulders that both they and their child should fit into societal and cultural expectations. Look at any parent website and the burden of anxiety about getting things 'right' is clear. Parenting per se is a goldfish bowl experience in which pretty much everyone from family members to neighbours through to teachers and even strangers who frequent the local supermarket feel they have the right to express a view.

Inclusive leaders need to consider parents who are told right from the beginning that their child is going to be 'different'. Stories about being informed that 'your child has Down syndrome' or that 'your baby has a profound hearing loss' suggest that for these parents a period of mourning may well be needed – mourning for the child they were expecting compared to the one they now have and mourning for themselves as they come to terms with forever being seen as different in some way. Feelings of fear for an uncertain future, worry about whether or not they are up to the job and for some, fear of family or community isolation because they no longer belong to the tribe of 'normal' parents. Depending on what or how they have been told, parents may feel a range of emotions about the opportunities ahead for their child, and for some this is expressed in a determination to fight for the best possible provision for their daughter or son, whose uniqueness and personality they do not yet know.

For the parent who comes to a gradual awareness that their child is not achieving the prescribed milestones as expected, or whose needs are manifesting themselves in ways that are as yet unexplained, the fear factor relating to the possibility that their child is 'different' can be equally great. It is no wonder then that the complexity of emotions experienced by parents who find themselves either suddenly, or over time in this 'different' situation from their peers, are often displayed by the flight fight, or freeze responses recognised by neurobiologists who are increasingly able to describe the complex workings of the brain (Roelofs, 2017).

For parents to engage fully in the opportunities that an inclusive early years' environment can offer their child, they need firstly to feel that both they and their child belong. McNamara *et al.* (2017) talks about the importance of connectedness as central to the physical, social, cognitive and emotional development of children. Similarly, it could be argued that parents who are on a journey of discovery need this same connectedness to develop the attributes for effective parenting as their crucial role takes shape. They need a secure framework within which honest, open conversations can develop. These must be based on a shared belief that their child is a valued individual and that they are a genuine partner in the problem-solving conversations that inevitably will need to happen between themselves and professionals. In some cases, parents need to be given the language with which teachers are familiar so that they can engage as equals. They need to know that their perspectives are essential, as are the views and feelings of their child in whatever ways they can be gathered. They need to have as much knowledge as possible about the early years' environment, the way the setting or nursery works, the methods professionals use to support and monitor children's development, along with the intricacies of provision and the ways in which it can be adapted. Knowledge can limit uncertainty and give greater choice and control, and having a sense of control can in turn contribute to a reduction in anxiety, thus opening up real possibilities for practical dialogue.

Strong, inclusive leaders are good communicators and engage parents purposefully by using evidence-based tools: for example, use of structured conversations based on coaching methodology in which dialogue is paraphrased, understanding reflected back, main issues identified, small manageable steps noted and lines of communication established all within mutually agreed timeframes. Person-centred tools should also be actively used to gather parent perspectives and to generate co-produced plans which focus on the child's journey towards the destination of adulthood. Action should be taken now, not once a referral has been made to an external specialist, thus giving both the parent and the child confidence that best endeavours are underway and the early years' cycle of assess, plan, do, review is a present, ever-emerging reality. Parents need the reassurance – as does the child – that it is 'revisited in increasing detail with increasing frequency to identify the best way of securing good progress' (DfE and DoH, 2015:5.44).

Inclusive leadership: good practice principles

Early years' environments which build and sustain (DfE and DoH, 2015) the core attributes of respect, connectedness and active dialogue hold the keys to successful inclusive practice. The confidence of staff must be shaped by the leader, who promotes and celebrates positive experiences for both child and parent. Good leadership means opening a dialogue with parents based on genuine information exchange, and the use of observation to feed the assess, plan, do, review cycle. It must be supported by excellent professional development for staff, incorporating formal and informal training supported by coaching/mentoring and a genuinely child-centred approach in which successes are logged and 'behaviours' are interpreted in an iterative way. The underpinning rationale is to develop a problem-solving mentality which is flexible and responsive (Callanen *et al.*, 2017). If the provision is based on the ever-evolving knowledge of the child through the cycle of continual assessment, fit-for-purpose planning and detailed discursive review, then the transition process onward to school is already underway, and the baton can be transferred safely. An important factor in this process is consideration of the research showing that learning and social skills gained by the end of one academic year frequently take a dip during the holidays (Shizwell and Defeyter, 2017; Quinn and Polkoff, 2017). The implication of this is of huge importance to the early years' sector, not least on behalf of those who have additional challenges upon entering new and more formal educational environments. Good transfer of information may therefore be only part of the story. The rest is about ensuring purposeful scaffolding for each child and a further strengthening of the good practice approaches already embedded in the early years. Important too is that the connectedness with parents is transferred securely into the new environment so that an ambitious, problem-solving team approach can continue to drive the inclusive mindset for the child.

Conclusion

In conclusion, the skills required by leaders are centred on the critical analysis of key early years' theories, which lead to the creation of a community of belonging in which inclusive practices dominate (Jones and Pound, 2008; Briggs and Briggs, 2009). Leadership skills must be used to genuinely celebrate and value parents' views and experiences, embrace the uniqueness of each child and give confidence to colleagues by developing systems and structures that promote coherent communication. Incrementally honing these skills is an iterative process, and inclusive leaders know that by taking a brave and confident stance, research and discussion, strong team work, and a cycle of reflection and review will provide the building blocks for successful practice within which children with SEND can thrive.

Reflective questions

- Can a focus on developmental norms block a culture of inclusion in early years' settings?
- How can SENCOs in the early years develop clear-sighted, knowledgeable leadership of SEND strategy and practice?
- How can SENCOs in the early years create a culture of belonging for children with SEND and their parents?

References

Allen, K. and Cowdrey, G. (2012) *The Exceptional Child: Inclusion for the Early Years*. 7th edn. Boston: Wadsworth.

Allen, S. and Whalley, M. (2010) *Supporting Pedagogy and Practice in the Early Years*. Exeter: Learning Matters.

Boehm, A. and Weinberg, R. (1997) *The Classroom Observer: Developing Observation Skills in Early Years Settings*. 3rd edn. London: Teachers College Press.

Briggs, M. and Briggs, I. (2009) *Developing Your Leadership in the Early Years*. London: Continuum.

Brodie, K. (2013) *Observation, Assessment, Planning in the Early Years: Bringing it all Together*. Maidenhead: Open University Press.

Callanen, M., Anderson, M., Haywood, S., Hudson, R. and Speight, S. (2017) *Study of Early Education and Development: Good Practice in Early Education. Research Report*. London: DfE.

Department for Education (2019) *Early Years Foundation Stage Profile, 2020 Handbook*. London: DfE.

Department for Education, and Department of Health (2015) *Special Educational Needs and Disability Code of Practice: 0–25 Years*. London: DfE.

Desforges, C. and Aboucher, A. (2003) *The Impact of Parental Involvement, Parental Support and Family Education on Pupil Achievement and Adjustment: A Literature Review*. London: DfES.

Donaldson, M. (2006) *Children's Minds*. London: Harper Perennial.

Elkind, D. (2016) History. In Elkind, D., Gurewitz Clemens, S., Lewis, R., Brown, S., Almon, J., Ferrara, K., Hirsh-Pasek, K., Golinkoff, R., Schweihart, L., Grob, R. and Wardle, F. (authors no ed.) *The Wisdom of Play: How Children Learn and Make Sense of the World*. Available at: https://cdn.communityplaythings. com/-/media/files/cpus/library/training [Accessed 22.10.19].

Froebel, F. and Hailman, W. (1887) *The Education of Man*. New York: Appleton.

Gorard, S. and Siddiqui, N. (2017) *Stop Labelling Summer-born Pupils as SEN!* Available at: https://schools-week.co.uk/stop-labelling-summer-born-pupils-as-sen/#:~:text=It%20is%20well%20known%20 that,older%20children%20in%20their%20year [Accessed 23.10.19].

Green, E., Stroud, L., O'Connell, R., Bloomfield, S., Cronje, J., Foxcroft, C., Hurter, K., Lane, H., Marias, R., Marx, C., McAlinden, P., Paradice, R. and Vènter, D. (2015) *Griffiths Scales of Child Development*. 3rd edn. Oxford: Hogrefe.

Hampson, M., Patton, A. and Shanks, L. (2011) *Ten Ideas for 21st Century Education*. Available at: https://www.innovationunit.org/wp-content/uploads/2017/04/10-Schools-for-the-21st-Century_0.pdf [Accessed 14.12.20].

Harris, A. and Goodall, J. (2007) *Engaging Parents in Raising Achievement: Do They Matter?* London. DCSF.

Hattie, J. (2009) *Visible Learning: A Synthesis of over 800 Meta-analyses Relating to Achievement*. London: Routledge.

Hendrickx, S. (2015) *Women and Girls with Autism Spectrum Disorder: Understanding Life Experiences From Early Childhood to Old Age*. London: Jessica Kingsley.

Jones, C. and Pound, L. (2008) *Leadership and Management in the Early Years, From Principles to Practice*. Maidenhead: Open University Press.

Kirby, A. (2014) *The Co-occurrence of Learning Difficulties, Practical Implications, Ecological Approach* [PowerPoint Presentation]. Available at: https://www.dyslexiascotland.org.uk/sites/default/files/ SPLDs%20overl [Accessed 04.11.20].

Lawson, W. and Dombroski, B. (2017) Problems with object permanence: Rethinking traditional beliefs associated with poor theory of mind in autism. *Journal of Intellectual Disability – Diagnosis and Treatment*, 5(1), 1–6.

Locke, J. (1824) *Some Thoughts Concerning Education: The Works of John Locke*. Vol. 8. London: Rivington.

Long, R. (2015) *Summer Born Children Starting School*. Briefing Paper Number 07272. London: House of Commons.

Lucas, B. (2010) *The Impact of Parental Engagement on Learner Success*. Winchester: Centre for Real World Learning.

Luna Scott, C. (2015) The futures of learning 3: What kind of pedagogies for the 21st Century? *UNESCO Education Research and Foresight*. Working Paper Series No. 15. Paris: ERF.

McLeod, S. (2018) *Jean Piaget's Theory of Cognitive Development*. Available at: www.simplypsychology. org.piaget.htm1/ [Accessed 10.11.19].

McNamara, L., Colley, P. and Franklin, N. (2017) School recess, social connectedness and health: A Canadian perspective. *Health Promotion International*, 32(2), 329–402.

Montessori, M. (2007) *The Absorbent Mind*. Radford, VA: Wilder.

Ng'asike, J. (2014) African early childhood development curriculum and pedagogy for Turkana nomadic pastoral commonwealth of Kenya. *New Directions for Child and Adolescent Development*, 146, 43–60.

Pankin, J. (2013) *Schema Theory*. Available at: http://web.mit.edu/pankin/www/Schema_Theory_and_Concept_Formation.pdf [Accessed: 4.11.19].

Piaget, J. (1957) *Construction of Reality in the Child*. London: Routledge and Kegan Paul.

Piaget, J. and Inhelder, B. (1967) *Child's Conception of Space*. New York: Norton.

Prizant, B. and Fields-Meyer, T. (2016) *Uniquely Human: A Different Way of Seeing Autism*. New York: Simon and Schuster.

Quinn, D. and Polkoff, M. (2017) *Summer Learning Loss: What Is It and What Can We Do About It?* Available at: www.brookings.edu/research/summer-learning-loss-what-is-it-and-what-can-we-do-about-it/ [Accessed 10.11.19].

Roelofs, K. (2017) Freeze for action: Neurobiological mechanisms in animal and human freezing. *Philosophical Transactions of the Royal Society of London. Series B, Biological Sciences*, 372(1718), 1–10.

Sharp, C., George, N., Sargent, C., O'Donnell, S. and Heron, M. (2009) *International Thematic Probe: The Influence of Relative Age on Learner Attainment and Development*. Available at: https://assets.publishing.service.gov.uk/government/uploads/system/uploads/attachment_data/file/604978/0209_CarolineSharp_et_al_RelativeAgeReviewRevised.pdf [Accessed 06.08.20].

Shizwell, J. and Defeyter, M. (2017) Investigation of summer learning loss in the UK – Implications for holiday club provision. *Frontier in Public Health*. Available at: www.ncbi.nlm.nih.gov/pmc/articles/PMC5635200/ [Accessed 04.11.19].

Sykes, E., Bell, J. and Rodeiro, C. (2016) *Birthday Effects: A Review of the Literature from 1990-on*. Cambridge: University of Cambridge.

Trussler, S. and Robinson, D. (2015) *Inclusive Practice in the Primary School, A Guide for Teachers*. London: Sage.

Warnock, M. (1978) *Special Educational Needs: Report of the Committee of Enquiry into the Education of Handicapped Children and Young People*. London: Her Majesty's Stationery Office.

Wilson, D. and Gross, D. (2018) Parent's executive functioning and involvement in their child's education: An integrated literature review. *Journal of School Health*, 88(4), 322–329.

8 Social, emotional and mental health

Lisa O'Connor

Introduction

This chapter considers the implications of changing agendas in relation to the well-being and mental health of learners and the role of the SENCO within these processes. The implementation of the *Special Educational Needs and Disability Code of Practice: 0 to 25 years* (DfE and DoH, 2015) has led to a category change in terms of behaviour, emotional and social difficulties (BESD) becoming social, emotional and mental health (SEMH). This is a momentous change which is felt to have far-reaching implications in terms of the expectations on educational professionals when identifying and supporting this particular area of need. There are a wide range of areas to consider within this category, which include self-esteem, emotional well-being and mental health, all of which are intricately linked. The importance of this category is apparent in recent publications such as *Transforming children and young people's mental health provision: a green paper* (DHSC and DfE, 2017), *Mental Health and Behaviour in Schools* (DfE, 2018a) and the *Mental health and wellbeing provision in schools research report* (DfE, 2018b). Such publications highlight the need to ensure that all professionals working alongside vulnerable learners are aware of the importance of recognising and addressing SEMH. This has significant implications in terms of accountability within identification and support processes for learners with special educational needs (SEN). The issues emerging from this expectation present concerns from professionals when reflecting upon their own knowledge and understanding of the area of mental health and the lack of accessible training opportunities since the implementation of this new category. Saqipi and Korpinen (2013) discuss teacher professionalism as outlined by Webb *et al.* (2004), defining this concept as their responsibility to develop knowledge; it is further suggested that such development can occur in reaction to tensions around role requirements or changes to policy and practice. This clearly links to expectations now prevalent within education as a wide range of professionals strive to gain a clearer understanding of the mental health category outlined in updated policy, guidance and legislation. This is an area of concern for many, as it was initially suggested that training would be implemented to support identification of mental health needs. This lack of training could result in those supporting learners feeling ill-equipped to identify SEMH. However, in reality this change of category is in fact merely a change of language, as emotional health has been a dominant factor in the BESD category and is an area those supporting learners have engaged with over an extensive period of time.

Implications for SENCOs/colleagues

The move to an area of need encompassing mental health has resulted in an expectation of stronger partnerships between educational settings and the children and adolescent mental health services (CAMHS). Mental health responsibilities are now proposed to be managed through the CAMHS and the *Special Educational Needs and Disability Code of Practice* (DfE and DoH, 2015), requiring a process which significantly overlaps CAHMS and education. The expectations now placed on those supporting learners within schools, colleges and other educational settings, in terms of identification of need and provision for children and young people's mental health difficulties, can be viewed as blurring the lines between education and health professionals' roles. Recent evidence from Norwich and Eaton (2015) suggests that the differing approaches of education, social care and health could cause tensions when medical and social models of disability form part of the approach to planning, with one service possibly focusing on prescriptive planning approaches and the other on responsive planning approaches. This creates a scenario where a range of professionals use different assumptions and language, which could impact on how they work collaboratively to promote the mental health of a child or young person. Wolpert *et al.* (2013) discuss an earlier national mental health initiative suggesting that common language is absent within mental health and education; therefore, a barrier to provision and effectiveness is created.

Variances in such models could have an adverse effect on identification and support for learners identified as having SEMH needs. In essence the vision of a collaborative model is a positive approach; however, facilitating such a model with other agencies can result in negative experiences for a SENCO charged with leading this process, as it can be an extremely challenging task in attempting to bring services together in multi-agency meeting scenarios. This could lead to uncertainty in promoting a system across a setting when the SENCO is aware this may be flawed; however, there is an expectation that co-operation among education, health and social care services will be encouraged. There is no suggestion of a lack of commitment from SENCOs and professionals supporting learners, but that the systems surrounding our ability to facilitate this collaborative approach may be somewhat restricted. Practices around such systems investigated by Vostanis *et al.* (2013) highlight the lack of frameworks to facilitate a process of bringing services together in a co-ordinated way and, although there is a focus on this in the *Special Educational Needs and Disability Code of Practice* (DfE and DoH, 2015), the issue is the actual implementation of a process requiring engagement from a range of services. They further discuss how differences in professional culture, priorities and attitudes can have an adverse effect on a system at the forefront of national priorities. In contrast to this view, Evetts (2012) considers that different professionals may not be opposites but can be reinforcing, as professional values can result in the emphasis of a shared identity, whereby relations can be collaborative and supportive. This is in fact the intention of the *Special Educational Needs and Disability Code of Practice* (DfE and DoH, 2015) in bringing a wide range of professionals together, and it is the systems around expectations that create difficulties when attempting to implement such practices.

Changing perceptions in relation to the importance of identifying and addressing social, emotional and mental health needs

Recognition of the range of needs encompassed within the SEMH category is the first step to ensuring that effective provision is implemented. It is essential that all professionals supporting learners recognise the equal importance of learning and social and emotional needs. Although systems and expectations within education often focus on attainment and progression, there should be no priority between the two areas. Without one the other will suffer, and an emotionally well-balanced child in a harmonious environment creates opportunity for learning. There is a need to consider why social and emotional difficulties are not always effectively addressed and if it is simply a case of emotional issues being viewed as less important in the structures surrounding educational establishments. Khadka (2018) discusses issues related to the importance of human needs, suggesting that although well-being is currently viewed as a complex area to be addressed, there is a lack of evidence that this is prioritised. A lack of fulfilment of lower-order needs often results in a major barrier to the development and learning of children and young people, and it is therefore essential that addressing SEMH is emphasised.

In terms of this issue, a learner who may be experiencing social and emotional difficulties will need support and intervention to engage in other aspects of learning. The most important factor in this process is that professionals within educational settings have a clear understanding of the impact of these difficulties and develop approaches to address this within their classroom. Glazzard and Bligh (2018) reflect that positive teacher attitudes are critical to developing relationships in the classroom and lead to more effective learning. If SEMH is not addressed and given the attention required, there is a question of how adequately individuals with learning difficulties are being supported. There is a possibility that social and emotional difficulties contribute to learning needs and can lead to adverse behaviours including distraction, disruption and displays of withdrawal. Alongside this a fear of failure can lead to an unwillingness to be independent, which creates further problems in addressing the learner's difficulties. For a learner who may already feel isolated, due to acknowledgement of their difference/difficulties, a failure to recognise and directly address their emotional needs could lead to further barriers in both learning and relationships. When considering acceptance and rejection, McCallum and Price (2016) believe a focus on the evolution of relationships results in a sense of belonging for learners, which impacts positively on the formation of identity. McCallum and Price also suggest that perceptions within society exclude children and young people with additional needs, and this further marginalises them within educational practices.

The development of secure relationships between professionals and learners is therefore a crucial aspect in the process around identification and support for SEMH. Showing an understanding of a learner's difficulties and behaviour leads to the formation of positive relationships and a sense of belonging for learners, which impacts positively on SEMH. Effective communication among learners, parents and carers is an essential aspect of addressing SEMH needs, and recognition that professionals are willing to listen and value input from everyone involved in the process leads to the establishment of effective relationships. The encouragement and evolution of strong and trusting relationships can lead to higher levels of engagement within support and intervention processes and result in the establishment of a cohesive approach to addressing the learner's needs. It is imperative that this approach becomes embedded as routine practice within the system of supporting learners with SEMH.

Co-ordinating support/whole-school approach

The co-ordination of a whole-school approach to SEMH begins with the development of collaborative relationships with a range of professionals. A shared vision can lead to motivation within a setting, and the development of such effectual relationships promotes a collaborative culture. Daniels (2006) believes that professional individualism is seen as an obstacle which has been caused by organisational structures, discouraging a culture of interaction and knowledge sharing, when in fact effective communication and collaboration create compelling inclusive provision. It is imperative that a collegial approach is encouraged to promote a positive environment and build relationships and partnerships between school and community. The SENCO's role in the implementation of effective collaborative processes can impact positively on these wide-ranging relationships, resulting in efficient support and provision for learners with SEMH. Devecchi and Rouse (2010:7) reflect on the benefits of established collaboration, describing an effective model as 'a mutual space for reflection', which can result in an understanding of shared responsibility and collegiality in a process. This should then lead to increased staff perceptions of accountability in relation to supporting learners with a range of needs including SEMH. A collaborative approach would also result in a greater understanding of the processes and procedures that need to be adhered to in order to ensure that all involved are addressing the needs of learners with SEMH.

The link between parents/carers and school is vital when implementing support for learners with a range of needs, so it is therefore essential that SENCOs develop strategies to ensure effective parental/carer collaboration takes place. In relation to this policy, legislation and guidance such as the Lamb Inquiry (DCSF, 2009) has investigated improving parental confidence in the current special educational needs provision system. The report states that strengthening relationships among all those involved in an individual's education will enhance outcomes for learners with special educational needs. The Children and Families Act 2014 and the *Special Educational Needs and Disability Code of Practice* (DfE and DoH, 2015) place parents at the centre of their own child's education, and schools are required to consult with them regarding their expectations from the setting. Hornby and Lafaele (2011) examine the barriers that can be created when parents' perceptions of a setting includes opinions that staff are reluctant to involve them in processes. Promoting a collaborative approach involving parents would give them confidence that their voice is valued in a process related to the implementation of provision to support learners with SEMH. The findings of Lamb (DCSF, 2009) and the *Support and Aspiration* Green Paper (DfE, 2011) subsequently led to current legislation and guidance in the form of the Children and Families Act 2014 and the *Special Educational Needs and Disability Code of Practice* (DfE and DoH, 2015). The findings, recommendations and expectations of this wide range of literature impact upon the role of the SENCO in relation to ensuring that all relevant stakeholders are involved in processes related to assessment and support. The implementation of systems encouraging effective collaboration with parents leads to a recognition that the profile of special educational needs (SEN) is prominent in their child's setting and instils confidence that the person leading SEN values their input when implementing effective support for learners. Tucker and Schwartz (2013) support this finding in suggesting that parents value authentic relationships with a leader willing to negotiate with a range of stakeholders, ensuring provision is effective.

These collaborative approaches forged between professionals and parents/carers would then impact upon multi-agency relationships. There is a need for greater involvement and communication among all stakeholders to ensure that a shared vision is present. This can be achieved through a focus on building stronger relationships with everyone involved in the processes surrounding a learner who is experiencing social and emotional difficulties. Evidence of the importance of such approaches appear in the Green Paper: *Support and Aspiration* (DfE, 2011), which focuses on bringing together all agencies involved, ensuring provision is implemented for a learner with SEN. Tucker and Schwartz concur: 'interactions between schools, professionals and families influence the dynamics of the working relationship' (2013:4). This approach should lead to a much more succinct process which ensures that all voices are captured when reviewing and implementing provisions for learners. There are obviously obstacles in attempting to execute this in terms of areas related to potential differences in working practices, opportunities for collaboration and the structures surrounding a variety of services. However, if compelling partnerships can be formed, there is the potential to overcome some of these issues.

Kearns (2005) reflects on the SENCO role as a collaborator promoting effective approaches to teaching and learning whilst engaging staff in developmental processes, a vital element in implementing provision and promoting efficient inclusive practice. A crucial aspect of this process is the raising of the SENCO profile in educational settings, as this can result in a higher level of impact when introducing initiatives and encouraging a whole-school approach. The SENCO potentially has the authority and capacity to enhance practice by ensuring that colleagues are aware of their responsibilities to learners. Collaboration is crucial in ensuring learners' needs are met, and the SENCO can expertly facilitate and promote change. An essential element of the National Award for SEN Co-ordination requires evidence that staff development is prominent on the SENCO's own agenda within their setting. Watkins *et al.* (2011) recognise the obstacles professionals can face in attempting to influence colleagues in a range of roles whilst promoting change in a pre-existing culture. This can be achieved not only through high-quality training but also when continually disseminating relevant information in order to support colleagues. A technique such as this leads to recognition that there is a supportive approach within the setting and can result in a more collegial environment when attempting to implement initiatives. This then allows an opportunity to discuss appropriate teaching and intervention, allowing for the development of a focused approach to SEMH. A further consideration within the process is the acquisition of the knowledge, strengths and development needs of all members of staff in terms of SEMH experience. This highlights the SENCO's willingness to acknowledge that there is a need to develop skills within this area and can decrease the apparent apprehension around the terminology of this category. A process encompassing a clear collaborative approach would also impact on ensuring SEMH is a priority to all staff rather than often being misconstrued as only the SENCO's responsibility. This would then ensure that all involved acquire a greater awareness of learners' needs and promote a supportive culture within a whole-school approach.

Alongside establishing a supportive training and development process, other mechanisms could be considered in order to ensure that all colleagues within the setting are aware of expectations. It would be useful to produce a SEMH policy or guidance document accessible to both staff and parents. This would provide clear guidelines outlining support processes and expectations within the setting. A document containing essential information related to support and intervention would then become a point of reference for all stakeholders and highlight the collegial approach the school is striving to achieve when supporting learners. The SEND information report could be a forum for this and include signposting for both professionals and parents in supporting learners with SEMH.

Supporting colleagues and learners

Learners with SEMH needs often face challenges that they do not have the ability to address, so relationships between adults and children are the key to achievement. In encouraging a classroom ethos of acceptance and empathy, it is possible to begin to effectively address needs. In attempting to implement a supportive culture, it is essential to encourage learners to express emotions, which can be achievable through targeted activities. Interventions should be considered as more than an opportunity for a class discussion or a child being given extra support on a daily basis; they can be used in a variety of contexts. An example of this could be the implementation of a whole-school initiative which addresses the needs of the community rather than singling out individuals. Such initiatives can begin with staff development activities, which the SENCO may facilitate as part of their role, in relation to ongoing continuing professional development for colleagues. An approach such as this can initially centre around discussion related to SEMH needs within the classroom and the concerns colleagues may have around supporting learners. This provides an opportunity to highlight gaps in knowledge and levels of confidence of a variety of staff who are expected to deliver interventions. When attempting to implement changes within a setting, there often can be concerns with colleagues feeling undermined or challenged by the need to address these issues, as they may feel this is a criticism of their own classroom practice. Alleviating these concerns and addressing them openly in a supportive context can lead to a much more collegial approach to a whole-school process. It may be that some colleagues feel there is less need for this particular approach in their own classroom; however, promoting the positive impact SEMH support can have on all learners is a crucial aspect of driving forward a whole-school approach.

To encourage engagement in this process, it may be useful for the SENCO to begin by providing staff with initial materials suitable to age phases or year groups. Accessibility of materials could potentially be the first obstacle colleagues face, and taking this concern out of the equation would be viewed as supportive and potentially encourage teachers/support staff to take the initiative in locating additional materials. This should in fact be a specific request within the process; although they may be provided with a bank of activities to use on a daily/weekly basis, there is an expectation that they would add to this through examples of their own practice and the acquisition of further ideas to use within these activities. It may even be useful to timetable a weekly session with a focus on SEMH, and this approach would then also highlight senior leaders' commitment to addressing the emotional needs of learners. Such an approach ensures that issues are regularly addressed within settings, and it is likely that this will happen on a daily rather than a weekly basis. Intervention should not be the sole responsibility of the class teacher; encouraging collaboration among all adults within the classroom can lead to the initiation of extra activities when necessary for learners displaying signs of SEMH needs. By working together in this way, it ensures that responsibility lies with all adults within the setting and leads to creating a positive environment.

A wide range of resources are available to support this area of need, which can be promoted to colleagues addressing SEMH in schools. There is no expectation that SENCOs must provide original resources, and taking some time to engage with available materials, in order to decide which are most effective for the needs of your setting, is an important approach. Online resources are readily available and accessible from organisations such as the Mental Health Foundation, displaying a wide range of accessible content for pupils, parents and carers, and teachers. It may be useful to direct colleagues to such forums, as they will contain case studies, podcasts and input from a variety of professionals who staff would easily identify with. Such support mechanisms not only equip colleagues with a range of materials but also provide an in-depth understanding of the issues faced by learners, parents, carers and professionals offering support to children and young people. This is a crucial element of promoting a whole-school approach, with those involved gaining an understanding of the potential barriers that learners with SEMH, parents and carers experience. Figure 8.1 is a diagram of one large hexagon with six smaller hexagons attached to each of the large hexagon's edges. The large hexagon contains the text: 'Promoting positive mental health'. Starting with the top hexagon and moving clockwise, the six smaller hexagons are labelled: Access information on symptoms and signs of mental health. Ensure opportunities to reflect on emotions are present. Incorporate mental health focus into daily or weekly timetable. Ensure opportunities exist for learners to build peer relationships. Provide examples of how to deal with emotions. Promote a positive environment – praise, encourage and listen.

It is also important to ensure that children and young people understand that it is a normal process to talk about feelings and worries to teachers, support staff and their friends. This can be approached in a variety of ways such as initiatives and interventions but also with simple displays or posters around educational settings which attempt to normalise emotions. Learners often do not have the confidence to express emotions such as feeling scared, frustrated, upset, angry or worried, as such emotions can lead to situations where they feel vulnerable. Providing

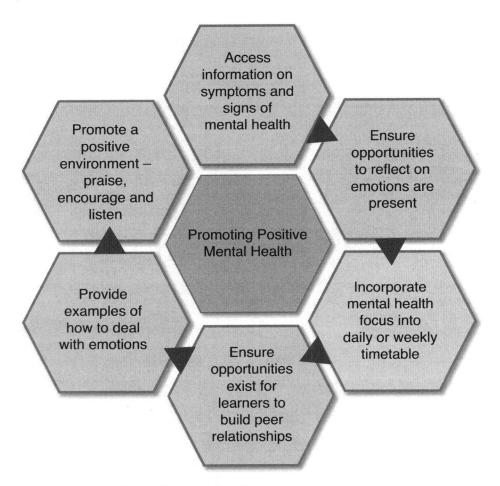

Figure 8.1 Steps to promoting positive mental health

opportunity for learners to express emotion is vital to promoting a safe and open environment. Alongside this the incorporation of an SEMH focus within their daily/weekly routines alleviates apprehension if they do need to discuss or express emotions.

Conclusion

In considering the topics outlined in this chapter, it is clear that the most important aspect of the SENCO role relates to leadership and the ability to create a culture based on collaboration. This extends beyond the school setting, and in order to facilitate this, SENCOs must see themselves as leaders representing their individual learners, colleagues and educational setting. The development of leadership skills is an important aspect of the role itself and in turn raises the profile of the SENCO within individual settings.

The leadership elements of the SENCO role encompass a variety of areas, and it is imperative that they remain central to the development of relationships within educational settings. This ensures a clear understanding of addressing SEMH needs is present and leads to the evolution of positive attitudes within the process. In establishing themselves as leaders in this way, the development of secure and positive relationships among learners, parents and professionals can become instiled in the culture of a setting. Leadership within the role is clearly not just related to co-ordination and implementation of processes but encompasses a range of areas such as interaction and knowledge sharing. It is therefore imperative that as a leader the SENCO facilitates a range of development mechanisms and promotes the implementation of specific interventions/processes to support SEMH needs.

The importance of developing colleagues' knowledge related to both the area of need and the expectations, in terms of supporting these specific needs, leads to more effective collaboration. Such collegial approaches build relationships between a wide range of stakeholders, which impacts positively on inclusive provision and establishes the SENCO as a leader within the process.

Reflective questions

- How might collaborative partnerships related to SEMH be strengthened?
- How might SENCOs influence perceptions regarding the importance of addressing SEMH in the classroom?
- What steps could be taken to promote a shared vision?

References

Children and Families Act 2014. London: HMSO.

Daniels, H. (2006) Rethinking intervention: Changing the cultures of schooling. *Emotional and Behavioural Difficulties*, 11(2), 105–120.

Department for Children, Schools and Families (DCSF) (2009) *Lamb Inquiry Special Educational Needs and Parental Confidence*. Nottingham: DCSF.

Department for Education (DfE) (2011) *Support and Aspiration: A New Approach to Special Educational Needs and Disability: A Consultation*. London: DfE.

Department for Education (2018a) *Mental Health and Behaviour in Schools*. London: DfE.

Department for Education (2018b) *Mental Health and Wellbeing Provision in School: Review of Published Policies and Information Research Report*. London: DfE.

Department for Education and Department of Health (DoH) (2015) *Special Educational Needs and Disability Code of Practice: 0 to 25 Years*. London: DfE and DoH.

Department of Health and Social Care (DHSC) and Department for Education (2017) *Transforming Children and Young People's Mental Health Provision: A Green Paper*. London: DHSC and DfE.

Devecchi, C. and Rouse, M. (2010) An exploration of the features of effective collaboration between teachers and teaching assistants in secondary schools. *Support for Learning*, 25(2), 91–99.

Evetts, J. (2012) Professionalism in turbulent time: Changes, challenges and opportunities. Paper presented at: *Propel Inaugural Conference: Professional Learning in Turbulent Times: Emergent Practices and Transgressive Knowledges*. Stirling University 9–11 May. Available at: www.stir.ac.uk/media/schools/sass-ed/propel/2012/JuliaEvetts-FullPaper.pdf [accessed 6 June 2019].

Glazzard, J. and Bligh, C. (2018) *Meeting the Mental Health Needs of Children 4–11 Years*. St. Albans: Critical Publishing.

Hornby, G. and Lafaele, R. (2011) Barriers to parental involvement in education: An explanatory model. *Educational Review*, 63(1), 37–52.

Kearns, H. (2005) Exploring the experiential learning of special educational needs coordinators. *Journal of In-service Education*, 31(1), 131–150.

Khadka, S. (2018) Conceptualizing child well-being in Nepal as fluid hierarchy of multi-dimensional basic needs. *Child Indicators Research*, 1–22.

McCallum, F. and Price, D. (2016) *Nurturing Wellbeing Development In Education*. Oxon: Routledge.

Norwich, B. and Eaton, A. (2015) The new special education needs (SEN) legislation in England and implications for services for children and young people with social, emotional and behavioural difficulties. *Emotional and Behavioural Difficulties*, 20(2), 117–132.

Saqipi, B. and Eira Korpinen, T. A. (2013) Understanding the context of teacher professionalism in education systems undergoing transition – Kosovo case. *Social and Behavioural Sciences*, 112(2014), 635–646.

Tucker, V. and Schwartz, I. (2013) Parents' perspectives on collaboration with school professionals: Barriers and facilitators to successful partnerships in planning for students with ASD. *School Mental Health*, 5(1), 3–14.

Vostanis, P., Humphrey, N., Fitzgerald, N., Deighton, J. and Wolpert, M. (2013) How do schools promote emotional well-being among their pupils? Findings from a national scoping survey of mental health provision in English schools. *Child and Adolescent Mental Health*, 18(3), 151–157.

Watkins, K. E., Lyso, I. H. and Demarrais, K. (2011) Evaluating executive leaderships programs: A theory of change approach. *Advances in Developing Human Resources*, 13(2), 208–239.

Webb, R., Vulliamy, G., Hämäläinen, S., Sarja, A., Kimonen E. and Nevalainen, R. (2004) A comparative analysis of primary teacher professionalism in England and Finland. *Comparative Education*, 40(1), 83–107.

Wolpert, M., Humphrey, N., Belsky, J. and Deighton, J. (2013) Embedding mental health support in schools: Learning from the Targeted Mental Health in Schools (TaMHS) national evaluation. *Emotional and Behavioural Difficulties*, 18(3), 270–283.

9 Pupils with social, emotional and mental health (SEMH) needs

The role of the Special Educational Needs Co-ordinator (SENCO) in meeting the inclusion challenge

Dr Dennis Piper

Introduction

Within the area of special educational needs (SEN), the inclusion of pupils with SEMH/BESD (behavioural, emotional and social difficulties) has frequently been reported as particularly problematic for teachers (Armstrong, 2014; Dyson *et al.*, 1998; Ofsted, 2006), and is predominantly accompanied by negative teaching attitudes (Centre for Social Justice, 2011; Gibbs, 2007), consequently making it a significantly difficult area for SENCOs when leading on inclusion. Unlike other pupils with SEN, pupils with SEMH/BESD are just as likely to be placed in 'specialist' provision now as they were 30 years ago (DfE, 2014; Graham *et al.*, 2019). MacFarlane and Woolfson (2013) suggest that, rather than solely focusing on 'the pupil' as 'the problem', investigating the determinants of teachers' attitudes is crucial in improving teaching practices and informing the role of the SENCO in leading on the effective inclusion of pupils with SEMH needs (DfE, 2014, 2016, 2019; Sharples *et al.*, 2015).

As Hinsdale (2016:7) so expressively states:

> If we accept that each person is a unique mystery and that we are each the Other to those around us . . . then we must recognize that the teaching relationship is minimally peopled by two Others. As the student is Other to the teacher, so the teacher is to the student. The space between these two Others is where the power of the relationship lies. It is a space of difficulty, but it is also a space of possibility if only we can act ethically within it.

Oldfield *et al.* (2017) have identified ongoing areas of concern which SENCOs need to be aware of as 'leaders of change' (Fullan, 1993) when working with pupils with SEMH needs and their class teachers (CTs). These include: definitions; teacher perceptions of pupils labelled SEMH/BESD; headteacher, teacher and parent roles; teachers' emotional well-being (EWB); the importance of self-efficacy and empathy. These topics are now explored.

Definitions

Conceptual frameworks in the field of SEMH remain a major concern (Norwich and Eaton, 2015). As Peaston (2011:6) states:

> With definitions that are so-context dependent, it is not surprising to find that categorisation of children varies from school to school.

The importance of 'definitions' to researchers, teachers, parents and young people cannot be underestimated, not least because of the SENCO and CT's role in identification (Goodman and Burton, 2010), problems of 'stereotyping' (Adera and Bullock, 2010) and 'labelling' (Sheffield and Morgan, 2017). Additionally, the link between vague and shifting definitions and their role in rapid policy changes remains problematic (Strand and Lindorff, 2018).

A number of studies have identified the need for initial teacher training (ITT) and continuous professional development (CPD) with different foci, but agreeing that teachers need increased understanding of pupils with SEMH/BESD. Whilst some highlighted opportunities to improve 'within teacher' attributes, particularly empathy (Westling, 2010), others advocated skills in delivering interventions (Oldfield *et al.*, 2017), utilising underpinning theories such as relational pedagogy (RP) (Reeves and Le Mare, 2017) or the theory of planned behaviour (TPB) (MacFarlane and Woolfson, 2013) in explaining attitude-intention behaviour relations. However, this remains controversial as Piper (2018:46), echoing Koger and Winter (2010), re-iterates "there is no confirmation that intentions always lead to actions" and monitoring "intention to enaction" is becoming increasingly significant for SENCOs in meeting the inclusion challenge.

Teachers' roles, perceptions, working relationships and the challenge for SENCOs

Goodman and Burton (2010) reported an intriguing finding that teachers with less than two years' experience had the most positive outlook concerning including pupils labelled SEMH/BESD. The reasons why and how more experienced teachers become less willing to teach pupils labelled SEMH/BESD remain an area of debate (Heikonen *et al.*, 2017). Issues identified include: high level of staff turnover, excessive workloads, lack of understanding by the senior management team (SMT) of the time pupils with SEMH/BESD and their families need, lack of colleagues' support and parents who blamed CTs for their children's difficulties.

Whilst Cole (2015) identified headteachers' reluctance to admit pupils with SEMH/BESD and Adera and Bullock (2010) identified their lack of understanding of 'role overload', contrasting viewpoints by Peaston (2011), MacFarlane and Woolfson (2013) and Piper (2018) identified a *key* factor supporting longer-serving teachers in working with pupils with SEMH/BESD – namely, a *positive inclusive attitude* by the headteacher, with *support* from the SENCO.

Adera and Bullock (2010) also identified the *isolation* felt by American teachers responsible for pupils with SEMH/BESD. However, in the UK, whilst "every teacher is a teacher of special educational needs" (DfE/DoH, 2015:6.36), frequently the SENCO has overall responsibility for managing these pupils and suggesting alternative solutions to support the CT in order to maintain the pupil in school. For example, Peaston (2011:13) quoted a SENCO, stating:

> If it's far more appropriate for the child to be working in a small group on their social skills rather than tearing the classroom apart and stopping other children learning then so be it.

The role of parents and the challenges for the SENCO and CT

According to Birenbaum-Carmeli (1999) and Peaston (2011), parents can be either a source of stress or support to SENCOs and CTs. With the Children and Families Act (2014) and SEND CoP (DfE/DoH, 2015) placing the child and parent at the centre of all school actions, SENCOs and CTs have begun to express unease in 'working with parents' on an equal partnership basis (Smaill, 2015). Minke *et al.* (2014) point out that, because the 'personal' and 'high stakes' nature of education are often highly emotional, blame and guilt are a frequent outcome. Graue (1999) warned of the dangers of failure by policy makers when promoting policies which impact on power relations, highlighting Lareau's (1989) study concerning the greater degree of leverage available to white middle-class parents and its emergence in emotionally charged situations as "the dark side of parental involvement" (Lareau, 1989:7).

Parent-school links extend well beyond the 'school gates'. The pivotal role of the family 'shapes' children's behaviour and its multifarious effect on the 'parent-child-school dynamic'. O'Connor and Scott (2007:28–29) conclude in their study of *parent-child relationship quality*:

> the more *extreme* the parenting environment, the *worse* the child outcome and/or the likelihood of *clinical disturbance*, for example aggressive behaviour and delinquency, depression, anxiety and other internalising problems.

Underscoring this point, Shaffer and Kipp (2013) highlight the family's critical role in *shaping* children's behaviour, by observing the behaviour of their *attachment figures*. These internal models or *cognitive-affective filters* subsequently have a profound influence in how pupils, particularly those with complex SEMH needs, respond to 'the other' (i.e. CTs) and how they see themselves in the social world. Therefore, understanding the complexities and tensions that can develop within power relations, including the impact of the teacher-parent-child dynamic, is critical to the SENCO's role in leading on positive and relational parent-school partnerships within an *inclusionary* framework (Ewing *et al.*, 2018).

SENCOs' and CTs' EWB, self-efficacy, motivation and emotional attunement

Armstrong (2014) raised the issue of teachers' sense of self-efficacy and motivation. This can be linked to Humphrey's (2013:141) argument for research to focus on teachers' 'will and skill', especially when working with pupils following social emotional learning programmes (Wolpert *et al.*, 2015).

As Cole and Knowles (2011:13) state:

> A single child's actions can cause extreme and long-lasting stress to staff, inducing feelings of inadequacy, anger and, at times, despair.

As early as 2000, Wearmouth *et al.* highlighted the negative impact of pupils with EWB needs on teachers' well-being when she stated that there must be *overt* recognition of the demands made on the CT:

> Criticising teachers for apparent weaknesses in classroom organisation and teaching approaches is easy . . . it is much more difficult to sustain enthusiasm and patience with pupils, some of whom may have arrived in school troubled and aggressive or withdrawn . . . for lessons every day.
>
> (Wearmouth *et al.*, 2000:60)

Whilst Soini *et al.* (2010) raised similar concerns, since Wearmouth *et al*'s. 2000 research, no major study has focused specifically on *how teachers feel about their own EWB*, including its impact on developing inclusive practices whilst working with pupils with SEMH needs. Claxton (1999) also suggests that providing the necessary balance to both teach and care for pupils with SEMH/BESD is what makes teaching problematic. For SENCOs and CTs, in loco parentis, judging this balance depends partly on 'emotional attunement' (Kimes Myers, 1997). This involves understanding how another person processes emotion, recognising his or her emotional state and responding accordingly.

Emotional attunement is crucial if teachers are to recognise and respond effectively to pupils' emotional states, because *how* pupils engage with teachers in educational activities *outweighs* the activities themselves (Bingham and Sidorkin, 2004; Piper, 2017, 2018). It is also consistent with person-centred working, and Article 12 "Respect for the views of the child" (UNCRC, 1989; Muscutt, 2020). Middleton (2019:169–170) underscores this, characterising the inclusive teacher as,

> driven by a *moral imperative* . . . utilising *relational thinking* and exemplifying a *relational compassion* predicated on . . . a belief that 'education is a human right'.

The importance of sensitivity and empathy

Westling (2010) highlighted the need for teachers to have high levels of sensitivity and empathy, because people who are best at identifying others' emotions are more successful in their working relationships and interactions with others.

Empathy involves understanding the other's feelings through processes such as role-taking, switching attention to take another's perspective or responding non-egocentrically. Empathy is a core component of emotional intelligence (EI) and includes cognitive and affective elements

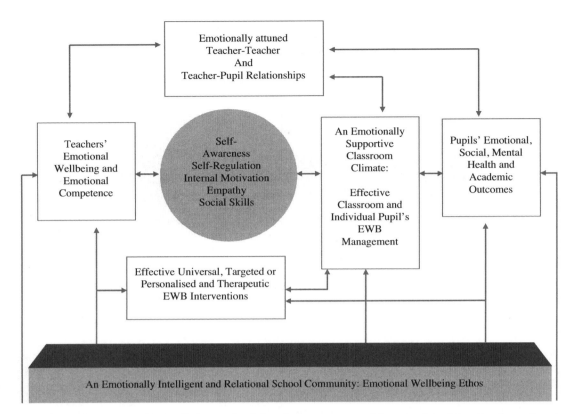

Figure 9.1 An emotionally intelligent and relational classroom model: a model of teachers' emotional well-being and emotional competence in relation to classroom and pupil outcomes, underpinned by an emotionally intelligent and relational school's ethos (Piper, 2017), adapted from Jennings and Greenberg (2009)

(Goleman, 1995). The cognitive component of empathy has been referred to as using 'theory of mind' (Baron-Cohen, 1995). This involves setting aside one's own current perspective, attributing a mental state to the other person (Leslie, 1987), and then inferring the likely content of their mental state, given the experience of that person.

Cooper (2011) provides a comprehensive description and classification of empathy at work in teaching and learning, revealing it as a complex phenomenon, closely associated with moral development, developing over time with frequency of interaction and highly dependent on the 'actors' and context of the interaction. Cooper describes the powerful effects of profound empathy[1] on self-esteem, relationships and learning. Empathetic teachers are revealed as highly moral individuals who 'attach' themselves mentally and emotionally to their pupils, generating emotional reciprocity modelling and evoking morality in their personal interactions with pupils and high-quality engagement in learning and behaviour. SENCOs are in a unique position and ideally placed to act as role models of this highly ethical inclusive practice within the classroom, underpinned by promoting an emotionally intelligent and relational school's ethos (see Figure 9.1).

Relational pedagogy, care, empathy and teachers' thoughts and feelings

As an RP theorist, Noddings (2012) suggests we should understand care as empathy, or as receptivity – open to someone's feelings, feel with someone; share a feeling and an understanding. Vygotsky (1986:10) reminds us of the importance of the interrelated nature of affect and cognition and the inadequacy of a merely cognitive approach, as:

> their separation is a major weakness . . . since it makes the thought process appear as an autonomous flow of 'thoughts thinking themselves'. Every idea contains a transmuted *affective* attitude toward the bit of reality to which it refers.

According to Cooper (2011), an attitude of care in teaching and learning emerges through 'profound empathy' in one-to-one relationships. Showing that you care profoundly facilitates a person-centred climate in which pupils, especially those with SEMH needs, learn most effectively, as the interconnectedness of personal and academic development underpin the learner's academic achievements.

Childerhouse (2017) and Hinsdale (2016), when advocating RP, argue that the curriculum and 'outcomes-driven' assessment appear to act as powerful factors in limiting teachers' ability to employ their empathy to best effect in meeting their pupils' needs, particularly those with SEMH needs. Vygotsky's (1986) early warning about the dangers of the separation of affect and cognition also applies to the divide between 'pastoral' and 'academic'. Failure of policy makers to recognise the significance of the affective is a factor that has led to the oppressive examination and testing regimes of recent years and subsequently had a profound effect on both pupils labelled SEMH/BESD and their teachers, who are often placed in an ongoing dilemma of attempting to address the EWB needs of those pupils alongside the pressures of achieving specific and or prescribed academic outcomes (Ofsted, 2019).

Findings from neuroscience and trauma-informed practice (Perry and Szalavitz, 2017) reaffirm the emphasis placed on affect by the earlier psychological literature (Damasio, 1994) and suggest strongly that *all learning is affective* in nature. Thus, the role of teacher empathy as a key constituent of the teaching and learning process and, as exemplified in RP, is deemed to be crucial to promoting affective, and by its nature, inclusive learning.

Many pupils who present with SEMH needs have experienced 'adverse childhood experiences' (ACEs) (Perry and Salovitz, 2017), which frequently impacts negatively on their learning and relationships with teachers. Damasio (1994) points out that the 'memory' of each interaction in a learning context is mapped both in the brain at an emotional level and throughout the body and remembered as a feeling. Consequently, interaction and associated learning is affective in nature. Noddings (2012) suggests that time is needed for real caring relationships to develop through the taught curriculum, including normal conversations and interactions that affirm and recognise pupils as valued individuals.

SENCOs as 'leaders on inclusion', when supporting teachers in applying Vygotsky's zone of proximal development, need to remind CTs and support staff that it involves both cognitive support and *emotional scaffolding*. Direction, support and intervention are vital to ensure pupils' progress at a sufficient pace, to help motivate and encourage them in their tasks and thinking. Formative assessment, which is at the very heart of learning, needs to be both emotional and cognitive, both personal and academic, and therefore poses the significant challenge for every teacher to underpin their formal and informal interactions with pupils, with both fundamental[2] and profound empathy. It is an integral part of the SENCO role to provide support and guidance in these vital areas. One way forward is to support teachers in recognising and understanding how their conceptual frameworks can either help or hinder the all-round progress of pupils with SEMH needs. One ongoing study which has focused on teachers' conceptual frameworks over time is encapsulated in the PIPER Model (Piper, 2017).

The PIPER Model – emergence and theoretical underpinnings

Between 2010 and 2015, 20 primary schools involving SENCOs, CTs, TAs and SMTs participated and collaborated in developing an evidence-based practice approach (DCSF, 2010; Wolpert *et al.*, 2015) to assist in the development of a three-step child-centred EWB intervention known as the PIPER Model to address pupils' social, emotional and behavioural needs (see Figure 9.2).

The PIPER Model's approach viewed 'behaviour as communication', necessitating the adoption of more holistic strategies and a concerted departure from the 'deficit' medical model of behaviour – *the child needs fixing* (Piper, 2017). The model originally utilised the Mental Health Foundation Risk and Resilience Framework (MHF, 1999) and has, over time, via an ongoing collaborative process with SENCOs leading group discussions, developed into an interactive four-field map with the 'school' as an additional key domain (Piper, 2017). The theoretical basis of the four-field map is underpinned by research into risk and resilience (Masten and Powell, 2003). Cooperative and *reflective* (Schön, 1991) completion of the four-field map constitutes Step 1 of the PIPER Model – Risk and Resilience Profiling (R&R).

Step 2 of the PIPER Model involves the application of a Tension Model (TM) and the collaborative production of a Reducing Anxiety Management Plan (RAMP), which includes the 'voice

STEPS (1a and 1b): R&R profiling:
Using the 4-field map - identify the child in question and begin profiling him/her on the basis of risk or resilience factors using the risk and resilience (protective factors) templates to record information. Underpin these judgements with a strong mutually agreed evidence base (at least 3 pieces of evidence) i.e. observable behaviour in and/out of class or school.

STEP (2a):
Read and discuss all aspects of the 'Tension' Model. Look carefully at pupil behaviours and teacher responses at each level. Notice that the pupil can move between levels (or states); identify the 'threshold between rational and irrational behaviours' i.e. Agitated State. Think carefully about what occurs within each level or 'state of tension'; e.g. 'Controlled' or 'Anxious' and begin to 'contextualise' the information in preparation for Step 2b - Creating a Reducing Anxiety Management Plan (RAMP)

STEP (1): Looking at the Risk and Resilience 4-Field Map:
The core group discuss the 'Risk and Resilience' (R&R) interactive 4-field map - agree an 'operational' definition for each characteristic / factor. A collective consensus is vital to 'benchmarking' at this First stage of provision mapping for Emotional Wellbeing.

STEP (2b): Creating a Reducing Anxiety Management Plan (RAMP):
Using the 'Tension' Model as a 'baseline measure' i.e. reference point, create your own 'operational' model - RAMP for the child - taking into account his/her behaviours at each level, his or her self-calming strategies and your agreed responses. This should create a 'tension' profile with which to begin devising a full risk assessment; this based on recognition of a combination of risk and resilience (protective) factors and the levels of tension or stress that may impact on the child's emotional wellbeing and, in turn manifest itself in a variety of presenting behaviours within each of the 5 'tension' levels or 'states'.

NEXT STEPS:
Once the provision map is collectively agreed, understood and approved, the information should be disseminated to ALL staff to ensure consistency and to create an optimum whole school inclusive and relational environment for the child to succeed/demonstrate evidence of progression. At review, evidence should be collated and presented to ascertain whether strategies have been effective in producing successful and measurable outcomes. At evaluation, a priority question should be - has the Provision Map (based on the R&R profile and RAMP) reduced (to any measurable degree) any risk factors and/or increased any number of resilience (protective) factors?

STEP (3): Creating a 3-Wave Provision Map
Using all the collated information from Steps 1-4 begin devising a 3-wave 'intervention' provision map. Take into account risk factors (health and safety) at each wave 'setting', your response - preventive measures / strategies, positive reinforcement (reward) when the child engages or achieves and define success criteria i.e. measurable outcomes. You may define this mapping process in 3 ways: (1) Intervention, (2) Risk Assessments and Preventive Measures and (3) Impact. It is vital you agree on a Start and Review date. Head teacher approval/signature for implementing the provision map is also necessary.

Figure 9.2 The PIPER Model – Personalised Interventions Promoting Emotional Resilience (a three-step guide)

of the child'. Both the TM and the RAMP are based on theories that underpinned psychological and psychotherapeutic research into emotions and anxiety-driven behaviours (Ellis and Joffe Ellis, 2011).

Step 3 of the PIPER Model involves combining the knowledge elicited from Steps 1 and 2 to create a personalised/child-centred three-wave Provision Map (PM), based on the policies and practices originally endorsed by Ofsted (2009) and the Equality Act (2010). This would enable the pupil to access a 'needs-led' curriculum predicated on *personal/child-centred* learning theories.

Within the context of delivering the IDP (DCSF, 2010), TaMHS (Wolpert *et al.*, 2015) and NASENCO (TDA, 2009), the PIPER Model emerged and continues to present as a researched, school-level evidence-based exemplar of an effective personalised, child-centred, cross-cultural and holistic approach to promoting emotional resilience in pupils with EWB needs and skills underpinning relational-based teaching in teachers (Ashman, 2017; Hanfstingl and Piper, 2018; Sanderson, 2019; Weingant *et al.*, 2019). Consequently, given its approach, the PIPER Model has, over time, presented itself as an ideal vehicle for helping to explore SENCOs' and CTs' evolving thoughts, feelings and actions and in keeping with current SEND policy and practice (DfE/DoH, 2015), promoting child-centred personalised interventions for pupils with SEMH needs via the assess, plan, do, review process.

Additionally, the PIPER Model assists SENCOs in becoming leaders of the in-school SEMH team around the child (SEMTAC) – a critical and challenging strategic role, supporting vulnerable pupils with deep-seated SEMH needs. SENCOs need to feel empowered by *a strong sense of agency and moral purpose* (Fullan, 1993) to facilitate proactive and inclusive approaches at every level of interaction; these exist via 'emotional connections', predicated on a nurturing and relational ethos, promoting the EWB of the school community and embracing the notion that "education is a human right" (Middleton, 2019). Creating an in-school SEMTAC exemplifies "SENCOs as relational change agents in schools" in meeting the inclusion challenge.

A SEMTAC should consist of teachers and support staff known as 'significant others' coordinated by the SENCO as *lead professional*, with the mutually agreed aim to collaborate, in order to support pupils with SEMH needs given their prior or current experience of them. Working within six core ethical principles – inclusion, compassion, empathy, self-awareness, self-reflection and child-centredness – SEMTAC should place the emphasis firmly on the needs ('risk' factors) and strengths ('resilience' or 'protective' factors) of the child or young person, rather than on those of organisations or other service providers. This is in keeping with 'the child's voice being heard' (DfE and DoH, 2015) subsumed within the Children and Families Act (2014), including article 3: *"The best interests of the child must be a top priority in all things that affect children"* and article 12: *"Every child has the right to have a say in all matters affecting them, and to have their views taken seriously"* (UNCRC, 1989) and (Muscutt, 2020).

A SEMTAC is about having a clear vision bolstered by strong leadership empowered to develop appropriate, resourced, preventive and evidence-based targeted interventions, within personalised provision maps, agreed and intended outcomes for children with SEMH needs. However, this will *not* be effective or thrive within a whole-school community, without an underpinning desire from *all* staff to actively 'include' vulnerable pupils with chronic complex needs, whose behaviours are driven by consistently high levels of anxiety and 'risk' in their daily lives.

Conclusion

In exploring the challenges facing the SENCO as a pivotal 'leader on inclusion' and CTs of including pupils with SEMH needs, it would appear that relatively few studies specifically focus on CTs' perceptions of pupils labelled SEMH/BESD and even fewer do so from a teacher-pupil relationship or RP perspective. Of those studies, none intensively follow teachers' statements from intentions to actual actions (Feucht *et al.*, 2017). Also, it is acknowledged that the area is complex (Oldfield *et al.*, 2017) and would benefit from a greater use of case studies (Armstrong, 2014:7), generating more research-informed and relationally underpinned inclusive practice. This is an area where SENCOs, participating in the NASENCO programme, are ideally placed to develop as 'teacher-researchers'.

In relation to teachers, it is suggested that a specific focus on teacher support and well-being, self-efficacy and empathy is likely to create a greater and better understanding of what enables experienced SENCOs in guiding CTs to provide positive engagement for pupils labelled SEMH/BESD rather than resort to exclusion for the 'greater good' of the school.

Considering teacher efficacy in relation to pupils labelled SEMH/BESD, it has been suggested that targeting specific individuals 'may be the most effective way to reduce behavioural difficulties' and further suggested that SEMH interventions need to draw on cognitive and behavioural approaches, including a greater understanding of how protective factors work within a risk and resilience context. Encapsulating the notion of *relationally underpinned inclusive practice*, the PIPER Model (2017), created collaboratively with SENCOs in a *strategic* role, CTs as *reflective practitioners* and *supportive* senior managers, provides a cost-neutral, evidence-based, positive and effective way forward, addressing many of the barriers identified (within the vast array of underpinning literature) when rising to the challenge of using evidence-informed, person-centred practices to meet the inclusion challenge and maintain pupils with SEMH needs in mainstream schools.

Reflective questions

- What SENCO-initiated school training has taken place in the school concerning SEMH needs? What impact has it had on the pupil, class teacher and other children in class?
- How are parents and/or carers enabled to 'work in partnership' with the school and other agencies to support a pupil with SEMH needs?
- What 'conceptual frameworks' are used in the school to understand and support pupils with SEMH needs?

Notes

1 Profound empathy encompasses a rich understanding of others in their social, historical and relational contexts. Hence, one-to-one or small group teaching naturally is more likely than large classes to produce profound empathy. Teachers who show profound empathy create an extremely rich mental model of individuals in their minds which they can relate to closely, both emotionally and cognitively. They draw on all their own experience and experience of other people and the clues emanating from pupils to interpret their feelings and understanding.
2 Fundamental empathy consists of the basic characteristics and means of communication which are needed to initiate empathetic relationships. For example, being accepting and open, giving attention, listening, being interested, taking a positive and affirmative approach, showing enthusiasm via appropriate facial expression and interaction, gestures, body language and movement, height, and distance, language and tone of voice. Over time and with frequency of interaction, fundamental empathy can develop into profound empathy.

References

Adera, B. A. and Bullock, L. M. (2010) Job stressors and teacher job satisfaction in programs serving students with emotional and behavioral disorders. *Journal of Emotional and Behavioural Difficulties*, 15(1), 5–14.

Armstrong, D. (2014) Educator perceptions of children who present with social, emotional and behavioural difficulties: A literature review with implications for recent educational policy in England and internationally. *International Journal of Inclusive Education*, 18(7), 731–745.

Ashman, S. (2017) *The Escalating Mental Health Crisis in English Secondary Schools: An Overview of Inclusive Pedagogies and Approaches to Improve the Emotional Wellbeing and Outcomes for Children and Young People with Social Emotional and Mental Health Difficulties.* Unpublished research paper (NASENCo), MMU.

Baron-Cohen, S. (1995) *Mindblindness: An Essay on Autism and Theory of Mind.* Cambridge, MA: MIT Press.

Bingham, C. and Sidorkin, A. M. (2004/2010) Manifesto of relational pedagogy: Meeting to learn, learning to meet. In Bingham, C. and Sidorkin, A. M. (eds.), *No Education without Relation.* Oxford: Peter Lang.

Birenbaum-Carmeli, D. (1999) Parents who get what they want: On the empowerment of the powerful. *The Sociological Review*, 199, 62–90.

Centre for Social Justice. (2011) *No Excuses: A Review of Educational Exclusion*: A Policy Report. London: Centre for Social Justice.

Childerhouse, H. (2017) *Supporting Children with Social, Emotional and Behavioural Difficulty (SEBD) in Mainstream: Teachers' Perspectives.* Unpublished PhD Thesis, Sheffield Hallam University.

Children and Families Act 2014. Chapter 6. London: Her Majesty's Stationery Office.

Claxton, G. (1999) *Wise Up: Learning to Live the Learning Life.* London: Bloomsbury.

Cole, T. (2015) *Mental Health Difficulties and Children at Risk of Exclusion from Schools in England: A Review from an Educational Perspective of Policy, Practice and Research, 1997 to 2015*. Oxford: University of Oxford.

Cole, T. and Knowles, B. (2011) *How to Help Children and Young People with Complex Behavioural Difficulties: A Guide for Practitioners Working in Educational Settings*. London: Jessica Kingsley.

Cooper, B. (2011) *Empathy in Education: Engagement Values and Achievement*. New York: Continuum.

Damasio, A. R. (1994) *Descartes' Error: Emotion, Reason, and the Human Brain*. London: Harper.

Department for Children Schools and Families (2010) *Inclusion Development Programme, BESD*. London: HMSO.

Department for Education (2014) *Children with Special Educational Needs 2014: An Analysis*. London: HMSO.

Department for Education (2016) *Mental Health and Behaviour in Schools: Departmental Advice for School Staff*. London: HMSO.

Department for Education (2019) *Permanent and Fixed Period Exclusions in England: 2017 to 2018*. London: Department for Education.

Department for Education and Department of Health (2015) *Special Educational Needs and Disability Code of Practice: 0 to 25 Years*. London: HMSO.

Dyson, A., Clark, C. and Millward, A. (1998) *Theorising Special Education*. London: Routledge.

Ellis, A. and Joffe Ellis, D. (2011) *Rational Emotive Behavior Therapy*. Washington: American Psychological Association.

Equality Act 2010. London: HMSO.

Ewing, D. L., Monsen, J. J. and Kielblock, S. (2018) Teachers' attitudes towards inclusive education: A critical review of published questionnaires. *Educational Psychology in Practice*, 34(2), 150–165.

Feucht, F. C., Brownlee, J. L. and Schraw, G. (2017) Moving beyond reflection: Reflexivity and epistemic cognition in teaching and teacher education. *Educational Psychologist*, 52(4), 234–241.

Fullan, M. (1993) Why teachers must become change agents. *Educational Leadership*, 50(6), 12–17.

Gibbs, S. (2007) Teachers' perceptions of efficacy: Beliefs that may support inclusion or segregation. *Educational and Child Psychology*, 24, 47–53.

Goleman, D. (1995) *Emotional Intelligence*. London: Bloomsbury.

Goodman, R. L. and Burton, D. M. (2010) The inclusion of students with BESD in mainstream schools: Teachers' experiences of and recommendations for creating a successful inclusive environment. *Emotional and Behavioural Difficulties*, 15(3), 223–237.

Graham, B., White, C., Edwards, A., Potter, S. and Street, C. (2019) *School Exclusion: A Literature Review on the Continued Disproportionate Exclusion of Certain Children*. London: Department for Education.

Graue, M. E. (1999) *Representing Relationships between Parents and Schools: Making Visible the Force of Theory*. Research Paper: Reconceptualising Early Childhood Education Conference, January 7, 1998. Honolulu.

Hanfstingl, B. and Piper, D. (2018) *The PIPER Model in Time-Out Classrooms: A Pilot Project Proposal; Evaluation of the PIPER Model in Carinthia, Austria*. Institute of Instructional and School Development Alpen-Adria-Universität Klagenfurt Austria. Presentation: June 2018, International Inclusion Conference, University of Wuppertal, Germany.

Heikonen, L., Pietarinen, J., Pyhältö, K., Toom, A. and Soini, T. (2017) Early career teachers' sense of professional agency in the classroom: Associations with turnover intentions and perceived inadequacy in teacher-student interaction. *Asia-Pacific Journal of Teacher Education*, 45(3), 250–266.

Hinsdale, M. J. (2016) *Relational Pedagogy*. Oxford Research Encyclopedia of Education. Oxford: Oxford University Press.

Humphrey, N. (2013) *Social and Emotional Learning: A Critical Appraisal*. London: Sage.

Jennings, P. A. and Greenberg, M. T. (2009) The prosocial classroom: Teacher social and emotional competence in relation to student and classroom outcomes. *Review of Educational Research*, 79(1), 491–525.

Kimes Myers, B. (1997) *Young Children and Spirituality*. London: Routledge.

Koger, S. and Winter, D. N. N. (2010) *The Psychology of Environmental Problems*. New York: Psychology Press.

Lareau, A. (1989) *Home Advantage: Social Class and Parental Intervention in Elementary Education*. Lanham, MD: Rowman and Littlefield.

Leslie, A. M. (1987) Pretence and representation: The origins of theory of mind. *Psychological Review*, 94, 412–426.

MacFarlane, K. and Woolfson, L. (2013) Teacher attitudes and behavior toward the inclusion of children with social, emotional and behavioral difficulties in mainstream schools: An application of the theory of planned behavior. *Teaching and Teacher Education: An International Journal of Research and Studies*, 29, 46–52.

Masten, A. S. and Powell, J. L. (2003) A resilience framework for research, policy, and practice: In Luthar, S. S. (ed.), *Resilience and Vulnerability: Adaptation in the Context of Childhood Adversities*. Cambridge: Cambridge University Press.

Mental Health Foundation (1999) *The Risk and Resilience Framework*. London: Department of Health.

Middleton, T. (2019) Thought piece – The inclusive teacher: Values and (com)passion in a wicked world. *Practice*, 1(2), 169–172.

Minke, K. M., Sheridan, S. M., Ryoo, J. H. and Koziol, N. A. (2014) Congruence in parent-teacher relationships: The role of shared perceptions. *The Elementary School Journal*, 114(4), 527–546.

Muscutt, J. C. (2020) Child rights, disability and educational psychology and inclusion. In Nastasi, B. K., Hart, S. N. and Nasser, S. (eds.), *International Handbook on School Psychology and Children's Rights*. Switzerland: Springer.

Noddings, N. (2012) The caring relation in teaching. *Oxford Review of Education*, 38(6), 771–781.

Norwich, B. and Eaton, A. (2015) The new special educational needs (SEN) legislation in England and implications for services for children and young people with social, emotional and behavioural difficulties. *Emotional and Behavioural Difficulties*, 20(2), 117–132.

O'Connor, T. G. and Scott, S. B. (2007) *Parenting and Outcomes for Children*. York: Joseph Rowntree.

Office for Standards in Education (Ofsted) (2006) *Inclusion: Does it Matter Where Pupils are Taught? Executive Summary*. London: HMSO.

Office for Standards in Education (Ofsted) (2009) *An Evaluation of National Strategy Intervention Programmes*. London: HMSO.

Office for Standards in Education (2019) *Framework for Inspections*. London: Ofsted.

Oldfield, J., Humphrey, N. and Hebron, J. (2017) Risk factors in the development of behaviour difficulties among students with special educational needs and disabilities: A multilevel analysis. *British Journal of Educational Psychology*, 87(2), 146–169.

Peaston, H. (2011) *Mainstream Inclusion, Special Challenges: Strategies for Children with BESD*. Nottingham: National College for Leadership of Schools and Children's Services.

Perry, B. D. and Salovitz, M. (2017) *The Boy Who Was Raised as a Dog: And Other Stories from a Child Psychiatrist's Notebook – What Traumatized Children Can Teach Us About Loss, Love, and Healing*. New York: Basic Books.

Piper, D. (2017) *The PIPER Model: Personalised Interventions Promoting Emotional Resilience in Children with Social, Emotional and Mental Health Needs*. London: Routledge.

Piper, D. (2018) *An Exploration of Primary School Teachers' Evolving Thoughts, Feelings and Actions Towards a Pupil with Emotional Wellbeing Needs, Labelled as Having Behavioural, Emotional and Social Difficulties: Utilising the PIPER Model as a Personalised 3-Step Emotional Wellbeing Intervention*. Unpublished EdD thesis, University of Manchester.

Reeves, J. and Le Mare, L. (2017) Supporting teachers in relational pedagogy and social emotional education: A qualitative exploration. *The International Journal of Emotional Education*, 9(1), 85–98.

Sanderson, D. (2019) *How Can We Build an Embedded Culture that is Centred on an Inclusive, Relational Pedagogy; One that Celebrates All Successes Including Curriculum Provision that Enables All Children and Young People to Succeed and Prepares them to be Successful, Independent Well-rounded Adults?* Unpublished research paper (NASENCo), MMU.

Schön, D. (1991) *The Reflective Practitioner: How Professionals Think in Action*. London: Routledge.

Shaffer, D. and Kipp, K. (2013) *Developmental Psychology: Childhood and Adolescence*. Boston: Cengage Learning.

Sharples, J., Webster, R. and Blatchford, P. (2015) *Making Best Use of Teaching Assistants.Guidance Report*. London: Education Endowment Foundation.

Sheffield, E. L. and Morgan, G. (2017) The perceptions and experiences of young people with a BESD/SEMH classification. *Educational Psychology in Practice*, 33(1), 50–64.

Smaill, E. (2015) How much is too much? Partnerships and power relationships between parents and schools. *Journal of Initial Teacher Inquiry*, 1, 62–64.

Soini, T., Pyhältö, K. and Pietarinen, J. (2010) Pedagogical well-being: Reflecting learning and well-being in teachers' work. *Teachers and Teaching*, 16(6), 735–751.

Strand, S. and Lindorff, A. (2018) *Ethnic Disproportionality in the Identification of Special Educational Needs (SEN) in England: Extent, Causes and Consequences*. Oxford: University of Oxford.

Training and Development Agency (2009) *Standards for the National Award of SEN Coordination*. London: TDA for Schools.

United Nations Convention on the Rights of the Child (1989) *Article 12*. UNICEF, UK.

Vygotsky, L. S. (1986) *Thought and Language*. Cambridge, MA: MIT Press.

Wearmouth, J., Edwards, G. and Richmond, R. (2000) Teachers' professional development to support inclusive practices. *Journal of In-Service Education*, 26(1), 49–61.

Weingant, V., Hanfstingl, B., Tremschnig, I. and Piper, D. (2019) Das Piper-Modell – personalised interventions promoting emotional resilience. In Kastner, Monika, Donlic, Jasmin, Hanfstingl, Barbara and Jaksche-Hoffman, Elisabeth (Hrsg.), *Lernprozesse über die Lebensspanne: Bildung erforschen, gestalten und nachhaltig fördern*. Leverkusen, Germany: Budrich.

Westling, D. (2010) Teachers and challenging behavior – Knowledge, views and practices. *Remedial and Special Education*, 31(1), 48–63.

Wolpert, M., Humphrey, N., Deighton, J., Patalay, P., Fugard, A. J., Fonagy, P., Belsky, J. and Vostanis, P. (2015) An evaluation of the implementation and impact of England's mandated school-based mental health initiative in elementary schools. *School Psychology Review*, 44, 117–138.

10 Medical conditions

Lorna Hughes

Encountering some form of medical incident or condition is unavoidable in a school context, whether this is relatively minor, through to more complex situations. It may be that a child or young person has a minor illness or injury that needs treatment. They may experience trauma or have an ongoing medical condition, otherwise known as a chronic illness, that may need support in managing. It could also mean supporting a child with a life-threatening condition such as cancer, or life-limiting conditions that are incurable and will shorten their lifespan. The responsibility for managing and leading on the support for children with medical conditions may not be directly attributed to the Special Educational Needs Co-ordinator (SENCO) role in policy. However, in practice, some schools will appoint the SENCO as the designated staff member to lead on this area. Additionally, in all schools, the SENCO will have some level of involvement in supporting learners with medical conditions due to the nature of their position as leaders for inclusive practice in schools.

Since the introduction of the Children and Families Act 2014, schools have statutory duties in supporting children with medical conditions. This is outlined in the key document *Supporting pupils at school with medical conditions* (DfE, 2015:5), with a central aim to ensure that 'all children with medical conditions, in terms of both physical and mental health, are properly supported in school so that they can play a full and active role in school life, remain healthy and achieve their academic potential'. The impact of medical conditions and chronic illness is not only likely to be detrimental to their education academically, but the effects may go beyond this to include difficulties with maintaining friendships, self-esteem and even psychosomatic symptoms leading to school phobia (Closs, 2000). Ongoing medical appointments or periods of hospitalisation can mean that children's opportunities to socialise with peers and feel part of a group in school can be adversely affected. In some cases, school can be a place that can offer a sense of normality and escape from the challenges of illness and ongoing medical treatments. Even for children with more serious medical conditions, maintaining attendance at school can be an essential to avoid a feeling of isolation or difference (Closs, 2000).

Managing the treatments for medical conditions can be challenging, and when working with children and young people, there will be occasions where they will need additional support, whether this is remembering appointments, taking medication, accessing therapies or other forms of support. This is especially so for young children or young people who may not be in a position cognitively to fully understand triggers, symptoms or treatments for their condition, and the implication when this is not managed effectively. Therefore, the leadership team at a strategic level, and any member of school staff on a practical level, may be in a significant position to ensure children's well-being.

Alongside the duty on schools to ensure there is appropriate access to education for children with medical conditions, there has been a reduction in the medical professionals available to support in schools. In 2015 The Royal College of Nursing (RCN) and National Association of Head Teachers (NAHT) reported there were just 1186 qualified school nurses to meet the needs of 8.4 million pupils (Henshaw, 2015). This presents challenges regarding access to medical expertise in an educational context. The commissioning for this service has now been allocated to local authorities rather than the National Health Service, which presents further issues due to local government cuts to budgets. The number of children with life-limiting or life-threatening illnesses in England is double what it was at the millennium (Robinson *et al.*, 2018), illustrating a greater need for expertise to be available.

With such a limited resource available, it may lead to limitations on providing support for staff training or sharing of essential knowledge regarding triggers, signs, symptoms and treatments for medical conditions. On a practical level, this could impinge on meeting the requirement that school leaders should 'consult health and social care professionals' to ensure that medical conditions are understood and supported (DfE, 2015:4). The NAHT general secretary, Russell Hobby, referred to the challenges in accessing critical services in school and noted the lack of resource 'makes it incredibly difficult to ensure that children with medical conditions receive the high levels of care they deserve' (Henshaw, 2015:318).

Some medical conditions will also be classified as disabilities as defined in the Equality Act 2010. For example, a child with very severe asthma who requires long-term use of a nebuliser frequently at different times throughout the day is going to have a substantial impact on their ability to perform day-to-day activities. In instances such as this, the child or young person would need provisions planned that are in line with guidance on medical conditions (DfE, 2015), as well as consideration of the statutory requirements for people with disabilities, such as positive discrimination and implementing reasonable adjustments.

Children's development can be affected differently at different stages, and it is expected that medical conditions and chronic illness will impact on a child's education, possibly resulting in special educational needs. Close (2000:30) acknowledged that if a child is diagnosed with a condition when they are younger rather than older, there is some evidence they will be 'more likely to experience learning difficulties'. The SENCO, therefore, is a central staff member in school to ensure a 'holistic approach to children's education if it is to be effective' (Close, 2000:93) and to reduce barriers to learning as far as possible, to facilitate inclusive education.

Implementation in school

Essentially, the governing body or equivalent has the responsibility for meeting the duties schools must implement to support learners with medical conditions. In a context where the focus is predominantly on teaching, learning and assessment, school staff are increasingly having to consider a more holistic view of the child and young person. It is not only their learning that may need support, but also responsibilities for their medical needs, which may be new and unexpected. The challenges are not only understanding more fully the medical conditions children attending the school have, but also the responsibility on staff members for managing or recognising aspects of these conditions which will need intervention. The DfE (2015:5) identified that 'parents of children with medical conditions are often concerned that their child's health will deteriorate when they attend school'. This issue was recognised by a university cross-faculty research group with a focus on developing an interdisciplinary community of learning and research (Soan, 2013). Academics from education and health faculties visited contrasting professional settings to support their understanding of different professions and settings. One outcome was the observation that children were too often visiting accident and emergency departments in hospitals because medical conditions had not been managed effectively in school. In response, a pilot medical training programme was delivered to support professionals working in education in developing an improved awareness and management of children's health and well-being (Hughes *et al.*, 2016). All staff have a responsibility to safeguard children, and the SENCO may also hold the position of Designated Safeguarding Lead (DSL) in schools. The implications of the new duties within education mean that if children face more severe health consequences when their medical conditions are not managed effectively, this involves consideration of safeguarding with regards to a school's duty of care.

School policy

Schools need to have a medical conditions policy which is reviewed regularly and is accessible to staff and parents. It is important to ensure the policy meets the requirements in *Supporting pupils at school with medical conditions* (DfE, 2015), because a range of aspects should be considered, from ensuring there is a procedure for briefing supply staff through to effectively managing transitions. There is guidance for developing and implementing the school's medical conditions policy (DfE, 2015:8–9), and it may also be useful to consult with medical professionals. As with the development of all school policies, it is important to involve wider stakeholders to fosters a collaborative approach. Those involved may understand the policy better and take some ownership, which could help embed important processes within school.

Individual Health Care Plans

Individual Health Care Plans are a statutory requirement and need to be in place for children with medical conditions that could fluctuate, or if high-risk emergency assistance might be required. The guidance recommends plans may be useful for managing other conditions too and outline that the decision to create an Individual Health Care Plan should be taken collaboratively between the parent or carers, school staff and medical staff, because not all children will require a plan (DfE, 2015). The Individual Health Care Plans must be reviewed annually at a minimum, but may be reviewed more frequently, and guidance on the process is included in Annex A (DfE, 2015:28). Generic templates are available from the Department for Education website, but owing to the level of information required for managing some conditions, the form can be adjusted. In some cases, organisations or charities will provide templates that are more in line with specific conditions such as diabetes etc.

Ensuring the information on an Individual Health Care Plan is clear and easily accessible is paramount. When communicating this essential information, it might be useful to consider:

- Clarity of information: Can the plan be followed/understood easily?
- Sufficient information/detail: Is there enough information to support the medical needs?
- Actions: Does the plan include the actions to be taken, e.g. in an emergency?
- Layout: How clear is the information set out?
- Medical terminology: Are relevant, clear terms used or defined?

Staff responsibilities

Within the guidance, 'headteachers have overall responsibility for the development of individual healthcare plans' (DfE, 2015:13), although it is likely a staff member will be appointed to lead on the provisions, support and implement the policy effectively. This can be 'conferred on a governor, a headteacher, a committee or other member of staff as appropriate' (DfE, 2015:7). The SENCO may take on this role because it is to be expected there will be involvement supporting children with medical conditions and certainly if they have a disability and or a special educational need.

In addition to leadership, any staff member in school might be involved in supporting a child or young person with medical conditions, and so appropriate or specialist training in specific areas may be required. It is necessary that 'sufficient staff have received suitable training and are competent before they take on responsibility to support children with medical conditions' (DfE, 2015:12). This does not mean that staff who hold a first-aid certificate should be called on, because their training and knowledge would not equip them with the required understanding of chronic or life-limiting illnesses, for example, epilepsy, diabetes, muscular dystrophy or cancer.

Case Study

To consider issues that might arise in school, the following fictional case study will be discussed, with a focus on how this relates to aspects of leadership.

School Scenario

Joshua is a student in Year 8 with significant cognition and learning needs. Cognitively he is at a much lower level than his peers (in line with a child aged six years), and he has difficulties with short-term and working memory. He has joined the school partway through the year due to the family relocating and has been attending for just a couple of weeks. Joshua has Type 1 diabetes, which was diagnosed four years ago and is managed with an insulin pen. He is supported well at home and self-medicates with support from an adult. The Individual Health Care Plan was provided by his previous school and notes he should be accompanied by a staff member at break and lunch to organise his medicine and oversee him self-medicating. Joshua's parents discussed his needs in a transition meeting with the SENCO. The diabetic nurse was unable to attend, but in the past had provided basic training to staff at the school and offered some further advice over the phone.

Shortly after joining the school, Joshua's parents confirmed that Joshua would be moving to a new type of insulin pen, and the procedure was slightly different. There would be more onus on Joshua in counting carbohydrates to ensure the correct allocation of insulin. As a result, a meeting was called to review the Individual Health Care Plan, but this was delayed because the diabetic nurse was not able to attend, yet the medication changed that day.

Staff supporting Joshua with self-medicating were concerned over the changes and worried over their responsibilities, especially as this was a new process and they did not feel sufficiently knowledgeable or competent. They felt that Joshua was not always sufficiently capable of remembering what he had eaten or reliably counting the carbohydrates due to his educational needs. They felt that the onus would be on them to ensure that the correct amount of insulin was administered, which they did not feel appropriately trained to do.

When the SENCO eventually arranged the meeting with the diabetic nurse, training was provided which appeased staff fears and anxieties. The nurse reassured staff of the process, and although this was a different method of administering medication, the principle was the same. There was further support on what signs staff should look for if a child was experiencing a hyper or hypo episode, as well as the procedure for managing this, so they had a better understanding of the procedures outlined on the Individual Health Care Plan.

Leadership

Managing the support for learners with medical conditions is a responsible position, and appointing a 'senior member of school staff' (DfE, 2015:28) to oversee this duty will be prudent. Some aspects of the statutory requirements for meeting the needs of learners with medical conditions relate very closely to the demands a SENCO will be enacting in schools. In this case study, a SENCO has been chosen to lead effective implementation, provide a strategic overview and deliver on the requirements.

The case study illustrates a range of challenges leaders might face in practice, including timely access to information, misconceptions over treatments, health services being stretched, lack of appropriate training opportunities and anxiety over professional identity and boundaries. Some aspects will be beyond the school's control, but understanding these tensions and issues can, to some degree, mitigate the risks because anticipation of potential issues may aid planning for preventative measures. Statutory duties extend beyond the operational and require strategic leadership to:

- effectively communicate information;
- lead on multi-agency working;
- ensure relevant staff training;
- implement a whole-school policy.

Each of these aspects will be explored based on the case study to consider some of the wider implications in school.

Effectively communicate information

Ensuring there are effective systems for communication across the whole school will be essential because children's well-being, health and even lives may be at risk if relevant information is not shared or sufficiently accessible. Implementing and maintaining systems and processes may be operational, but overseeing these systems to ensure they are effective and meet statutory duties requires strategic leadership and demands a high level of responsibility. The SENCO in the case study is the key point of contact for parents, holds responsibility for updating and communicating the changes to the Individual Health Care Plan, as well as organising further relevant information and training for staff. This range of capabilities requires a professional who can effectively communicate, coordinate, plan and deploy resources.

Facing situations when there is a gap in services or lack of knowledge regarding children's needs can occur in practice. Access to relevant information can be challenging when this is held by different services, because consent to sharing information would need to be sought unless a child was at risk of harm (DfE, 2018). As in the case study, the parents and carers can sometimes be the first to inform the school of a medical condition or a change to the treatment. Within the guidance, 'other healthcare professionals, including GPs and paediatricians, should notify the school nurse when a child has been identified as having a medical condition that will require support at school' (DfE, 2015:14). However, not all schools have direct access to a school nurse, and schools without access may need to complete a referral to obtain medical information, which then involves further delays.

The case study demonstrates the difficulties a leader may face in managing a situation where information is limited or delayed. Robinson *et al.* (2018) presented findings on the difficulties teachers reported in accessing support from the health service. This included issues over knowing who to contact to gain the required knowledge as well as delays in accessing the necessary information. A statutory duty being placed on schools (DfE, 2015), without sufficient resources or access to the relevant services, will lead to frustration and may ultimately impact negatively on working relationships across services. Even for a SENCO, who may be in a position of advantage in their understanding of referral requirements and access to wider external services, does not negate the challenges when services may be negligible. As in the case study, the barrier of 'getting everyone to a multi-disciplinary meeting' to share information can be an obstruction (Robinson *et al.*, 2018:62). Limited access to services, and finding ways to manage situations when this occurs, requires the ability to draw on other resources and adopt flexible solution-focused approaches.

Within the *Special Educational Needs and Disability Code of Practice: 0–25 Years* (DfE and DoH, 2015), the roles of the Designated Medical Officer (DMO) and Designated Clinical Officer (DCO) are local authority positions to ensure the health system is fully supporting children with SEND. The DMO supports the Clinical Commissioning Group by providing advice and 'a point of contact for local partners, when notifying parents and local authorities about children and young people they believe have, or may have, SEN or a disability' (DfE and DoH, 2015:50). The DMO would usually be a paediatrician, but if the role is undertaken by a 'nurse or other health professional', the role would be the DCO (DfE and DoH, 2015:51).

It is unlikely the DMO or DCO would be directly involved in planning or assessment for individuals, but they may support schools with their duties to meet the needs of children with medical conditions. However, as these roles are non-statutory, there can be considerable variation (CfDC, 2019), which could impact on how effectively the support is implemented. Fortunately, in the case study there is existing involvement from the diabetic nurse and therefore consent to share information was in place, but for other medical conditions this may not be the case, so further barriers may persist. Despite these barriers, the SENCO would need to communicate the most relevant and current information available across the school, alongside the need to ensure this information is updated as necessary.

Lead on multi-agency working

Liaising with a range of professionals to facilitate and lead on multi-agency working is key in meeting the needs of children with medical conditions. The SENCO will generally already have contacts with a wide range of health professionals and experience of working in multi-agency collaborations and therefore be in the position to effect a holistic approach to meeting needs.

The case study illustrates how quickly professional identity and boundaries can be called into question. The teaching profession focuses on pedagogy and children's learning, yet in the case study school staff are administering medication and monitoring health conditions, which is evidently beyond their expertise. It seems the responsibilities being placed on teachers and school staff are calling into question where professional boundaries lie as well as personal confidence and competence in performing tasks outside areas of expertise. Robinson *et al.* (2005:175) posed the question 'When is a Teacher not a Teacher?' in the title of the paper exploring 'identity transformation for professionals in multi-agency teams' (Robinson *et al.*, 2005:175). This leads to questions over professional values and ideologies which may be challenged, especially as initial training for professional roles (such as teacher or nurse) typically involve developing expertise in a specific area. When this specific knowledge is shared in multi-agency teams, it may place professionals in a position of questioning the boundaries of their role. In the case study, the teaching staff are dependent upon the medical professionals for expertise. Research conducted by Robinson *et al.* (2018) identify possible insecurities in teachers' perceptions of working with others when the knowledge required is outside of the discipline. Two-thirds of teachers in their study 'hope to turn to health care professionals to supplement their understanding of the medical and non-medical needs of pupils' (Robinson *et al.*, 2018:62). Concerns over professional boundaries was also evident because two-thirds of participants were reluctant to take on a healthcare role and would have preferred to rely on healthcare professionals for support in meeting their duties.

Ensure relevant staff training

SENCOs are leaders in inclusive learning, teaching and assessment, focusing on ways in which they can support teachers to reduce or remove barriers which impact on learning. Ensuring appropriate training is accessed by staff is an important aspect of implementing inclusive practices and securing the best possible outcomes for learners. In the case study, access to training to support the child with diabetes is essential, not only to support and protect the child but also to ensure that staff are competent. Otherwise, lack of appropriate knowledge of medical procedures could lead to dangerous consequences.

Staff in the case study had basic training in supporting children with diabetes, but due to the complex nature of changes to medication for a more vulnerable individual, it could be questioned if the training was sufficient. School staff should not administer 'prescription medicines or undertake healthcare procedures without appropriate training' (DfE, 2015:18). Ekins *et al.* (2017) highlight the anxiety school staff may experience due to lack of confidence with managing medical conditions in schools.

Standard 5 of the *Teachers' Standards* requires teachers to 'adapt teaching to respond to the strengths and needs of all pupils' (DfE, 2011:11), but this is specific to teaching and does not refer to administration of medication or procedures to support health and well-being. The word 'health' does not feature in the *Teachers' Standards*, and children's well-being is only referred to twice in the wider professional responsibilities. Yet, good standards of health are essential to children's development. *The United Nations Conventions on the Rights of Disabled Persons* notes an individual's 'right to the enjoyment of the highest attainable standard of health' (UN, 2006:18), and as such, this aspect cannot be ignored by the teaching profession.

Acknowledgement that a 'range of factors can inhibit pupils' ability to learn' (DfE, 2011:11) may encompass medical conditions in a broad sense; however, many conditions will demand specific knowledge to be developed, and training may be necessary for teaching and school staff. An important consideration is that although any staff member could be requested to provide support for a child or young person with medical conditions, 'they cannot be required to do so' (DfE, 2015:14). As in the case study, this could present difficulties for the SENCO when there is a change which needs to be acted upon in a short period of time. It is important to recognise the weight of responsibility being placed on school leaders in implementing their statutory duties as well as the weight of responsibility on teachers and school staff in administering treatment or specialised support. Some school staff may be affected emotionally when supporting children with more complex needs, and it is important they feel supported and are not placed in situations which could lead to higher levels of anxiety or stress. Robinson *et al.* (2018:57) raise this issue and call for 'a whole school approach that protects and promotes teachers' emotional well-being'.

Implement a whole-school policy

The implementation of a whole-school policy will require strategic oversight and on a practical level a good understanding of current legislation in relation to health, safety, data protection and confidentiality. A whole-school policy must address the ways in which the school will support children with medical needs, but there should also be consideration of the support for staff, as evident in the case study. Keeping staff appropriately informed, trained and motivated to meet duties in line with the school's policy lies with 'a named person who has overall responsibility for policy implementation' (DfE, 2015:8). However, it is not one person's responsibility to implement the support and provisions, so a school culture should be fostered where there is shared responsibility and support for staff in understanding that 'supporting a child with a medical condition during school hours is not the sole responsibility of one person' (DfE, 2015:12). The importance of collaborative working is not just key for working across different sectors, but also crucial for school staff in working together effectively to support operational systems and processes. The SENCO is in a position of understanding school leadership and governance and can inform the school policies and priorities to support an inclusive ethos and foster working together in a collegial way (Ekins and Grimes, 2009).

Conclusion

Allocation of resources and the level of support for schools to meet duties related to supporting children with medical conditions (DfE, 2015) continues to be a challenge. Since the introduction of the requirement, there are ways in which practice has been developing to address some of the challenges explored in the chapter, such as emerging models for up-skilling professionals and in some cases an emphasis on pre-service training for school staff. Further areas of development could include consideration of initial teacher training and the development of whole-school policies, which account for staff well-being as well as children's well-being.

In response to training needs, models for up-skilling education professionals have been trialled. Lee (2018) outlined the success of health professionals in designing and delivering a city-wide training service for school staff to improve understanding of children's medical conditions. Hughes *et al.* (2016) found that 94% of participants who attended a pilot medical training programme for school staff were in favour of a future medical conditions day to raise awareness of managing medical conditions in schools. This demand for training raises the issue of school staff not having the required knowledge. The SENCO may hold the responsibility for leading on professional development and arranging relevant training to ensure the needs of the children in their context are met.

There is a clear indication that more needs to be done in meeting the training needs of professionals from the earliest stages of their training. There could be further focus of multi-agency working in initial teacher training to facilitate improved professional competencies with meeting all children's needs in a holistic way, recognising our own areas of expertise and when we need to call on the expertise of others. SENCOs may be able to raise awareness of the benefits of multi-agency working with staff in schools. This may be crucial in fostering improved confidence and competence in the areas in which we are working and understanding the professional boundaries in which we are operating.

Adopting whole-school policies which foster collaborative and supportive approaches across the school may help all staff in meeting their statutory duties. Robinson *et al.* (2018) raise the importance of incorporating acknowledgement of staff well-being in managing more challenging and emotional experiences of working with children with more complex medical conditions within policies school leaders are implementing.

Robinson *et al.* (2018:67) claim the findings from their study 'suggest that asking teachers to extend their role by relying on obtaining information, skills and training from parents, children and other professionals might be inadequate'. Education and health professionals are continuing to foster effective practice in supporting children and young people (Hughes *et al.*, 2016; Lee, 2018), yet this tends to be pockets of good practice and is not always funded sufficiently to sustain ongoing support, resulting in challenges which continue to persist in practice.

Reflective questions

- What can make school policies for meeting the needs of children with medical conditions more accessible to staff and parents?
- In what ways can strategic leadership foster effective systems for communication to support children's well-being and health?
- How can SENCOs and professionals work together to reduce the concerns over professional boundaries in meeting their duties for children with medical conditions?

References

Children and Families Act 2014. London: Her Majesty's Stationery Office.

Closs, A. (2000) *The Education of Children with Medical Conditions*. London: David Fulton Publisher Ltd.

Council for Disabled Children (CfDC) (2019) *Designated Medical/Clinical Officer Handbook*. Available at: https://councilfordisabledchildren.org.uk/sites/default/files/uploads/DMO%20DCO%20Handbook%20-%20revised%20edition%202019.pdf [Accessed 1st April 2020].

Department for Education (2011) *Teachers' Standards Guidance for School Leaders, School Staff and Governing Bodies*. Available at: https://assets.publishing.service.gov.uk/government/uploads/system/uploads/attachment_data/file/665520/Teachers__Standards.pdf [Accessed 1st December 2019].

Department for Education (2015) *Supporting Pupils at School with Medical Conditions*. London: Crown Copyright. Available at: www.gov.uk/government/publications/supporting-pupils-at-school-with-medical-conditions-3 [Accessed 1st December 2019].

Department for Education (2018) *Information Sharing Advice for Practitioners Providing Safeguarding Services to Children, Young People, Parents and Carers*. Available at: https://assets.publishing.service.gov.uk/government/uploads/system/uploads/attachment_data/file/721581/Information_sharing_advice_practitioners_safeguarding_services.pdf [Accessed 1st December 2019].

Department for Education (DfE) and Department of Health (DoH) (2015) *Special Educational Needs and Disability Code of Practice: 0–25 Years*. Available at: www.gov.uk/government/publications/send-code-of-practice-0-to-25 [Accessed 1st December 2019].

Ekins, A. and Grimes, P. (2009) *Inclusion: Developing and Effective Whole School Approach*. London: McGraw-Hill Education.

Ekins, A., Robinson, S., Durrant, I. and Summer, K. (2017) *Educating Children with Life-Limiting Conditions: A Practical Handbook for Teachers and School-based Staff*. Abingdon: Routledge.

Equality Act 2010. London: Her Majesty's Stationery Office.

Henshaw, P. (2015) Only 1186 qualified school nurses for 8.4 million pupils. *British Journal of School Nursing*, 10(7).

Hughes, L., Durrant, J. and Le Moine, G. (2016) Skilling up for health and well-being – the professional development challenge. *Professional Development Today*, 18(4), 16–25.

Lee, D. (2018) School nurses lead training for school staff members across the city of Stoke on Trent. *British Journal of School Nursing*, 13(7).

Robinson, M., Anning, A. and Frost, N. (2005) 'When is a teacher not a teacher?': Knowledge creation and the professional identity of teachers within multi-agency teams. *Studies in Continuing Education*, 27(2), 175–191.

Robinson, S., Ekins, A., Durrant, I. and Summers, K (2018) Teachers communicating about life-limiting conditions, death and bereavement. *Pastoral Care in Education*, 36(1), 57–69.

Soan, S. (2013) *An Exploration Through a Small Number of Case Studies of the Education Provision for Looked After Children Who Have Experienced Early Life Abuse or Neglect*. PhD thesis, Canterbury Christ Church University.

United Nations (2006) *Conventions on the Rights of Persons with Disabilities*. Available at: www.un.org/disabilities/documents/convention/convoptprot-e.pdf [Accessed 1st April 2020].

11 Person-centred approaches

Angela Scott

Introduction

This chapter explores the theory and practice underpinning the use of person-centred approaches in schools and settings. It is designed to provide a balanced view of the history and use of person-centred practices in order to introduce new perspectives and further strengthen inclusive leadership.

Background and history

The history of person-centred approaches goes back 60 years and is attributed to the psychologist Dr Carl Rogers (1902–1987) where, as part of his focus on mental health, he explored the notion of a 'fully functional person'. To help conceptualise this he created a meta-theoretical framework based on his belief that people have an inherent tendency for growth and development (Rogers, 1951, updated edition 2003). This idea is in stark contrast to a world in which increasing medicalisation and diagnosis could be said to define or limit people's potential. His theories were based on the notion that change through therapeutic means is achievable via a holistic approach in which experience and personality at its simplest are the drivers (Sanders and Joseph, 2016).

The journey of person-centred approaches initially grew from theory to practice through the psychotherapy route of counselling. Used in this way, the counsellor would show empathy for and acceptance of a person based on the belief that fulfilment of personal potential comes through 'the need to be with other human beings and a desire to know and be known by other people' (The Person-Centred Association, 2019:1). Crucially, the underlying theory promoted a non-directive approach in which openness to experience, being both trusted and trustworthy, having curiosity, creativity and compassion were all perceived as core building blocks. As the power of person-centred approaches was realised, Rogers and his colleagues sought to extend its reach by promoting it as a concept suitable for use in child care, education, management, patient care and resolution of conflict (The Person-Centred Association, 2019).

It could be hypothesised that Roger's theories provide an exciting challenge to the increasingly diagnostically driven world of special educational needs and thus are an essential tool for inclusion. Murphy and Joseph (2018:1) suggest that its radical theory is premised on a 'pedagogical discourse and not a mental illness discourse and that it addresses personal and structural power and the dialectical relation between self and society'. Translated, this could mean the promotion of a set of principles through which people are appreciated and valued within their culture, and that regardless of others' values, beliefs and ideas, each person has the right to make choices for themselves. For Special Educational Needs Co-ordinators (SENCOs), the need to fully understand and utilise the power of person-centred approaches is an essential 'must' and should be placed at the heart of the school or setting's inclusive agenda.

The person-centred approach gained traction in educational settings over time and through various means. In 2007, a study by Gatongi sought to review its potential as a method through which to improve disruptive behaviour in classrooms. He questioned whether it could be seen as a way of 'understanding and solving issues of relationships, emotional development and ethical behaviour' (Gatongi, 2007:1). Two years later, Freiberg and Lamb's focus on its use in classroom management suggests that person-centred classrooms promote better achievement and contribute to an environment where teacher-pupil relationships become more positive. In addition, their work highlighted evidence of better 'school connectedness', a more dynamic and positive classroom climate and importantly, observable improvements in 'student self-discipline' (Freiberg and Lamb, 2009:1).

The key driver for its use in education developed initially in the 1980s, gaining further ground in the early 2000s through the introduction of person-centred planning as a way of organising everything around one person in order to define and ensure a better future for that person (Ritchie, 2002). The concept here was for a person who has been disempowered to gain the right support in order for them to engage in the life they want. Thus, the introduction of person-centred planning began to be trialled for children and young people with learning difficulties and disabilities in special schools. Here there was a particular focus on the statutory year 9 review point for those with a Statement of Special Educational Needs, the forerunner of Education, Health and Care Plans (EHCPs). It is at this point that discussions about the journey towards adulthood become central to the annual review process, and it is no accident that the *Special Educational Needs and Disability (SEND) Code of Practice* (DfE and DoH, 2015:9.184) stresses the importance of both seeking and recording the 'views, wishes and feelings of the child or young person' at this crucial time, continuing the original principle outlined in Chapter One of the Code (DfE and DoH, 2015:1.1).

Current context

From the early 2000s onwards, the person-centred approach was further developed through training, the creation of practical resources and exposure to a range of situations from special schools through to planning meetings for children in the care system and outwards into various therapeutic environments. Sanderson *et al.* (2002) began to distil the ideas into a mindset supported by a range of practical tools designed to help people 'think and plan for their life, direct their own support and identify and achieve their goals' (Helen Sanderson Associates, 2019:[online]).

It is useful to examine the core purpose of the *SEND Code of Practice* (DfE and DoH, 2015) before looking at the role of person-centred approaches within it. The document outlines statutory requirements and good practice guidance for special educational needs and/or disability from ages 0–25. Looked at as a whole, it provides a continuum of thinking aimed at destination adulthood. Along the way it conveys important messages about a child or young person's journey; for example, identification of needs must take into account the views and experiences of the child or young person no matter what their age and complexity of need (DfE and DoH, 2015:5.40, 6.45, 7.15). Leading on inclusion at this juncture is synonymous with planning and executing a high-stakes relay race. Teachers, SENCOs and others are the 'holders' in the relay race of life for each child and young person. They must perform their best, taking the baton forward and using their skills and professionalism to make sure it is securely handed over to the next person who will play their part on behalf of that child up and until adulthood is reached. The centrality of the child/young person and their family throughout this process can be effectively hosted by understanding Rogers' person-centred theory of the 'fully functional person': 'curious', 'creative' and 'open to experiences' (Rogers, 1962). This concept presents avenues of possibility for inclusive leaders by opening up innovative ways of thinking that can translate into good practice within schools and settings. First, however, there needs to be a clear understanding of person-centred approaches as a concept to avoid any risk of confusion.

Moving from concept confusion to concept clarification

Concept confusion is best described as difficulty disentangling concepts within similar themes. Each concept will have a theoretical underpinning and some common drivers. However, in conceptualising and seeking to operationalise them, they are incorrectly interrelated, leading to the fidelity of their core purpose being lost. Looking at this in detail requires an exploration of person-centred approaches in relation to pupil voice, pupil engagement and pupil participation. Each of these initiatives appears to raise the profile of children and young people within the educational process, but each is a discrete concept within itself.

Pupil voice, which is the first to be explored, is described variously as the influence and contribution of pupils through active participation in the systems and processes of schooling (Macbeath, 2006:1). In the vernacular, this can be described as 'having a say within the bounds of school convention'. Quaglia and Corso (2014:xiv) describe an operational view of pupil voice as 'occurring when students are meaningfully engaged in decision-making and improvement related processes in their schools'. The establishment of school councils would be one such example. The key emphasis is on the belief systems in schools and settings through which agreement on the value of pupil voice is reached. This is, in itself, a potentially controversial issue due to the finely tuned balance of power on which education systems are built. Opening the door to pupil voice would seem to be unleashing a collaboration of the unequal. This opens up questions about who is in charge of the situation and whose voice is heard. Giving pupil voice may facilitate greater democracy and enhance inclusion, but studies such as those by Fielding and Ruddock (2002) illustrate the practical dilemma of, for example, pupil evaluation of a teacher's lessons.

So, pupil voice is not unlike person-centred approaches in that it requires a platform for pupils to communicate. Where it diverges is its valuing of pupils within the hierarchy of schools, and a call to action to deliver transformative practice based on collaboration and democracy (Fielding and Ruddock, 2002). The concept is intended to give agency and voice to pupils in order to impact on the function and systems of classrooms and the wider school environment.

We move now to look at the concept of pupil engagement. Perhaps the best way to conceptualise this language is to reverse it and imagine pupil disengagement. When pupils disengage, they fail to benefit from the rich social interaction found in classrooms and the wider school context. When they disengage from learning, they are stereotypically described as 'challenging' and often fail to reach expected educational milestones. Pupil engagement is the complete reversal of this: it is purposeful interaction in the learning and the social environment of the classroom and the wider context of the school. Consequently, success and achievement are recognisable and measurable by whatever socio-political and contextual indicators are present at the time.

A deeper exploration of pupil engagement raises some important questions captured by Taylor and Parsons (2011). To engage fully, does a learner have to be proficient in a range of skill areas including but not limited to academic, intellectual, behavioural, emotional or social? As we come to recognise the power of technology over our lives and those of pupils in our schools, engagement might now be defined in a different, more technologically orientated way. The social purpose of being in school may, for example, have lost its function as more and more social communities develop through technological, virtual platforms, thus participation in the three-dimensional world of real people may be less engaging to children and young people than it was in the past. The learning experience may not be static, and the shape-shifting nature of our world may mean that the concept of pupil engagement cannot be securely defined. Contrast this to the meaning of person-centred approaches where the fixed position is the fulfilment of personal potential, where experience and personality are the drivers (Rogers, 1962).

The final theme to be explored within this subject of concept confusion is that of pupil participation. 'Children's participation has been of the most debated and examined aspects of the Convention on the Rights of the Child since it was adopted by the UN in 1989' (Lansdown, 2005, cited in Percy-Smith and Thomas, 2010:11). Children's participation has become synonymous with children's rights, and how these apply in different contexts and cultures is an ongoing challenge.

If children have a right no matter what their age or ability to express themselves and to be their own advocates, it is incumbent upon others, particularly adults, to engage in an active listening process. Without this, they will not be able to exercise their rights to 'be involved and taken seriously in decision making, and it requires governments to assure the realisation of this right to every child' (Lansdown, 2005, cited in Percy-Smith and Thomas, 2010:13). This is policy on a grand scale, which impacts variously on legislation and guidance for children and young people across the country. Lansdown (2005, cited in Percy-Smith and Thomas, 2010:20) defines three types of participation: (1) consultative, in which the adult seeks a child's views to gain knowledge and understanding of their lives; (2) collaborative, which can be defined simply as a partnership between child and adult aimed at maximising the decision-making processes; and (3) child-led participation in which the child initiates and the adult facilitates.

Hart's *Ladder of Participation* (1992) defines an incremental process in which the intensity of child participation increases. This one-dimensional model might generate the false belief that the ladder has to be climbed incrementally, with each step having been achieved. This is clearly not the case (Wetzelhütter and Bacher, 2015). The eight-stage process opens up a picture not of a journey but of a hearts and minds environment achievable through strong leadership fed by a collaborative and appropriately orientated belief system. Of the eight stages (Hart, 1992), it is clear to see that the thinking for an inclusive school supported by the leadership of the SENCO should be no lower than the fifth stage, which is that of informed participation. Without creating an environment where children are treated seriously, any attempt at introducing person-centred approaches is likely to fail.

Current context

The SEND Code of Practice heralds a moment of liberation from the more formulaic structures of the previous two codes (DfE, 1994; DfES, 2001). Schools and settings are gifted the opportunity to develop good practice systems and processes based on a set of core principles, for example: nursery schools must use their 'best endeavours', 'young people should be supported to participate in discussions about their aspirations, their needs, and the support that they think will help them best' (DfE and DoH, 2015:5.6, 7.13). Furthermore, 'it is up to schools to determine their own approach to record keeping' (DfE and DoH, 2015:6.72). The implication of flexibility within core principles creates opportunity for strong inclusive leaders to begin to think about innovative practices, and central to those is the implementation of person-centred approaches. In its first iteration, this may mean for many the introduction of a one-page profile or the reframing of the existing planning system to incorporate the first-person language of the child or young person. The journey of implementation which began in 2014 provided an exciting and sometimes daunting time for SENCOs. They were challenged by the call to reframe old ways of working, develop new ideas and reinvigorate inclusive approaches to SEN, centred on collaboration, participation and person-centredness. Activity levels in school were high as the new concepts were reflected upon ready for implementation. However, a major 'initiative clash' brought about by the launch of a new National Curriculum also timed for 2014 created tensions of both priority and capacity for many schools and settings. In addition to this, there may have been a lack of theoretical underpinning knowledge needed for the effective introduction of a radical concept that was conceptually different to pupil voice, pupil engagement and pupil participation. A renewed focus based on a secure understanding of theory combined with strong leadership skills might well be needed therefore to re-invigorate the power of person-centred approaches as a tool for leading on inclusion.

The SEND Code of Practice makes use of the term *person-centred approaches* only six times in the entirety of its 275 or so pages. In the main it only infers a person-centred approach, talking regularly about the 'participation of the child or young person in decisions', 'greater choice and control' and the 'views, wishes and feelings of children and young people' (DfE and DoH, 2015:1.1, 1.2, 5.40, 6.45, 7.13, 9.22). It could be said that this language mixes if not merges the two concepts of pupil participation and person-centredness, thus making opaque the true meaning of Rogers' initiative (1951, updated edition 2003). Parents are also expected to benefit from a fully participatory approach, which by implication might be suggestive of further and extended uses of person-centred approaches. However, this could be a possible cause for debate; for whom are person-centred approaches intended if in fact they are, in Rogers' original view, a therapeutic approach to helping an individual gain self-understanding based on a notion that 'we are the best experts on ourselves'? (Rogers, 1962, cited in Mcloed and McCormack, 2019:3). Hypothetically this could mean that at times there might exist a clash between the different voices who hold different perceptions, possibly resulting in a lack of clarity about how to agree on the direction of travel best placed to achieve destination adulthood. Where this is the case, the resultant action for SENCOs is to be secure in their knowledge of theories underpinning the concept of participation in equal measure to those of person-centred approaches. To know where they are distinct and different and to understand where they are dependent upon each other is the depth of knowledge required by SENCOs to lead the debate effectively.

Person-centred approaches might well provide a key to the door that unlocks the essential metacognitive and self-regulatory developments that are essential to learning and life. Who is it that will spend the whole of their life with themself? It is only and always that person. How vital is it then that each person knows as much as they can about themselves to 'do life' effectively, or in Rogers' words, to become that 'fully functional person'? (Rogers, 1951:[online]). Current interest in metacognition has been mainstreamed through the ongoing work of the Education Endowment Foundation (EEF, 2020). Larkin (2010:6) describes metacognition as 'second order thinking', in other words, the reflective part of thinking. She talks about the importance of 'mental state words' such as 'know', 'think', 'guess', believe', 'remember' as being central to the development of metacognition throughout childhood and on into adulthood (Larkin, 2010:7). When we compare these core concepts with the open-minded discursive approach designed to 'adjust to one's own thinking in order to become self-determining' (Sandvik and McCormack, 2018:3), we can begin to see some important links. In this transformative world of possibilities, metacognition, which could be described as a thinking about thinking, can open up the way for children and young people to begin to self-regulate. Where person-centred approaches can play a part in this is when by seeking to engage in discussion about self-determination, the right environment is set and the right tools are used to generate practical ideas about what works in helping learning and social interaction to take place successfully. This can generate discussion about the role of that individual in a first-person sense, from which the perceived role of supporting others can flow. This powerful combination can lead to purposeful action which defines and celebrates the child or young person as both instigator and driver.

Effective operationalisation of person-centred approaches

Operationalising any initiative, not least person-centred approaches, is predicated on having a strategy. This requires deep knowledge, a clear vision, a plan of action and the ability to mobilise appropriate resources both human and material. Effective operationalisation must be based on a cyclical process which aims to ensure that the implementation is evidence-based, purposeful, collaborative and sustainable (EEF, 2019). At an operational level a deep knowledge of all aspects of person-centred approaches must pervade. This in turn feeds the overall direction of travel and serves to underpin the leadership skills needed to work collaboratively in helping others to examine, question, validate and revise beliefs, values, attitudes and feelings in a transformative way (Mezirow, 1991 cited in Belanger, 2011).

At a practical level this means understanding that there are many ways to implement person-centred approaches, and the core theoretical principles must drive the practice. It means sharing a key message that person-centred approaches are in themselves not a 'one-off event', but in the spirit of all therapies, a discursive process aimed at the self-fulfilment of the focused individual.

Effective operationalisation requires some key actions, all of which require strong inclusive leadership skills. These are best summarised as:

- a commitment to gaining secure knowledge of the theory which underpins person-centred approaches and a belief in its power to help each child or young person achieve adulthood by being trusted, open to experiences and able to make the right choices for themselves;
- an understanding that the 'tools' employed need to be facilitative and not an end in themselves;
- sufficient knowledge and wisdom to use effective verbal and nonverbal communication in the pursuit of embedding meaningful person-centred approaches;
- an innovative mindset that seeks to establish a participatory environment where children and young people feel informed and respected because their opinions are valued and acted upon in appropriate ways;
- research-based thinking that embraces the value of the person-centred approach as a platform for developing children and young people's metacognition and self-regulation;
- a critically analytical stance through which to review what's working so that it can be further developed and remove that which is not, thus taking the lead from the SEND COP.

(DfE and DoH, 2015:6.77)

It is important to reflect on Sanders' and Joseph's view (2016) that Rogers is 'more than a footnote in history'. His therapeutic approach 'seemed respectful of people, foreshadowing the current trend towards mindfulness, acceptance and compassion with his emphasis on the differently named but similar concepts of congruence, unconditional regard and empathy' (Sanders and Joseph, 2016:1).

Establishing collaborative preparedness

The key proponents of person-centred approaches in the 21st century, such as Inclusive Solutions, Sheffkids, and Sanderson (Inclusive Solutions, 2019; Sheffkids, 2019; Helen Sanderson Associates, 2019), contribute frameworks and tools which provide a basis for collaborative preparedness. When introducing and using these in a flexible and tailored way, inclusive leaders must continue to uphold the outcomes-driven theories of Rogers, whose therapeutic methods provide a respectful positive psychology through which children and young people should become fully functional people. Collaborative preparedness must centre on the theories allowing the use of tools to be recognised as facilitative platforms for discussion. Entering into the discursive world of person-centred approaches does require practical tools with which to frame and guide the process. The word here is 'tools' as a plural in contrast to any one-size-fits-all approach, which may be counterintuitive to the theories put forward by Rogers. A note of reflection about the practicalities of using 'tools'; just as 'IEPs were never intended to be just bits of paper' (Gross, 2015:12), inclusive leaders should prepare the launch of person-centred tools in such a way that they are understood and owned by the children and young people, are dynamic and purposeful and do not in themselves default into becoming a bureaucratic paper-based exercise.

Establishing an effective style of reflective delivery

SENCOs and leaders of SEND should enter into the person-centred world expecting to be surprised by what they learn from children and young people. They need to hone their abilities to probe, listen, reflect back, paraphrase and enable joint reflection with individuals, many of whom are likely to have cognitive, communication and attention challenges, to name but a few. In the words of Sandvik and McCormack (2018:1), this is a reflexive approach in which the ability to 'facilitate a mutually respectful dialogue' is crucial. It is about 'being open and aware of the life-worlds of others' and it 'promotes authenticity, self-determination and reciprocity' (Sandvik and McCormack, 2018:1). The tools provided by the current proponents in the field (Helen Sanderson Associates, 2019; Sheffkids, 2019; Inclusive Solutions, 2019) are beneficial in facilitating processes that should be cyclical in nature and empowering to children and young people.

Working in a person-centred way must be truly meaningful, and tokenism – that is, delivering something that is of perfunctory or symbolic effort only – must be guarded against. The time commitment to achieve this is not to be underestimated. The Education Endowment Foundation (EEF, 2019) reflects that one of the main dilemmas in our school system is how to match the time required to launch a new initiative with the equal time needed to embed, sustain and further develop it. With teacher work-life balance ever in sharp focus (Ofsted, 2019; Sims and Jerrim, 2020), leading on person-centred work needs to have cognisance of this issue. If we start a process to which we do not return, or if a child or young person tells us there is something that would help them in some way or that something is important to them and we do not deliver, was it not better never to have opened that door than to disappoint? Sanders and Joseph (2016), reflecting on Rogers' work (1951, updated edition 2003), tell us that being both trusted and trustworthy are central tenets of the approach.

Conclusion: embedding and further developing good practice

Leadership theory (Kotter, 2012; Day and Sammons, 2014) supports the notion of valuing individuals, building teams, starting small and scaling up. Within these core theories lies the importance of empowerment and ownership, which lead to a joint approach of identifying and removing any obstacles, and most importantly, toward a distributive style of leadership. Within the work of person-centred approaches, distributive leadership means mobilising expertise at all levels. In practical terms this means children and young people talking to their teachers about what works in combination with parents sharing what enables them to have more good days than bad with their son or daughter. It means young people making short videos about themselves to give to their new teacher in preparedness for a change of class and/or school. It means children and young people leading staff meetings focusing on what helps them to self-regulate and entering into ongoing dialogue about how teachers can help them prepare and respond to changes in their environment. Embedding and further developing good practice is achieved by implementing systems designed to release a fully functioning individual on their journey towards their destination of adulthood. This is what should feed the moral imperative to develop sound discursive skills and seek out the structures and tools to best release the power of person-centred approaches.

What we establish and achieve by way of person-centred approaches for a diverse population of children and young people feeds the climate of inclusion in our schools and settings. The leadership of this initiative needs to start with good knowledge and strong belief combined with the participation of children and young people in trials of different methods and tools. Let them be the ones to drive the development of what works and be involved in the collaborative decision-making about removing that which does not, thus setting the scene for the strategic development of ever-more-inclusive practices in our schools.

Reflective questions

- What essential knowledge is needed for SENCOs to implement effective person-centred approached in schools and settings?
- Can person-centred approaches be used to help children and young people with SEND become 'the best experts of themselves'?
- What practical guidance can SENCOs give to colleagues on the day-to-day use of person-centred approaches?

References

Belanger, P. (2011) *Theories in Adult Learning and Education*. Leverkussen Opladen: Barbara Budrich Publishers. Available at: www.barbara.budrich.net

Day, C. and Sammons, P. (2014) *Successful School Leadership*. Reading: Education Development Trust. Available at: www.educationdevelopmenttrust.com [Accessed 17 August 2020].

Department for Education (DfE) (1994) *Code of Practice on the Identification and Assessment of Special Educational Needs*. London: DfE.

Department for Education (DfE) and Department of Health (DoH) (2015) *Special Educational Needs and Disability Code of Practice: 0 to 25 Years*. London: DfE.

Department for Education and Skills (DfES) (2001) *Special Educational Needs Code of Practice*. London: DfES.

Education Endowment Foundation (EEF) (2019) *Putting Evidence to Work: A School's Guide to Implementation*. London: Education Endowment Foundation.

Education Endowment Foundation (2020) *Metacognition and Self-regulation*. Available at: https://educationendowmentfoundation.org.uk/evidence-summaries/teaching-learning-toolkit/meta-cognition-and-self-regulation/ [Accessed 4 August 2020].

Fielding, M. and Ruddock, J. (2002) *The Transformative Potential of Student Voice, Confronting the Power Issues*. Paper presented at the BERA Conference at the University of Exeter. 12–14th September 2002. Available at: www.leeds.ac.uk/educal/documents/00002544.htm [Accessed 30 October 2019].

Freiberg, H. and Lamb, J. (2009) Dimensions of Person-Centred Classroom Management. *Theory Into Practice*, 48(2), 99–105.

Gatongi, F. (2007) Person-centred Approach in Schools: Is It the Answer to Disruptive Behaviour in Our Classrooms? *Counselling Psychology Quarterly*, 20(2).

Gross, J. (2015) *Beating Bureaucracy in Special Educational Needs*. Abingdon: Routledge.

Hart, R. A. (1992) *Children's Participation from Tokenism to Citizenship*. Florence: Innocenti Essays, Unicef International Child Development Centre.

Helen Sanderson Associates (2019) *Helen Sanderson Associates Home*. Available at: http://helensandersonassociates.co.uk/ [Accessed 30 October 2019].

Inclusive Solutions Website (2019) *Inclusive Solutions*. Available at: https://inclusive-solutions.com/ [Accessed 30 October 2019].

Kotter, J. (Ed.). (2012) *Leading Change*. Cambridge: Harvard Business Review Press.

Larkin, S. (2010) *Metacognition in Young Children*. Oxon: Routledge.

Macbeath, J. (2006) Finding a Voice, Finding Self. *Educational Review*, 58(2). Available at: www.tandfoline.com.doi/abs/10.1080/00131910600584140 [Accessed 30 October 2019].

McLoed, S. and McCormack, B. (2019) *Person Centred Therapy: Reflections on the Process*. Available at: https://doi.org/10-19043/ipdj.82.008 [Accessed 25 October 2019].

Murphy, D. and Joseph, S. (2018) Contributions from the Person-centred Experiential Approach to the Field of Social Pedagogy. *Cambridge Journal of Education*, 49(2).

Ofsted (2019) *School Inspection Handbook*. London: Ofsted.

Percy-Smith, B. and Thomas, N. (Eds.). (2010) *A Handbook of Children and Young People's Participation: Perspectives from Theory and Practice*. Oxon: Routledge.

The Person-Centred Association (2019) *What Is a Person-Centred Approach?* Available at: www.the-pca. org.uk/ [Accessed 25 and 30 October 2019].

Quaglia, R. J. and Corso, M. J. (2014) *Student Voice: The Instrument of Change.* London: Corwin. A Sage Company Publication Ltd.

Ritchie, P. (2002) A Turn for the Better. In O'Brien, J. and O'Brien, C. (Eds.), *Implementing Person Centred Planning.* Toronto: Inclusion Press, 11–24.

Rogers, C. R. (1951 updated in 2003) *Client Centred Therapy Its Current Practice, Implications and Theory on Personal Power, Inner Strength and Its Revolutionary Practice.* London: Constable and Robinson Ltd.

Rogers, C. R. (1962) *Towards Becoming a Fully Functional Person in Perceiving, Behaving and Becoming. A New Focus for Education. Yearbook 1962 Ed.* Available at: www.centerfortheperson.org/pdf/toward-becoming-a-fully-functioning-person.pdf [Accessed 30 October 2019].

Sanders, P. and Joseph, S. (2016) *An Organismic Positive Approach to the Problems of Living and Helping People Flourish. Person Centred Psychology.* Available at: www.researchgate.net/publication/320282854_Sanders_Joseph_PCT_Positive_psychologyFINAL_copy [Accessed 8 April 2020].

Sanderson, H., Kennedy, J., Ritchie, P. and Goodwin, G. (2002) *People, Plans and Possibilities, Explaining Person Centred Planning.* Edinburgh: SHS Ltd.

Sandvik, B. M. and McCormack, B. (2018) *Being Person-Centred. Qualitative Interviews. International Practice Development Journal.* Available at: www.fons.org/library/journal/volume8-issue2/article8 [Accessed 31 October 2019].

Sheffkids (2019) *Website.* Available at: www.sheffkids.co.uk/adultsite/pages/resources.html?LMCL=mkG5oR [Accessed 31 October 2019].

Sims, S. and Jerrim, J. (2020) *TALIS 2018: Teacher Working Conditions, Turnover and Attrition. Statistical Working Paper.* London: DfE & Government Social Research.

Taylor, L. and Parsons, J. (2011) Improving Student Engagement. *Current Issues in Education*, 14(1). Available at: https://cie.edu/osj/index.php/ceiatasu/article.download.745/162/ [Accessed 31 October 2019].

Wetzelhütter, D. and Bacher, J. (2015) *How to Measure Participation of Pupils at School. Analysing Unfolding Data Based on Hart's Ladder of Participation.* Available at: https://mda.gesis.org/index.php/mda/article/download/2015.004/19 [Accessed 30 October 2019].

12 The SENCO role

Leading on assessment

Tracy Edwards and Mhairi C. Beaton

'There's a pupil in my class who I think really needs an assessment of SEND. Could I put in a request for one?'

'What is the assessment data telling us about the overall progress of our SEND pupils?'

'How can we assess Chloe in French? She doesn't have the literacy to access the test paper.'

'I was actually surprised when I assessed their learning from the previous lesson. He had remembered so much more than I expected.'

Introduction

As the prior quotations show, notions of 'assessment' underpin many of those day-to-day encounters with colleagues that are a key part of the SENCO role. Such notions, however, can be extremely varied in nature, reflecting a wide range of perceptions of what assessment is and what a SENCO 'does'. It is not unusual, for example, for the term 'assessment' to be interpreted differently in the context of SEND and reserved for reference to diagnosis and identification. In other situations, 'assessment' in the context of SEND may become a synonym for 'data', requiring the design of systems and processes to quantify the progress made by pupils or the identification of 'trends' relating to SEND cohorts. At times, the term 'assessment' may be used to refer to activities such as 'record keeping' or 'evidencing'; activities that are not assessment per se but are processes which merely support assessment.

This chapter will examine the SENCO's role in leading assessment processes and how a SENCO's promotion of both formative and summative assessment might enhance inclusion. Following a consideration of the difference between formative and summative assessment, this chapter proposes two 'paired principles' for guiding SENCOs in making effective strategic decisions around curriculum and assessment within their schools. These 'paired principles' of 'critical triangulation' and 'opportunistic innovation' are illustrated through references to recent policy changes and can be utilised when considering and implementing assessment practice which all pupils, including pupils with SEN, might benefit from.

Formative and summative assessment: what is the difference and what does this mean for pupils with SEND?

Much assessment activity that takes place in schools is described as 'summative'. Summative assessment describes assessment taking place at particular points of time, such as at the end of the academic year or key stage. Summative assessment may be used to provide a snapshot of the achievement or attainment of individual pupils, often in order to report pupil progress to parents (Black and Wiliam, 1998). Additionally, summative assessment enables schools to generate data on large groups of pupils to inform analysis and maintain accountability. This activity can also inform whole-school strategic planning, processes such as timetabling or the appraisal of teachers. On a local authority or national level, data from summative assessments, collected from all schools, may hold wider stakeholders accountable and shape wider policy decisions.

Inclusive and high-quality education, including effective SEND provision, is contingent on a school and its educators knowing their pupils, the barriers they encounter and the teaching strategies they tend to respond well to, in addition to the strategies that support them personally to face challenges (Deluca and Bellara, 2013). Formative assessment is therefore used by educators to enhance their knowledge and understanding of pupils (Black and Wiliam, 1998; Black *et al.*, 2003). This can be done through a variety of methods, including the marking of written work, question-and-answer sessions within lessons, or the use of close observation techniques to explore an individual's experience of lessons (Wiliam, 2011).

Unlike summative assessment, formative assessment is a continual and ongoing process. Its overall role is to enable greater personalisation of teaching and learning, informed by elicited insights into pupils within a classroom. The use of purposeful formative assessment ensures that educational provision is no longer generic. As teachers note the responses of pupils to learning opportunities through formative assessment processes, small refinements and adaptations are being made all the time (Black *et al.*, 2003). This has obvious value to any pupil with SEND, who like all pupils, require teachers who are not passive in their practice, but actively interacting with their unique learning differences.

The implementation of the 'graduated approach', as outlined in the 2015 SEND Code of Practice, would be impossible without the use of formative assessment. The term 'graduated approach' refers to a four-stage cycle of assess/plan/do/review that should be successively followed in relation to pupils identified as requiring 'SEND support'; this term being used to identify pupils with needs that have been recognised by a school but are not deemed as yet to require the drafting of a legally binding Education, Health and Care Plan. Alongside outlining the graduated approach, the Code of Practice also emphasises that 'quality first' teaching is central to SEND provision (0–25 SEND Code of Practice, section 1.24). Formative assessment is a key contributor to giving teaching this 'quality'.

In leading assessment, therefore, SENCOs have a role to play in facilitating practitioner reflections on practice and building a culture of professional enquiry around learners, which use formative assessments as a starting point (Rudduck and McIntyre, 2007). One example of how this might be achieved is through the use of 'lesson study', through which teachers conduct joint observations and planning, and collaboratively interpret formative assessment data such as that derived from question-and-answer sessions, close pupil observations, or discussion activities (Norwich and Ylonen, 2015). Using this method of lesson study permits the implementation of the graduated approach representing a 'spiral of enquiry' or a 'spiral of support' around each pupil. Whilst residing at the centre of the enquiry process, each rotation of the assess/plan/do/review cycle around the child enables provision to 'wrap around' them more tightly and become increasingly supported within the classroom.

However, in contrast to this productive use of assessment processes to enhance learning and teaching for all, anecdotal evidence would seem to suggest that many SENCOs in the English policy context are spending time on tasks such as comparing predicted attainment against actual or the progress of SEND pupils with the progress of a year group as a whole. Whilst entirely worthwhile activities, this comparative use of summative assessment data emulates the 'big data revolution' that has been taking place within technology and industry; the collection and analysis of statistics on vast populations to support the identification of trends, the customisation of products and services, and the targeting of marketing.

The Finnish educationalist, Pasi Sahlberg, however, presents a powerful case for educators to instead be primarily guided by 'small data'. For Sahlberg (2017), 'big data' can often be too simplistic, enabling evaluations that are limited to a superficial level. 'Small data', however, is more qualitative, providing richer insights into the learning of individuals. Only by interacting with the more nuanced 'small data' can SENCOs discover what is really going on for pupils and lead colleagues to teach in transformative ways that do not merely reproduce the usual patterns of success and failure.

The leadership of SEND provision, however, does not involve the wholesale rejection of any one type of assessment. Leading SEND provision is likely to involve both 'big' and 'small' data, use formative and summative assessment processes, and contribute to delivery of assessment, which is both subject specific within the curriculum and non-subject specific around holistic goals relating to emotional well-being, engagement or independent living skills. Inclusive education settings will also be concerned with capturing those significant 'small steps' of progress made by lower-attaining learners whilst maintaining sight of those 'big steps' being ultimately worked on, such as those relating to the aspirational outcomes outlined within Education, Health and Care Plans. It is not surprising, therefore, how hybrid the word 'assessment' has become, with it seemingly referring to a wide range of expectations of SENCOs as leaders of learning.

Inclusive assessment as 'critical triangulation'

Whatever approach to assessment is being used, and whatever the type of data being collected, it is important that it reflects the *evaluation* of learning and progress, rather than the *demonstration* of it. SENCOs offer far less value to schools if they are preoccupied with gathering evidence to 'show' the impact of provision on the achievement of SEND pupils. Instead, SENCOs' focus must lie on enabling staff to confidently identify what is working well within their educational provision and what may need to change. It could be easily argued that some 'types' of assessment and data collection are more facilitative of this goal. It is also the case, however, that the evaluation of learning and progress might be strengthened through the first 'paired principle' that underpins the core arguments within this chapter: 'critical triangulation'.

Critical triangulation is the use of a range of assessment systems, methods and approaches with an openness to the possibility that they may each reveal different things about the learning undertaken. Critical triangulation, therefore, requires professionals to interpret data subjectively with a degree of scepticism. Critical triangulation is an alternative to assessment that is based entirely on a single method or system with uncritical fidelity. Although Critical triangulation may incline us to work more with formative rather than summative assessment, it does not require us to make a simplistic binary choice between one approach and another.

Critical triangulation of assessment approaches is integral to the leadership of those cultures of professional enquiry within schools that strive to *evaluate* learning and progress rather than *demonstrate* it. The interpretation of varied and possibly conflicting data requires dialogue and interaction with pupils with SEND, their families (Laluvein, 2010; Oostdam and Hooge, 2013), teachers, teaching assistants and other professional agencies (Head, 2003; Rose, 2011). Through critical triangulation approaches, SENCOs have the ability to collaborate with all relevant stakeholders to make sense of the experiences of each individual pupil. This logically offers greater transformative potential than the uncritical use of a single assessment approach through which single data sets are presented with assumed unambiguity and authority.

Depending on priorities for pupils, and a school's circumstances, a wide range of assessment tools exist that can play a role in critical triangulation. For example, a primary school may report in relation to the pre-key stage standards for mathematics, reading and writing, when assessing pupils working significantly below age expectations. Alongside this, they may also use tools such as the 'Thrive' approach to assess social and emotional development (www.thrive approach.com) or 'Mapp' to track personalised learning intentions, including those that relate to aspirational outcomes within Education, Health and Care Plans. They may also find themselves adapting the Engagement Model (DfE, 2020) to develop setting-specific assessment processes which address complex barriers to learning and participation.

Inclusive assessment as 'opportunistic innovation'

Within the English policy context and going in the direction of travel taken by recent governments, resistance from SENCOs and schools to adoption of more inclusive and creative approaches to assessment is understandable. In recent years, middle and senior school leaders shaping inclusive education provision in England have become used to implementing statutory approaches to assessment with its emphasis on 'big data' rather than applying the principles often outlined in policy to shape approaches for pupils within their setting.

Any suggestion that schools might exercise the autonomy to choose and interpret a range of assessments with criticality, therefore, may be met with any entrenched 'learned helplessness' within a school's culture, that can represent a barrier to its development (Kerkha, 1995). There would also seem to be an inbuilt concern that giving educational professionals the agency to innovate can incite scepticism, fear or 'innovation' that is moulded within old paradigms that ends up lacking in innovation.

Various features of current national policies relating to curriculum and assessment in schools do raise questions around inclusivity and learning differences: replacing levels with age expectations, the 'knowledge-rich' emphasis on content within the National Curriculum, exam-only GCSEs, the 'Progress 8' scoring of secondary schools and its apparent impact on arts subjects. However, for the SENCO within a school, these very same policies can be embraced as an

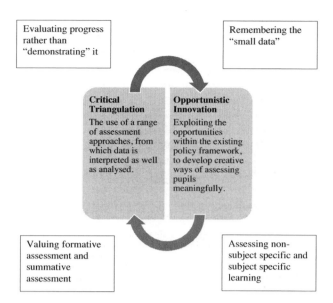

Figure 12.1 Principles for leading inclusive assessment in schools

invitation to 'opportunistic innovation' and the leadership of personalised curriculum planning that drives improved outcomes for SEND pupils.

In relation to inclusive assessment, opportunistic innovation can be defined as positively exploiting elements of national policies frameworks so that they underpin a rationale for the inventive design of new approaches through which pupil need can be addressed with sincerity. Examples of opportunistic innovation for SENCOs might be leading a working party to write a set of assessment objectives related to developing independent living skills for living in a small town for a school which was working to teach skills such as safely waiting at a bus stop, to vulnerable pupils with a diagnosis of Severe Learning Difficulties. Another example of opportunistic innovation might be through the development of social skills groups in a primary school, through which pupils work on personal learning intentions related to turn taking or losing a game.

It is through such opportunistic innovation that the SENCO leadership role becomes an active pedagogical one, leading inclusive teaching and learning towards its continual improvement. The opposite of opportunistic innovation might be termed 'cautious compliance': an assumption that schools can only possibly work within perceived expectations and that any alternative ways of assessing pupils are therefore not viable.

Figure 12.1 summarises the 'paired principles' of critical triangulation and opportunistic innovation as ways of providing assessment processes that enhance learning and teaching within schools.

Inclusive assessment and curriculum policy for SEND

Having considered how each of our 'paired principles' might support the leadership role of the SENCO in relation to assessment processes within their educational contexts, the chapter's focus now moves on to consider inclusive assessment approaches in relation to recent education policy within the English context, and the SENCO's leadership role in implementing this policy in ways that enhance the educational experience of all pupils.

Whilst not without its tensions, the 2014 National Curriculum for England and Wales, alongside accompanying changes to statutory assessment, was viewed as a key milestone enabling educators to 'critically triangulate' their assessments and be 'opportunistically innovative' in relation to SEND pupils. For example, the replacement of National Curriculum levels with age expectations enabled some schools to creatively shape their own internal assessment systems upon which to base their evaluations.

Perhaps more importantly for some SENCOs, supplemental to the 2014 National Curriculum, the Rochford Review (Standards and Testing Agency, 2016) made recommendations for the assessment of pupils working below age expectations. The very first of these recommendations was the removal of 'P-Scales', otherwise referred to as 'P-Levels' (p. 10). The 'P-Scales' were devised for the assessment of pupils attaining below 'Level 1' under the former National Curriculum (Ndaji and Tymms, 2010; Imray, 2013). Since publication of the Rochford Review (Standards and Testing Agency, 2016), pre-key stage standards have been introduced for mathematics, reading and writing to be implemented in primary education settings.

It has been noted that, unlike the P-Levels, the brevity of the pre-key stage standards results in teachers finding it challenging to break them down into 'small steps' for interim assessment. That this is the case is not an oversight but an intentional part of their design. The pre-key stage standards have been devised to be broad and that pupils be required to achieve each element of a standard, resulting in pupils remaining on the same standard for many years. For example, a pupil who is proficient at sight-reading familiar words but is not decoding any words using phonics will remain on Standard 2 for reading even if they have achieved all other aspects of Standards 3, 4 and 5. Although this initially appears somewhat unjust and seems not to capture the achievements made, it must be remembered that reporting against the standards is primarily summative in purpose – populating national data sets rather than labelling the pupil. Nevertheless, it must also be noted that if assessment is viewed in an 'opportunistically innovative' manner, SENCOs can encourage staff to consider more holistically the progress being made by the pupils *within* a standard.

Particularly, when used as part of critical triangulation with other assessments, teachers can be encouraged by SENCOs to distinguish between true achievement and progress and merely moving from one standard to another. Concentrated efforts to 'show' movement within and between P-Levels led to many schools breaking them down into pages of sequential 'small steps' for pupils to work through to 'demonstrate' progress term-by-term. The published guidance to pre-key stage standards, however, emphasises that they are not a 'formative assessment tool' (Standards and Testing Agency, 2020a:2). Instead, they exist to enable reporting at the end of Year 2 and Year 6 and do not prompt teachers to place the demonstration of progress above evaluating it.

The Rochford Review (2016) also addresses the issue of 'non-subject specific learning', giving credibility to assessment practices with pupils with complex learning needs, permitting focus to be placed on developmental priorities rather than the subjects within the National Curriculum. The Rochford Review (2016) references the seven 'indicators of cognition and learning' established through the Complex Learning Difficulties and Disabilities Research Project (Specialist Schools and Academies Trust, 2007). This informed the eventual publication of the Engagement Model, based on the following five areas of engagement (Standards and Testing Agency, 2020b:10):

- Exploration
- Realisation
- Anticipation
- Persistence
- Initiation

This Engagement Model is based on a recognition that 'engagement' is an essential dimension to learning and encourages close observation of pupils around the five indicators. Such observations are an example of the use of 'small data' to generate insights into individual pupils which inform planning and enable the refinement of provision. Rather than have a basis in subjects such as Maths and English, these indicators facilitate more holistic assessment.

The Rochford Review (2015) was concerned with assessment at Key Stages 1 and 2, but its broad principles may be applied to all phases of education and school contexts. Although the Review recommended the statutory use of this 'non-subject specific' assessment for only a tiny proportion of pupils in the school system, it likely has value in supporting any pupil for whom there are broader barriers to being 'engaged' in learning, including those with social, emotional and health difficulties.

One final key message of the Review (2016) was to avoid permitting assessment to drive the curriculum. Arguably, this occurred previously when some schools and teachers broke down P-Scales into exhaustive lists of tasks to be sequentially worked through. Such lists were often conducive to pupils being required to 'perform' rather than 'master' knowledge and skills; to 'do' something in the moment so that a box could be ticked rather than embed their learning sustainably. For learners in Key Stages 4 and 5, this has also arguably often been the case across the accreditations landscape.

Opportunistic innovation and the 2019 OFSTED Framework

Deep and sustainable learning resides at the very heart of the new framework for OFSTED inspections. Unlike previous frameworks, the new OFSTED Framework (2019) has a 'Quality of Education' grading category within which the curriculum is central. Through this process, data that appears to 'show' progress will play a much more marginal role in upholding the accountability of any school. This apparent change of emphasis in the new OFSTED Framework is a response to possible previous incentives for schools to significantly narrow their curriculum offer, to the detriment of those who would benefit the most from having the broadest range of alternatives. Using the new OFSTED Framework, inspectors are now required to assess and evaluate the three I's:

- Intent: the purpose and design of a school's curriculum
- Implementation: the structure and organisation of learning
- Impact: results, pupil destinations, reading

The emphasis on curriculum 'Intent' enables schools to make bold decisions to establish the most meaningful education package for their pupils. For example, this may mean compromising subjects such as science by giving an extra hour a week to the Duke of Edinburgh Award Scheme for pupils at risk of exclusion. In other circumstances it may also involve extending curriculum time for subjects such as science or maths or anything else that addresses priorities for individual pupils.

In focusing on the 'Implementation' of the curriculum, the new OFSTED Framework (2019) emphasises evaluation of the sequencing of programmes of study – the order in which things are taught and the cumulative building of knowledge upon the foundations made during previous learning. This represents a departure from what was termed the 'OFSTED Lesson' and judgements based on snapshots at specific points of time. The new OFSTED Framework places more emphasis on where each lesson fits into the bigger picture of the curriculum and the role it plays in wider visions for the long-term progress of pupils. The framework also has an interest in how knowledge is being maintained and strives to move away from notions that a 'lesson' can be 'good' in isolation. Under this system, it is also not satisfactory for secondary schools to use the accreditation being followed as a curriculum. The subject in question (the 'intent') is what is being taught, and the accreditation is part of the assessment of this (the 'impact'). Thus, curriculum should be driven by intent, rather than by the requirements of any qualifications.

These changes have exciting implications for the SENCO role. They enable opportunistic innovation around assessment, which interacts with the reality of a pupil's point of learning, needs and experiences. SENCOs may lead, for example, in implementing systems for evaluating pupil progress in relation to life skills, engagement or health and well-being; establishing clear synergy, for example, between what is 'taught' and what is outlined within an Education, Health and Care Plan. SENCOs may also play their part in navigating the 'deep dives' that are now part of the inspection process: focused explorations by inspectors of particular aspects of a school's curriculum via scrutiny of pupil work, visits to a sample of lessons and discussions with senior and middle leaders, teachers and pupils. Rather than be something to dread, these 'deep dives' might be viewed as opportunities to articulate pupil-centred decision-making informed by collaborative formative assessment.

The new OFSTED Framework should permit SENCOs to focus on such activities as 'intent' for SEND pupils rather than demonstrating that small steps of progress have been made via a series of ticked boxes. Indeed, it should be noted that under the new OFSTED Framework schools are not required to show any internal tracking data. Supporting the organisation of learning in ways that support the maintenance and building of knowledge (implementation) enables the SENCO to build considerations around barriers to doing effective learning, resulting in the development of inclusive curricula across the school. Through this process, the SENCO can be a leader of authentic assessment and pedagogy as opposed to a leader of alleged 'assessment' and bureaucracy.

Enhancing inclusive assessment through the SEND Code of Practice (2015)

The SEND Code of Practice (2015) is often viewed as the primary policy document impacting on the work of the SENCO in England. In relation to assessment practices, the SEND Code of

Table 12.1 Convergent and divergent assessment-for-learning

	Convergent	Divergent
What does the teacher want to achieve?	Teacher wants to 'know' if learners can come up with the 'right' answer.	Teacher strives to elicit rich insights into how their pupils learn, e.g. how they approach problem-solving activities, their strengths and misconceptions they hold.
	Learner responses are predictable and match what teacher anticipated.	Surprise is planned for.
How are lessons planned?	Teachers passively follow a scheme of work.	Planning is active and responsive.
Example 1: Year 10 Science	Pupils are asked to hold up mini-whiteboards at the end of a lesson, with a one-word answer to the question 'What colour will the solution turn if proteins are present?' [Answer: Purple]	Teacher asks pupils to think about their dinner last night and how it would respond in biuret test; what reasons do they give from their answers?

Practice (2015) in many ways aligns with other government policy documents, such as the Rochford Review (2016) and new OFSTED Framework (2019). It should be noted, however, that the Code of Practice (2015) policy on assessment also has the potential to be interpreted in ways that would be detrimental to learners with SEND.

For example, the 'graduated approach' outlined in the Code of Practice (2015) for pupils identified as 'SEND support' might be merely viewed as a record keeping or accountability tool, through which SENCOs can 'evidence' that they have 'tried something' before putting in a formal request for an Education, Health and Care Plan. However, when viewed alongside the new OFSTED Framework (2019), one can view the graduated approach cycle of assess/plan/do/review more positively, as a framework for iterative and inclusive teaching.

Florian and Beaton (2018) utilise Pryor and Crossouard's (2008, 2010) distinction between 'convergent' and 'divergent' assessment-for-learning activities in outlining a clear and exciting vision for inclusive formative assessment in schools. Whereas 'convergent' approaches focus on the effective transmission of knowledge from teacher to learner, 'divergent' approaches are interactive, open and facilitate a deeper dialogue around learner development. According to Florian and Beaton (2018), teachers can use divergent formative assessment to allow themselves to be taken by surprise, and thereby challenge misperceptions they may hold, such as presumptions about a pupil's level of ability.

The use of the Engagement Model (Standards and Testing Agency, 2020b), published following the Rochford Review (Standards and Testing Agency, 2016), exemplifies this type of divergent formative assessment offering voice and agency to pupils who may not have verbal language to communicate their experiences of learning. Using the five areas of engagement within the model, practitioners are provided with a scaffold for carefully observing pupils, analysing their responses and considering any unintentional communication that may inform refinements to the learning environment to further maximise engagement.

For other pupils, divergent approaches to assessment have proved to be beneficial, as pupils take ownership of their learning as they develop a more informed understanding of themselves as learners (Reay and Wiliam, 1999).

Table 12.1 outlines the distinction between divergent and convergent formative assessment, giving examples.

Conclusion

This chapter has focused on the SENCO's leadership role in enabling assessment practices that facilitate a better educational experience for all pupils. Following a discussion on the different purposes of summative and formative assessment, it was proposed that the use of 'critical triangulation' and 'opportunistic innovation' can support schools to assess pupil progress more effectively. Both 'paired principles' were then examined within the context of current government education policy in England.

In conclusion, it should be noted that effective critical triangulation of assessment is reliant on having confident professional judgement and pedagogy, as is the capacity to accept the invitations from policy, to engage in related, meaningful opportunistic innovation. To truly enact our two paired principles, education professionals need to be able, for example, to select, summarise, interpret and synthesise data from a range of sources (Deluca and Bellara, 2013). This makes the SENCO role, in relation to the leadership of assessment, a highly important one, involving the development of systems, processes and staff.

In addition to strong leadership, pedagogy and creativity, both critical triangulation and opportunistic innovation require investments in resources and time. Collecting small data via close pupil observations can be highly time-consuming, requiring staff who could be otherwise supporting learning more directly. Using several assessment tools simultaneously could arguably add onerously to workload. These entirely valid concerns make it imperative that, in developing inclusive assessment, schools genuinely break away from old ways of working and move into new. Changes cannot simply be implemented on top of previous practices. Schools need to boldly cease assessment activity which may not be contributing to enhanced participation of all pupils in learning and instead introduce new methods of assessment which have been demonstrated to be more ethical and effective.

Reflective questions

- How can more individualised and bespoke assessments approaches be directed to feed into wider evaluations of provision, at a whole-school and local authority level?
- Are there existing assessment practices, ongoing in many schools, that could be easily abolished to make way for newer, more authentic ones?
- How can assessment information based on small data be succinctly captured for reporting purposes?

References

Black, P., Harrison, C., Lee, C., Marshall, B. and Wiliam, D. (2003) *Assessment for Learning: Putting It Into Practice*. Buckingham: Open University Press.

Black, P. and Wiliam, D. (1998) *Inside the Black Box: Raising Standards Through Classroom Assessment*. London: King's College.

Deluca, C. and Bellara, A. (2013) The current state of assessment education: Aligning policy, standards, and teacher education Curriculum. *Journal of Teacher Education*, 64(4), pp. 356–372.

DfE (Department for Education) (2020) *The Engagement Model*. London: DfE.

Florian, L. and Beaton, M. (2018) Inclusive pedagogy in action: Getting it right for every child. *International Journal of Inclusive Education*, 22(8), pp. 870–884.

Head, G. (2003) Effective collaboration: Deep collaboration as an essential element of the learning process. *Journal of Educational Enquiry*, 4(2), pp. 47–62.

Imray, P. (2013) Can the P scales give a sufficient and accurate assessment of progress for pupils and students with severe or profound and multiple learning difficulties? Is it reasonable for such pupils to be judged on the same precepts as all other children in the education system? *The SLD Experience*, 66, pp. 17–25.

Kerkha, S. (1995) *The Learning Organization: Myths and Realities*. Washington, DC: ERIC Publications.

Laluvein, J. (2010) School inclusion and the 'community of practice'. *International Journal of Inclusive Education*, 14(1), pp. 35–48.

Ndaji, F. and Tymms, P. (2010) The P scales: How well are they working? *British Journal of Special Education*, 37(4), pp. 198–208.

Norwich, B. and Ylonen, A. (2015) A design-based trial of Lesson Study for assessment purposes: Evaluating a new classroom based dynamic assessment approach. *European Journal of Special Needs Education*, 30(2), pp. 253–273.

OFSTED (2019) *The Education Inspection Framework*. London: Office for Standards in Education, Children's Services and Skills.

Oostdam, R. and Hooge, E. (2013) Making the difference with active parenting; forming educational partnerships between parents and schools. *European Journal of the Psychology of Education*, 28, pp. 337–351.

Pryor, J. and Crossouard, B. (2008) A socio-cultural theorisation of formative assessment. *Oxford Review of Education*, 34(1), pp. 1–20.

Pryor, J., and Crossouard, B. (2010) Challenging formative assessment: Disciplinary spaces and identities. *Assessment and Evaluation in Higher Education*, 35(3), pp. 265–276.

Reay, D. and Wiliam, D. (1999) "I'll be a nothing": Structure, agency and the construction of identity through assessment. *British Educational Research Journal*, 25(3), pp. 343–354.

Rose, J. (2011) Dilemmas of inter-professional collaboration: Can they be resolved? *Children and Society*, 25, pp. 151–163.

Rudduck, J. and Mcintyre, D. (2007) *Improving Learning through Consulting Pupils*. Abington, Oxon: Routledge.

Sahlberg, P. (2017) *Finnish ED Leadership: Four Big, Inexpensive Ideas to Transform Education*. London: Corwin.

Specialist Schools and Academies Trust (2007) *The Complex Learning Difficulties and Disabilities Research Project Developing Pathways to Personalised Learning*. London: iNet.

Standards and Testing Agency (2016) *The Rochford Review: Final Report*. London: UK Gov (Standards and Testing Agency).

Standards and Testing Agency (2020a) *2019/20 Pre-Key Stage 1: Pupils Working Below the National Curriculum Assessment Standard*. London: UK Gov (Standards and Testing Agency).

Standards and Testing agency (2020b) *The Engagement Model*. London: UK Gov (Standards and Testing Agency).

Wiliam, D. (2011) *Embedded Formative Assessment*. Bloomington: Solution Tree Press.

13 Education, Health and Care Plans

Louise Arnold and Janet Hoskin

Introduction

Dominant narratives of childhood and disability have impacted the way in which children with Special Educational Needs and Disability (SEND) have been historically excluded from having a voice in their education. In particular, children with SEND can be marginalised or viewed as unable to compete in a marketised, neo-liberal system. The SEND Reforms of 2014 aimed to bring about radical changes in the way that we support children and young people to be more aspirational about the future, although recent reports suggest that this has not in fact taken place. The key focus of this chapter is Education, Health and Care Plans (EHCPs), the 'single plan' that has replaced Statements of Special Educational Needs. This chapter will explore the process in which these plans sit and to what extent they can support children and young people and their families to get the lives and outcomes they want. Theoretical perspectives and practical strategies for co-producing plans with children and young people with SEND and their families will be shared.

The SEND reforms

In 2014 Edward Timpson promised that the new legislation would be the most significant reforms of their kind for over 30 years (Spivack *et al.*, 2014). 'The SEND Reforms', as they have become known, did appear to promise much change. Firstly, a single plan to be co-commissioned by education, health and care providers from 0–25 years aimed to ensure that accountability could not be shifted between different services. Secondly, a 'Local Offer' along with personal budgets would introduce an element of choice, in particular with regard to leisure and community activities, thus ending the 'blanket provision' that children and young people with SEND were often offered. Thirdly, a new chapter on Transition to Adulthood was to ensure that young people with complex needs no longer 'fell off the cliff' of children's services when they reached 18 years, but would experience a smooth shift into adult services. In support of this, the Care Act stated that where adult services had not begun to support young adults, children's services had a duty to continue with their provision. Overall, these changes are underpinned by two important principles: firstly, a new focus on outcomes for the young person rather than simply identifying their needs. This means being aspirational about the future and having expectations that young people with SEND wherever possible could reach normative benchmarks such as employment and independence. Secondly, that there was to be an emphasis on co-production, with the family and young person being 'at the heart of the assessment and planning process' (DfE and DoH, 2015:147). This introduced an emphasis on person-centred planning – a way of supporting people with additional needs to identify their personal hopes and aspirations, and in the context of Education, Health and Care Plans this usually means in the areas of education and employment, independence, community inclusion and health. The significance of this shift towards placing the child or young person in the centre reflects a positive move towards putting the individual at the heart of practice, with professionals working to support the individual to make decisions about their own lives.

Education, Health and Care Plans: the process

The Education, Health and Care Plan (EHCP) replaced the Statement of Special Educational Needs under the Children and Families Act 2014. The plan is for children who may need more support than can be provided with SEN Support at the school, and a needs assessment must be conducted by the local authority in order to determine eligibility. The core documents for understanding the process of applying for a needs assessment with a view to getting an EHCP are the Children and Families Act 2014 and the accompanying updated SEND Code of Practice (DfE and DoH, 2015). There is a clear timescale and process mapped out in the Code of Practice document, so this section will pick out key duties for the SENCO and other considerations that may need to be made through the year.

The right to request a needs assessment for an EHCP is held by the parent of a child, a young person (aged 16–25) or a professional from a school or college. Enabling parents to request a plan gives families new power as they are no longer reliant on the school if the school is not supportive of their request. Professionals should not usually request this without the consent of the parent or young person in question (DfE and DoH, 2015), though the bottom line is the assessment must not be sought unless the parent has been informed. Where positive partnerships are being maintained, informing parents rather than involving them in the process should be a last resort. The role of the SENCO when families are seeking or undergoing a needs assessment can include providing support for families, or signposting families to sources of support or information where it cannot be provided within the setting. The SENCO often takes a lead role in co-ordinating and collaborating with other professionals involved in supporting the child and family.

The local authority has six weeks to make a decision about whether or not to carry out a needs assessment and communicate their decision to the parent or young person (DfE and DoH, 2015); see figure 13.1 for more information. There is detailed information on the process in the SEND Code of Practice (DfE and DoH, 2015), but SENCOs should be aware of the legal status of the separate elements of the EHCP: the sections outlined in the SEND Code of Practice must be included and must be labelled as shown in the code (Sections A-K, labelled in this way, and not merged together). There is detailed guidance in the Code of Practice of what to include in each section, including where sections must link; for example, any need listed in part B (the child or young person's special educational needs) must have a corresponding entry in part F (the special educational provision required by

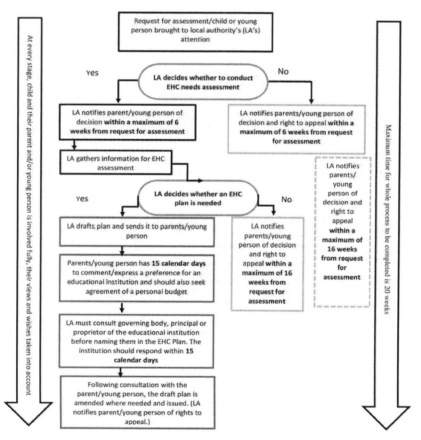

Figure 13.1 Flowchart showing the statutory timescales for Education, Health and Care needs assessment and plan development taken from the SEND Code of Practice (DfE and DoH, 2015:154)

the child or young person: what the provision will be, who will provide it, and how and how often this will be provided). Part A is where the young person and family are able to include their views and aspirations for the future, and this is an important step in the journey towards setting the outcomes that the EHCP should record. It is therefore important that time is taken before the meeting to discuss this both with the young person and their parents. For ideas, the Council for Disabled Children website provides examples of good practice for professionals.

EHCPs must be reviewed every 12 months, or earlier if requested by the parent, young person, the headteacher/governor of the school or setting attended by the child or young person, or the local authority (DfE and DoH, 2015). This can mean putting into place a timeframe for EHCPs in the school or setting, but being mindful that a review may be requested to take place earlier. This can be used as an opportunity to celebrate the progress that the child or young person has made, or to quickly review areas where more support can be put into place to move towards outcomes.

Success of the reforms

The introduction of the EHCPs was seen as a significant improvement in child-centred practice at the local authority level, but reception has been mixed. Despite some initial successes, with Pathfinder authorities reporting plans are of a higher quality, allowing professionals to see the child in a more holistic way (Spivack *et al.*, 2014), reports since have given a picture of delays and challenges. Initially, impact of the new legislation looked promising and evaluations from 'Pathfinder' local authorities (those areas that had trialled the reforms from 2011–14) and families who were transitioned to EHCPs early on were very favourable (Thom *et al.*, 2015; Skipp, 2016; DfE and MoJ, 2017). Sales and Vincent (2018) reported that participants in their small-scale study said there was now greater effort being made to gain child and parental input in the assessment process and development of plans, but noted that this commitment was not always shared by all professionals and that it may take longer to achieve the 'attitudinal changes' needed for this to happen. Similarly, Boesley and Crane (2018) interviewed SENCOs about the EHCP process, and some felt there was a lack of involvement from health professionals, with a key finding being that the process is experienced more positively when professionals work together and take opportunities to join meetings in person. There are also concerns that the outcomes presented in EHCPs are mainly focused around education, with Adams *et al.* (2018) finding that some plans had the health section left blank or with only educational outcomes listed.

Complaints from families to the Local Government Ombudsman (LGO) about EHCPs doubled between 2015–16 and 2016–17, and many councils failed to meet the legal deadline of April 2018 for transference to EHCPs from the old system of Statements of Special Educational Needs (LGO, 2017). Those plans that were created were often not within the 20-week deadline, resulting in some children with SEND being unable to start school on time. In just under one-third of the 30 local authorities they inspected between 2017–18, the Office for Standards in Education (Ofsted) and the Care Quality Commission (CQC) reported significant concerns about whether the local area was meeting its duties or securing better outcomes for children and young people with SEND (Ofsted and CQC, 2017). These reports also criticised the lack of coordinated services, lack of proper assessment, input of therapy, support from local Children and Mental Health Services and the lack of young people's voices in the SEND process (Local Government Ombudsman, 2017; Ofsted and CQC, 2017).

Moreover, stressful struggles for families that were supposed to have been removed through the new legislation have been highlighted by the recent House of Commons Select Committee report, which describes the SEND process as continuing to be framed by 'bureaucratic nightmares, buck-passing and a lack of accountability, strained resources and adversarial experiences' (HCESC, 2019). Of course, funding has played a role in the success of the reforms, and some have questioned the how radical changes can take place at a time of austerity (Norwich, 2014). Hunter *et al.* (2020) report that the number of EHCPs has risen by 35% since 2013, whereas the High Needs Funding budget (that resources EHCPs) has only increased by 12%. This means that there has actually been a decline in High Needs Funding of 20% in five years (Hunter *et al.*, 2020).

Perhaps not surprisingly, SEND Tribunals have overwhelmingly favoured parents, who have won 92% of cases concerning EHCPs (2018–19 statistics) against their local authorities (DfE, 2020). This indicates that provision should have been made initially, but families have had to take their local authority to a tribunal before they are able to secure support. As the recent House of Commons Education Select Committee's (2019) report on the first five years of the SEND Reforms noted, that as well as adequate resources, a 'systemic cultural shift' needs to happen in schools so that the hopes, dreams and aspirations of disabled young people and their families matter as much as those of students considered to be high achievers.

Theory that informs our practice

According to Burch (2017), the changes outlined in the new SEND Code of Practice construct a particular narrative of what success looks like for young people who have SEND. She argues that the four outcome areas highlighted in the SEND Code of Practice (that is, employment, independence, community inclusion and health) all serve to meet the needs of neo-liberal economic and social policy, rather than the individual aspirations of young people with SEND. Neo-liberalism is a system that places the market at the centre of everything and believes that unrestricted competition will bring about the best ways to live. Neo-liberalism has been popular in England and America since the 1980s and has introduced elements of competition and privatisation into the public sector. Goodley (2011) talks about how neo-liberalism constructs the 'ideal citizen' and pupil, which is an able-bodied individual who can contribute positively to the economy and is, as Lynch (2006) says, an 'economic maximiser'. According to Goodley *et al.* (2014), neo-liberalism is closely linked to ableism, which Liddiard (2020) explains is 'the material, cultural and political privileging of ability, sanity, rationality, physicality and cognition' (Liddiard, 2020:[online]).

Within a neo-liberal and ableist system, young people who have SEND can be viewed as 'non-marketable commodities' (Blackmore, 2000:385), who are unable to contribute efficiently to the needs of the society. Priestley (2003) argues that the benchmarks of adult success, such as employment and residential independence, are problematic for many disabled young people and that ideas such as 'transition' and 'adulthood' are socially constructed (Priestley, 2003). The SEND Reforms, with their focus on employment and independence, are therefore based on constructs of adulthood and success that either do not reflect reality for many young people with SEND, particularly those with complex learning impairments, or that ignore the dreams and aspirations of these young people in favour of supporting a market-driven society (Burch, 2017). According to Campbell (2009), no-one is able to live up to the expectations of ableism, which expects us all to be 'perfect and species typical', and therefore the ideal pupil exists in a world of 'compulsory able-bodiedness' (McRuer, 20013) as well as academic achievement.

Goodley *et al.* (2016) and colleagues explore the contradictions linked to the attraction of neo-liberal ideals for disabled people. Their framework of 'disHumanism' acknowledges the individual desire for the normative and the benefits that this brings, such as rights and a sense of belonging, but at the same time recognises that disability is disruptive to these norms and can challenge and shape the way we view them. So, for example, employment for a young person with learning disabilities may involve help from a job coach or it may mean working a shorter or more flexible week; living 'independently' for a young adult with a physical disability could include support from a personal assistant. Ultimately, they argue, this can transform the way we view what it means to be human, as perhaps life does not have to be about competition and isolation but rather interdependence and community (Goodley *et al.*, 2016).

The child at the centre of the Education, Health and Care Plan

Key to the ethos of the new legislation is Section 9 of the SEND Code of Practice, which states that children and young people with SEND and their families must be 'at the heart of the assessment and planning process' (DfE and DoH, 2015:147). We have a legal obligation to include children in the discussions and decisions around their aspirations, outcomes and support; the Children and Families Act 2014 states that parents of children and the young person must be involved, but the SEND Code of Practice (DfE and DoH, 2015) goes further to state that children must be involved and consulted throughout too, in accordance with the United Nations Convention on the Rights of the Child (UN, 1989).

Twenty years ago, children were not always seen as beings in themselves (Corsaro, 2011), but defined in relation to their capacity to act as an adult – with adulthood being the 'gold standard' (Tisdall, 2012:181). Shifting perceptions of children and their role in society have not always been afforded high status, however. With the introduction of the UN Convention on the Rights of the Child (UNCRC) and the developing Sociology of Childhood, children and young people are increasingly seen as human beings with their own ideas, preferences and rights rather than 'human becomings', waiting for their lives to happen.

UNCRC article 12 (UN, 1989) states that children should be consulted in all decisions made about their lives ('matters affecting them'), and Lansdown (2005) discusses 'emerging capacities' when thinking about how children are able to engage – with different levels of engagement depending on the child's level of understanding and maturity. This could, however, be problematic when considering disabled children – if their ability to understand and participate is underestimated by the person who is the gatekeeper to their participation, then it could lead to exclusion. Similarly, disabled people have historically been viewed as unable (or not encouraged and supported) to speak for themselves and have relied on professionals to help them make decisions about their lives. This has led to what we call 'othering', where disabled children and adults are viewed as less than human and reliant on other people to speak for them and make choices on their behalf. The creation of the social model of disability by the disabled people's movement in the late 1970s and early 1980s dispelled many of these myths and moved away from a deficit model of disability, instead arguing that disability is caused by:

> the disadvantage or restriction of activity caused by a contemporary social organisation which takes now or little account of people who have impairments and thus excludes them from mainstream of social activities.
>
> (UPIAS, 1976:14)

The social model has been key in achieving material rights for disabled people and led to important protective legislation such as the Equality Act 2010. This incorporates the duties of institutions such as schools, colleges and employers with regard to reasonable adjustments they must make so that a disabled young person can be included in that setting. This not only involves the physical environment, but the way in which the curriculum is delivered, any assessment is designed as well as policies about behaviour and communication (Equality Act, 2010).

For disabled children or young people, there can be a 'double jeopardy' (Lansdown, 2005) where they are viewed as non-adults and non-able. The impact of this for disabled children is that expectations of their ability, understanding and capacity can be significantly underestimated. This has been evident during the most recent period of austerity and funding cuts that disproportionately hit disabled people (Duffy, 2013) and unfairly affect the education of children with SEND (Children's Commissioner, 2019). The media reporting of these cuts has targeted children with SEND, with headlines that construct children with SEND as 'other' and taking resources away from the rest of the school. An example here is a headline from the *Times* (later amended): 'pupils lose out as £400 million schools funding diverted to special needs' (Hurst, 2019). Headlines such as this construct a competitive environment, pitting children and families against each other for limited resources, rather than focusing on the bigger issue of underfunding of the education budget.

Runswick-Cole and Hodge (2009) have argued that Special Educational Needs should be reframed as Educational Rights. After all, resources should not be dependent on schools' goodwill or work ethic but on the rights that the young person and family are due from legislation. The importance of our outlook as teachers and professionals working with children with SEND and their families cannot be overestimated. An understanding of the social model of disability is essential so that other staff are not viewing children with SEND as victims of tragedy but rather as individuals who have views and opinions like everyone else and aspirations for a fulfilled life.

Co-producing outcomes with young people and their families in practice

Despite the many concerns that we have discussed about the legislation's subtext with regard to what makes a good life, we have experienced some positive changes in the SEND process since 2014 for several reasons. Firstly, the shift to outcomes rather than needs and difficulties that were emphasised in statements of special needs could be seen as raising aspirations for many young people with SEND. Secondly, in comparison to the old system, effort has been made to include children and young people in SEND review meetings. This has worked most effectively when young people are given the opportunity to start meetings with short presentations about what is working well for them at the moment and what their future plans are. Some families, particularly if their child or young person has a complex health condition that can involve different services, or when the young person is non-verbal, may choose to use Wikis instead. A Wiki is a small secure website personal to the young person with SEND that can be used to store and share important information about the young person as well as record their hopes and aspirations. Wikis have been developed by the Rix Centre at the University of East London in partnership with adults and young people with SEND. The beauty of the Wiki is that they are usually owned by the young person and their family, who are able give access to and share information with professionals and anyone else important in the life of the young person. As well as photographs, audio and video clips, it is possible for families to scan and upload PDFs of any medical, educational and social care assessments, thus removing any difficulties professionals may have in sharing personal information. This puts the power into the hands of the family, who can join different services up on their Wiki by giving them access to the information stored there.

Using multi-media advocacy, which the Wiki is an example of, also has the advantage of potentially being more inclusive in the kinds of contributions that are shared from children and families in the process as well as the final EHCP. The legislation is clear that the child or young person must be consulted about decisions made about their lives (DfE and DoH, 2015), and their views must be represented in their EHCP. The ways that children and young people are involved may vary because of the preferences of the individual (i.e. whether they choose to attend the review meeting or not), but care must be taken to represent the child or young person's views however they communicate. This means in many cases, a non-verbal contribution will need to be sought, and the child or young person may need resources in order to give this, for example, sufficient time, an established communication partner, translator or advocate, communication aids or books. Good practice may see child, young person and parent contributions included in first person, in language that is accessible for the child or young person (Adams *et al.*, 2018).

Successful partnership working demands that partners are able to listen to and respect each other. This begins with how parents are addressed; there are parent-led movements advocating for recognition of parents as people by the use of names rather than 'mum' or 'dad' (Nimmo, 2019), with the principle being to ask rather than assume how a parent would like to be addressed. Respecting the knowledge a parent has about their child or young person is critical too; moving towards more triadic partnerships (where child, parent and professional are all involved and considered equal in knowledge and participation) ensures that information sharing is not one directional (i.e. from professional to parent, in the form of instruction or information), but parties work together to ensure meaningful and appropriate discussions take place (Arnold, 2018). Professionals also need to avoid viewing the child or young person's home life through a deficit lens; Callan and Morrall (2009) in the context of early years' provision relate this to considering what parents are not doing, or the input that a child or young person is not receiving. This can be harmful to partnership working and could alienate families.

In order to access resources for their child, many families will have had to endure a range of deficit assessments and fights on many fronts. It is therefore essential that professionals are aware of this unpaid labour and the impact it can have on families; it's also important to acknowledge that in most cases it is the families who understand their children best and who spend the most time with them. With this in mind, the use of solution-focused approaches can be extremely helpful when supporting a family and young person to think about what they need in their EHCP. These approaches come from ideas associated with Solution-Focused Brief Therapy that was developed by De Shazer and is based on four premises:

1   *Look for resources (rather than problems) a person has*
2   *Explore the person's possible and preferred future*
3   *Identify what is already working towards that future*
4   *Accept that the person is an expert of their own life*

(De Shazer *et al.*, 2007; Ratner *et al.*, 2012)

This helps everyone think about what a good future for the young person would look like and how to get there, rather than focusing on everything that hasn't worked so far. It also helps to see the young person and his/her family as having agency and expertise rather than as victims. As a professional, using solution-focused language and having a script of sentence starters can be very helpful when writing and reviewing the EHCP. Questions such as 'What are you pleased to notice about H's life now?', 'What is working well in H's life?' can be useful, as are questions like 'How have you managed that?' This can be quite counter-intuitive for those of us who are parents or experienced in working in schools, where we are often quick to identify the problem in order to tackle it. However, according to solution-focused thinking, in order to create real change it is essential that the young person and family are supported to identify where they want to get to, how they will get there and be invested in the journey.

For making future plans, and co-producing outcomes, being able to ask a young person and their family where they hope to be in five years is very useful. From here, move backwards to identify what needs to be in place in one year, in sixth months and in one month. This helps to make outcomes SMART (Specific, Measurable, Assignable, Realistic and Time-bound), as milestones can be established as well as who should be responsible for each one. Co-production with the family, school, health and social care services along with the local authority is essential and all resources costed. It is helpful to include as many people as possible into the young person's circle of support, or 'community circle' (Neill and Sanderson, 2012), so that the family feel supported. The website Preparing for Adulthood provides a very helpful summary of person-centred thinking tools for EHCP planning, and IPSEA (Independent Provider of Special Education Advice) have an excellent checklist that schools and families can use (IPSEA, 2014).

Planning for the future

Past reports from families and disabled adults have shown support through transition to adulthood has often been lacking in any expectation and direction, making it difficult for families to work out possible routes to employment or any sort of residential independence (Abbott *et al.*, 2013; Mitchell, 2015; Ofsted, 2010). Since 2014, the SEND Code of Practice now has a whole chapter dedicated to Transition to Adulthood, which is the time between the ages of 14–19 years. According to the SEND Code, every young person with SEND between the ages of 14–19 years has the right to discuss their future in terms of the four outcome areas: employment, independence, community inclusion and health. Although we can question the appropriateness of these normalised outcomes for all children (and several have), it is essential that we do see the paradigm shift that this is creating: rather than consigning young people with SEND to day centres or living in isolation at home, the guidance is suggesting that all young people should be supported to gain employment or independence if this is what they want. As Goodley *et al.* (2016) and colleagues have noted: 'Disabled children have been marginalised by or excluded from the expectations, opportunities and aspirations afforded to so called "typically-developing children"' (Goodley *et al.*, 2016).

In her review of post-16 provision, Sayce (2011) reported that the disabled young people she spoke to overwhelmingly had similar aspirations to their non-disabled counterparts in that they wanted to achieve training and employment. Furthermore, she suggests that people who work are healthier than those who do not, and employment brings with it many positives such as developing friendships, rather than just getting a job done. Of course, the new legislation has involved many obstacles to achieving these outcomes, but the introduction of programmes such as supported internships, along with more of an emphasis on traineeships and apprenticeships for disabled young people, has improved the likelihood of sustained employment (Hunter *et al.*, 2020). Therefore, it is essential that SEND professionals are aware of opportunities for work experience and paid employment that are suitable for young people who have SEND. Every borough should have at least one college that offers supported internships, which are courses linked to fixed-term work experience that lead to employment (Sayce, 2011). In some local authorities these may be franchised, such as Project Search, which offers training and work experience in hospitals, often with a job coach and education facilities onsite. Having imagination, a can-do attitude and high expectations are also essential qualifications for SEND professionals as making some of these arrangements work can often require a high level of juggling and a leap of faith. Have a look at the Preparing for Adulthood website for case studies presenting how young people have translated some of the outcome areas, for example, job-carving, supported internships and supported living.

Emergency Covid-19 legislation that affects SEND

As we are going to press, the 'unprecedented' world pandemic has meant changes to legislation that supports disabled adults and children. The emergency Coronavirus legislation passed in March 2020 will mean that local authorities have lower duties of care to disabled adults and children, which will impact particularly on those transitioning between different stages of their education and those who rely on social care. In particular, in Section F of the EHCP, the local authority no longer has an 'absolute duty' to provide Special Educational provision but rather must make 'reasonable endeavours' to do so. Although this is a short-term measure, it has left many families of children with SEND feeling abandoned or overlooked, and highlights the precariousness of being disabled during a world crisis. We are concerned that this reflects ableist values and risks disadvantaging children and families who already experience significant marginalisation.

Conclusion

We conclude this chapter by supporting many of the original intentions of the SEND Reforms and in particular changes to EHCPs. We are pleased to hear that for many children and young people with SEND, support is now planned and implemented using person-centred approaches. It is also good to see that employment opportunities for disabled young people are increasing. However, we are disappointed that far too many families are still having to battle for necessary resources, and we believe this means that aspirations for the future will remain low for many young people with SEND. We are concerned that this is caused by an underlying ableism in society that privileges those who are non-disabled, viewing those with SEND as 'other' rather than as part of an inclusive and diverse society. We have used theoretical perspectives of childhood and disability to both make sense of the new legislation and to explore ways in which disabled children and young people can use it to transform how we view disability and society. We have also offered some practical strategies for working with children and young people with SEND and their families in planning for the future. Finally, we have noted the precarious times in which we live and the need for improved support during crises such as Covid-19, rather than reducing educational and social care at a time when families most need it.

Reflective questions

- Reflect upon the significance of the child at the centre of the SEND Reforms and the focus on outcomes and aspirations: what might this mean for children and young people and their families?
- Consider the SENCO's role in the production of the Education, Health and Care Plan: who might be key partners in creating and drafting the plan?
- Examine the way children and young people with SEND have been 'othered' and how this can impact upon their participation in decisions made about their lives: are there particular barriers and how could these be addressed?

References

Abbott, D., Carpenter, J. and Bushby, K. (2012) Transition to adulthood for young men with Duchenne muscular dystrophy: Research from the UK. *Neuromuscular Disorders*, 22(5), 445–446.

Adams, L., Tindle, A., Basran, S., Dobie, S., Thomson, D., Robinson, D. and Codina, G. (2018) *Education, Health and Care Plans: A Qualitative Investigation into Service User Experiences of the Planning Process.* London: DfE.

Arnold, L. (2018) Working with parents: Principles of engagement. In Crutchley, R. (ed.) *Special Needs in the Early Years: Partnership and Participation*. London: Sage, 25–43.

Blackmore, J. (2000) Can we create a form of public education that delivers high standards for all students in the emerging knowledge society? *Journal of Educational Change*, 1, 81–387.

Boesley, L. and Crane, L. (2018) Forget the health and care and just call them education plans: SENCOs' perspectives on education, health and care plans. *Journal of Research in Special Educational Needs*, 18(1), 36–47.

Burch, L. (2017) Governmentality of adulthood: A critical discourse analysis of the 2014 Special Educational Needs and Disability Code of Practice. *Disability and Society*, 33(1), 94–114.

Callan, S. and Morrall, A. (2009) Working with families and parent groups. In Robins, A. and Callan, S (eds.) *Managing Early Years Settings*. London: Sage, 125–143.

Campbell, F. (2009) *Contours of Abelism: The Production of Disability and Abledness*. London: Palgrave.

Children and Families Act 2014. London: Her Majesty's Stationery Office.

Children's Commissioner (2019) *UK Children's Commissioners' UNCRC Mid-term Review*. Available at: www.childrenscommissioner.gov.uk/wp-content/uploads/2019/11/cco-uk-childrens-commissioners-uncrc-mid-term-review.pdf [Accessed 13.08.20].

Corsaro, W. (2011) *The Sociology of Childhood*. London: Sage.

Department for Education (2020) *Special Educational Needs and Disability: An Analysis and Summary of Data Sources*. London: DfE.

Department for Education and Department of Health (2015) *Special Educational Needs and Disability Code of Practice: 0 to 25 Years*. London: DfE and DoH.

Department for Education and Ministry of Justice (2017) *Review of Arrangements for Disagreement Resolution (SEND)*. Research Report. London: DfE and MoJ.

De Shazer, S. and Dolan, Y. with Korman, H., Trepper, T., McCollom, E. and Berg, I. (2007) *More than Miracles: The State of the Art of Solution-focused Brief Therapy*. Binghamtom, NY: Haworth Press.

Duffy, S. (2013) *Briefing on How Cuts Are Targeted. Centre for Welfare Reform*. Available at: www.centreforwelfarereform.org/library/briefing-on-how-cuts-are-targeted.html [Accessed 13.08.20].

Equality Act 2010. London: Her Majesty's Stationery Office.

Goodley, D. (2011) *Disability Studies: An Interdisciplinary Introduction*. London: Sage.

Goodley, D., Lawthom, R. and Runswick-Cole, K. (2014) Disability and austerity: Beyond work and slow death. *Disability and Society*, 29(6), 980–984.

Goodley, D., Runswick-Cole, K. and Liddiard, K. (2016) The disHuman child. *Discourse: Studies in the Cultural Politics of Education*, 37(5), 770–784.

House of Commons Education Select Committee (2019) *Special Educational Needs and Disabilities. First Report of Session 2019*. Available at: https://publications.parliament.uk/pa/cm201919/cmselect/cmeduc/20/20.pdf [Accessed 28.07.20].

Hunter, J., Runswick-Cole, K., Goodley, D. and Lawthom, R. (2020) Plans that work: Improving employment outcomes for young people with learning disabilities. *British Journal of Special Education*, 47(2), 134–151.

Hurst, G. (2019) *Schools 'Struggling to Meet the Cost of Special Needs Support'*. Available at: www.thetimes.co.uk/article/schools-struggling-to-meet-cost-of-special-needs-support-r6d9rjvhp [Accessed 13.08.20].

Independent Parental Special Education Advice (2014) *Education Health and Care Plan Checklist*. Available at: www.ipsea.org.uk/Handlers/Download.ashx?IDMF=afd8d11f-5f75-44e0-8f90-e2e7385e55f0 [Accessed 13.08.20].

Lansdown, G. (2005) *The Evolving Capacities of the Child*. Florence: UNICEF.

Liddiard, K. (2020) Surviving ableism in Covid times. Only the vulnerable will be at risk . . . but your 'only' is my everything. *I-Human Blog, University of Sheffield*. Available at: http://ihuman.group.shef.ac.uk/surviving-ablesim-in-covid-times/ [Accessed 13.08.20].

Local Government and Social Care Ombudsman (2017) *Education Health and Care Plans: Our First 100 Investigations*. Coventry: LG and SCO. Available at: EHCP FINAL2 (1).pdf [Accessed 14.12.20].

Lynch, K. (2006) Neo-liberalism and marketisation: The implications for higher education. *European Educational Research Journal*, 5(1), 1–17.

McRuer, R. (2013) Compulsory able-bodiedness and Queer/Disabled existence. In Davis, L. (ed.) *The Disability Studies Reader*. 4th edn. Abingdon: Routledge, 369–378.

Mitchell, F. (2015) Facilitators and barriers to informed choice in self-directed support for young people with disability in transition. *Health and Social Care in the Community*, 23(2), 190–199.

Neill, M. and Sanderson, H. (2012) *Circles of Support and Personalisation*. Available at: http://includ-ed.eu/sites/default/files/documents/circlesofsupportandpersonalisation.pdf [Accessed 17.08.20].

Nimmo, S. (2019) Please don't call me mum. *British Medical Journal*, 367, 15373.

Norwich, B. (2014) Changing policy and legislation and its effects on inclusive and special education. *British Journal of Special Education*, 4(4), 403–425.

Ofsted (2010) *The Special Educational Needs and Disability Review: A Statement Is Not Enough*. Manchester: Ofsted.

Ofsted and Care Quality Commission (2017) *Local Area SEND Inspections: One Year On*. Manchester: Ofsted.

Priestley, M. (2003) *Disability: A Life Course Approach*. Cambridge: Polity Press.

Ratner, H., Evan, G. and Iveson, C. (2012) *Solution Focused Brief Therapy: 100 Key Points and Techniques*. London: Routledge.

Runswick-Cole, K. and Hodge, N. (2009) Needs or rights? A challenge to the discourse of special education. *British Journal of Special Education*, 36(4), 198–203.

Sales, N. and Vincent, K. (2018) Strengths and limitations of the education, health and care plan process from a range of professional and family perspectives. *British Journal of Special Education*, 45(1), 61–80.

Sayce, E. (2011) *Getting in, Staying in and Getting On: Disability Employment Support Fit for the Future*. London: Department for Work and Pensions, The Stationery Office.

Skipp, A., Hopwood, V. and ASK Research (2016) *Mapping User Experiences of the Education Health and Care Plan Process: A Qualitative Study*. Research Report. London: DfE.

Spivack, R., Craston, M., Thom, C. and Carr, C. (2014) *Special Educational Needs and Disability Pathfinder Programme Evaluation. Thematic Report: The Education, Health and Care (EHC) Planning Pathway for Families that Are New to the SEN System*. Research Report. London: DfE.

Thom, G., Lupton, K., Craston, M., Purdon, S., Bryson, C., Lambert, C., James, N., Knibbs, S., Oliver, D., Smith, L. and Vanson, T. (2015) *The Special Educational Needs and Disability Pathfinder Programme Evaluation. Final Impact Research Report*. London: DfE.

Tisdall, E. (2012) The challenge and challenging of childhood studies? Learning from disability studies and research with disabled children. *Children and Society*, 26(3), 181–191.

Union of the Physically Impaired Against Segregation (1976) *Fundamental Principles of Disability*. London: The Disability Alliance.

United Nations (1989) *Convention on the Rights of the Child*. Available at: www.ohchr.org/en/professional interest/pages/crc.aspx [Accessed 13.08.20].

Part III SENCOs' leadership role in multi-disciplinary practice

14 Multi-professional meetings

SENCOs' reflections on the empty chairs at the table

Helen Ackers

Meetings (between professionals) have to be right. You are talking about these meetings having a potentially massive impact on a child's life. We need to get that right.

(*SENCO from the North of England*)

Introduction

This chapter will consider the nature of multi-professional meetings and the efficacy of establishing frameworks of human activity based on trust and effective communication. Multi-professional meetings can be complex, however; for example, professionals may hold potentially conflicting points of view reflecting their differing professional backgrounds and protocols, and professionals may not be able to consistently attend meetings. An empty chair at a meeting room table can be seen to represent a visual metaphor that the human activity involved within multi-professional meetings is not functioning effectively. It may represent a lost opportunity to gain a holistic picture of a child or young person. Special Educational Need Co-ordinators (SENCOs) may find themselves in a position of leading the drive for communities to support and adopt inclusive approaches, but they cannot do this in isolation.

This chapter explores the use of structured frameworks of understanding; by involving reflection upon the voice of the parent/carer and pupil's voice, professionals can aim to achieve a holistic, shared understanding of children and young people. Drawing on interview data taken from SENCOs in the North of England, this chapter analyses the complexity of multi-professional meetings and the implications for SENCOs and their school/settings/communities. During this chapter, children and young people (CYP) with special educational needs and/or disabilities (SEND) will be referred to as SEND CYP.

Understanding the current landscape

The dialogue around multi-professional working is a well-trodden path reflecting a depth of guidance and legislation. Developments in the 1970s signalled a shift in the creation of special educational provision, with all children being entitled to an education that was deemed appropriate. The Warnock Review (DES, 1978) resulted in a key piece of legislation, the Education Act 1981, and the 'act affirmed the principle of integration' (Wearmouth, 2016:20). It included the concept of statements, later to be reconceptualised as Education, Health and Care Plans. The Act ensured, in relation to special educational support, a legal entitlement. The protection of children from experiencing negative difficulties within mainstream schools was firmly established.

This national perspective echoed an internationally shifting landscape. The move to acceptance of learners' differing needs entailed a shift to inclusion both in a sense of conceptualisation and practicality (Van de Putte *et al.*, 2018). The Salamanca Statement indicated 'the need to work towards "schools for all" – institutions which include everybody, celebrate differences, support learning, and respond to individual needs' (UNESCO, 1994:2). The United Nations Convention on the Rights of Persons with a Disability (United Nations, 2006) signalled the shift of viewing disabled persons as people who were subjects who had rights such as the right to an education of equal opportunity.

The consideration of multi-professional meetings within this shifting landscape has undergone a lengthy development. Milbourne *et al.* (2010) consider the establishment of Social Exclusion

Units in 1997, which signalled a change in ideological reasoning. It highlighted a lack of a joined-up response from services and departments that did not effectively work together (SEU, 2001). This need for professionals to co-operate with each other was again echoed in the Children Act 2004.

The Removing Barriers to Achievement Strategy (DfES, 2004) and Every Child Matters (DfES, 2003) policy shared the aim of making sure that children's needs were identified to ensure early support. It signalled a move towards a common assessment framework (CAF) capable of promoting a common language of SEND within multi-disciplinary teams, ensuring there was coordinated planning and delivery of integrated services. More recently, the Children and Families Act 2014 and the SEND Code of Practice: 0 to 25 years (DfE and DoH, 2014) outline the principles that professionals working with SEND CYP should consider. One of these is the collaboration and cooperation among education, health and social care. Support that is offered by professionals should remain person and family centred (Parkin *et al.*, 2020). SEN Support and Education, Health and Care Plans are identified as two routes within which support can be placed. The latter is identified as requiring a 'unified approach' (Parkin *et al.*, 2020:25).

Issues with health and social service provision in multi-professional meetings have been highlighted in various audit commission reports, including the Statutory Assessment and Statements of SEN: In Need of Review (Audit Commission, 2002) and the Audit Commission Report (2007) that found the Child and Adolescent Mental Health Services (CAMHS) to be insufficient. Such issues are further compounded by the postcode lottery to access services (Lamb *et al.*, 2018). Barnes (2008) reflected that geographical location is 'the single most overriding factor influencing access to multi-agency provision' (Barnes, 2008:233). This continues to be of concern, with Ofsted (2020:22) commenting, in relation to SEND: 'joint commissioning is a weakness in around a third of areas we have inspected to July 2019'.

SENCO voices

The interview extracts featured in this chapter were gathered having sought approval in line with a university research ethics policy. The extracts shine a light of understanding on the complexity associated with multi-professional working from the SENCOs' perspectives. Giving a public voice to SENCOs is considered particularly important. For as Clough and Corbett (2006) point out, the space is often dominated by academics who have the 'luxury of detachment', in comparison to SENCOs and other professionals who have to produce 'a workable structure to get them through each day' (Clough and Corbett, 2006:164). The SENCO interviews illuminate four particular points that were important to the SENCOs: time, continuity, efficiency and workload. Each theme is represented through a selection of the interview replies followed by points of discussion.

Time

A common theme amongst the SENCOs was the challenges associated with time.

> "You need advice from other professionals. But it takes so long".
> "It can be hard (to arrange multi-professional meetings) because say you want (Educational Psychologist) to attend, she has limited times. You put a date in. She can't do that. So, then you have to change, rearrange with the parents for different dates. It all takes time".
> "It needs to be the right people at the meeting and, well I suppose, the right amount of time to really solve the issues".
> "The meetings don't ever seem to have enough time. They may shine a different light on it, but the light soon goes out".

Discussion

The concept of time pressure was a recurring theme. One SENCO drew particular attention to the involvement of Educational Psychologists. The SENCO greatly valued the involvement of the Educational Psychologist in meetings. Psychological principles that lay at the heart of educational psychologist training can benefit multi-agency meetings by developing holistic views of children (Greenhouse, 2013; Gaskell and Leadbetter, 2009). However, interviewed SENCOs found the time it took to arrange meetings around the busy schedules of such professionals had a negative impact on their own leadership roles; time taken to rearrange meetings meant they could not undertake other aspects of their strategic SENCO role. Such busy schedules could be seen to illuminate a wider issue of a funding crisis (LGA, 2019).

Delays in organising multi-professional meetings could be detrimental to the process of identification and support, including the ability of schools and parents/carers to move forward with a request for an Education, Health and Care Plan assessment. This phenomena of issues with timescales is not new. Roaf (2002) reflected how there were often lengthy delays when trying to access the services from more than one agency, which can have far-reaching consequences:

> For example, a delayed diagnosis can impact on access to education. On a personal level, a delayed diagnosis denies a child or young person the opportunity to understand the factors that are causing them to respond in a specific way. For families this can create undue stress, with their child's response to the world often misinterpreted as poor behavioural issues.
>
> (Roaf, 2002:2)

Issues with funding and timeframes are also highlighted amongst health professionals. The British Medical Association recommends, for example, that action should be taken to ensure there is adequate funding to deliver health and educational support that is joined up, ensuring no child waits longer than three months for an initial autism spectrum disorder diagnostic assessment (BMA, 2019).

The lead professional and continuity

The SENCOs spoke of the need for a lead professional and also continuity.

> "*I don't really know if we (SENCOs) are the best person (to be the lead professional) but who else would have been the lead for some of them? Because very often not everyone comes to the meeting and very often the same people don't come to all the different meetings*".
>
> "*We have tried multi agency working. There's that multi agencies can't come to the same meeting, or come to subsequent meetings. We don't get that total and utter overview for a child*".
>
> "*In that one (multi-professional meeting) health may have been the better person to lead it (the meeting) but no one from health came to the meeting*"!
>
> "*If you get it wrong because someone does not turn up for a meeting, you don't get all the pieces of the jigsaw*".

Discussion

There can be benefits to having a key worker and/or lead professional at multi-professional meetings. Parents/carers consider this as a way services could be developed further, a way to overcome barriers to participation and a means to support parents/carers (Barnes, 2008). However, the SENCOs in the interviews reflected upon *who* was the best person to take on such roles. The Common Assessment Framework (CAF) and Education, Health and Care Plans identify the need for a key worker to take the lead in the agreement process with the learner/parent/carer. This question of who leads multi-agency meetings is worthy of further thought, as 1,318,300 pupils in England are identified as having special educational needs (DfE, 2019). This number represents 14.9% of all pupils in England, with 271,200 pupils in England having an Education, Health and Care Plan (DfE, 2019). Therefore, the understanding of how different professionals can come together to participate in effective multi-professional meetings is crucial. Questions and misunderstanding as to who should lead meetings and act as the lead professional/key worker may be due to a blurring of professional boundaries within meetings (Engestrom and Sannino, 2010). A lack of clarity as to the processes involved in how roles should be allotted may result in a default position that the responsibility should always be allocated to the SENCO.

The SENCOs interviewed reflected that although meetings may have the core aim to provide a collaborative approach, they can range from unstructured, simple short meetings between professionals to potentially lengthy, structured evaluation meetings. Such meetings require lead professionals/key workers who can competently use a range of skills. The interviewed SENCOs also commented upon the lack of consistency in professionals attending meetings. This is not a new phenomenon. Issues surrounding the retention of staff in the National Health Service (NHS) 'is and will remain a key issue for the NHS' (NHS Employers, 2019:2). The effectiveness of a multi-disciplinary group can be understood in terms of the effort of members and the development of strategies which draw upon the skills and knowledge of each member (Hackman, 2012). Consistent attendance at meetings could enable clearer identification of professional roles, responsibilities and accountability being established. By becoming more skilled in explaining each of their own areas of expertise, professionals could develop a mutual understanding of each professional's specialisms. Although the SENCOs interviewed did consider the contributions from other professionals at meetings were helpful and important in providing different opinions, knowledge, insight and advice, they reflected this often could not be achieved due to the lack of consistent attendance. There needs to be shared understanding and commitment among professionals to the rules and responsibilities of the multi-professional meetings (Engestrom, 2011). One of these may be an understanding of the importance of professionals attending subsequent meetings in order for joint decision-making to be monitored effectively.

Efficiency in meetings

SENCOs reflected on the efficacy of some meetings, which should also be set in a context of the first discussion on time.

> "We have had some meetings . . . I don't necessarily know how successful".
>
> "[Identified professionals] I know have said to parents we've done what we can for now. We can't do anything more for your child and then it comes back to school. . . . I feel it is always left to school to try to carry on and pick it up again".

Discussion

The concept of a system with no perceived joint accountability from all professionals involved was reflected upon by the interviewed SENCOs. They questioned the success of multi-professional practice and whether the SEN CYP, who were supposed to be the central focus of the meetings, eventually became lost in them. Simply having all the chairs around a meeting table full of the right people does not imply there will be successful outcomes for the SEN CYP. Each professional may have differing views as to what they consider to be the ultimate outcome of the multi-professional meeting, which will impact upon the efficiency of the meetings. Such difference in views can lead to 'tensions and a need to establish new ways of working' (Greenhouse, 2013:408). Each professional may have different responses to the reason why the meeting was called (Engestrom, 2011). This can result in conflicting motives, as each professional may have a differing viewpoint as to how the pathway to success can be achieved. The meaning for the meeting can be lost within the different interpretations of the professionals involved, resulting in conflicting outcomes for SEN CYP and their families/carers (Truss, 2008).

Greenhouse (2013) considers that professionals from sectors such as education, health and social services may construct differing interpretations as to how the objective of the meetings can be achieved. Different professionals may use differing tools to reach their viewpoint. NICE public health guidance (2015) recommends that services should be delivered that meet the individual and diverse needs of CYP. Strategic planning, commissioning and provision of services that are integrated with other professionals is emphasised.

The interviewed SENCOs reflected on whether the multi-professional meetings ever solved identified issues. Truss (2008) describes a gap between how the system should work for SEND CYP and the realities of how it fails to work, with CYP needing to fail for a long period of time before the systems responds. Successful multi-professional work depends on those involved both collaborating and cooperating with each other. If the communication between agencies is not effective, then parents/carers can find themselves 'fighting a system, not engaging with it' (Truss, 2008:372). A lack of interconnection from professionals can result in a holistic picture not being formed and therefore integrated systems not working efficiently (Morrison, 2002).

Workload

In conjunction with time and efficiency, the SENCOs referred to their workloads.

> *"Workload and complexity of cases is a big issue".*
> *"There is more and more we (SENCOs) are being asked to be responsible for and to lead."*
> *"And I think if I look back over years, not just as a SENCO but working in schools, there is more and more and more we are being asked to be responsible for and to lead."*

Discussion

In England, it is a statutory duty that every mainstream maintained or academy school appoints a SENCO (The Education (Special Educational Needs Co-ordinators) (England) (Amendment) Regulations, 2009). Although there has been statutory guidance which suggests the SENCO role responsibilities (DfE and DoH, 2014), there is a lack of clarity as to what the role should entail (Pearson, 2010). The national picture of SENCO workload indicates that 71% of SENCOs report that administration tasks accounted for the majority of their SENCO time in an average week (Curran *et al.*, 2018). Meetings, including liaison with external agencies, accounted for the second most time-consuming role. SENCOs consider they do not have enough time to meet the demands of the role (Curran *et al.*, 2018).

Several comments from the interviewed SENCOs focused upon whether the workload involved in multi-professional meetings is currently appropriate and manageable. The Lamb Inquiry (Lamb, 2009) highlighted issues with the reality of organisations working together and the need for a multi-disciplinary approach to support children and families/carers. However, the comments from the interviewed SENCOs cast doubt as to whether such a multi-disciplinary approach has been achieved yet. The SENCOs questioned if the workload of the multi-professional approach is fairly distributed. If the workload is not fairly distributed, then it could be questioned if 'all professionals working with a child should explicitly understand their responsibilities in order to achieve positive outcomes' (Laming, 2009:36) is being achieved. SENCOs find themselves working in highly complex environments where their ability to lead and develop inclusive cultures within their school communities is crucial; however, 'in many schools SENCOs have been overwhelmed by paperwork, presenting them with the conflicting demands of managing bureaucracy against the more crucial development of whole-school strategy' (Sweb, 2007:439–440).

Analysis of theoretical concepts

To aid the analysis of the interviews, three theoretical perspectives will be reflected upon. These theories consider effective dialogue, the restructuring of human activity and the trust professionals should aim to develop between each other. After reflection upon these theories, the current state of partnership working is considered.

Effective dialogue

Many discussions take place in schools: 'leaders need to learn how to make connections among all the peoples comprising the school community' (Stoll *et al.*, 2003:105). Reflecting upon Bohm (1985), it can be viewed that when professionals enter into discussion they will bring with them firmly held beliefs and practices. Bohm (1985) considered that when discussion moves to dialogue, then people are more willing to enter into a process of developing common thinking, leading to common course of action. They may not agree with each other, but they are able to meet at a common point. To reach a point of dialogue, professionals need to come to meetings with an open mind, moving beyond pre-held assumptions, enabling them to unite with others to develop inclusive practice. By choosing the right facilitator for a meeting, progress can be maintained as professionals continue with a dialogue rather than moving back to a discussion.

The restructuring of human activity

To achieve a better understanding of the complexity of multi-professional working, it can be useful to reflect upon Engestrom and Sannino's (2010) activity theory (AT). Greenhouse (2013:405) considers that AT 'provides a framework for the understanding how activity is restructured'. It considers the human activity that occurs when, in the context of multi-professional meetings, different professionals from different sectors come together to enable change to occur. Within the framework of AT, if the expertise of each professional at a meeting is shared, then positive collaboration can occur across the professional boundaries. Engestrom (2011) refers to this as expertise developing horizontally. In such circumstances, the role of the SENCO and their leadership potential could be strengthened as they increased their understanding of other professional practices. As many SEN CYP present with multiple needs, this strengthening professional knowledge of the SENCO will not only improve their ability to meet the needs of the SEN CYP but also improve their leadership ability as the acquired knowledge and understanding would influence future decision-making across the school community.

The interviewed SENCOs reflected that some meetings never appeared to achieve long-lasting outcomes. This could be partially attributed to the complexity of the situations the meetings are attempting to address. Within the framework of AT (Engestrom, 2011), there is a need for different professionals to share effectively their knowledge and working practices. When viewed through AT (Engestrom and Sannino, 2010), it can be regarded that the construct of the multi-professional meetings involve a division of labour, as each professional will come to the meeting with a background based in differing knowledge and ways of working. 'Some professionals may perceive their expertise and knowledge as superior to others, resulting in the loss of other expertise' (Greenhouse, 2013:409). Each professional needs to be aware of the importance of their role and that of others.

Trust

A barrier to efficient multi-professional practice could be the willingness of professionals to fully cooperate with each other due to a lack of trust. The interviewed SENCOs provided an insight into this issue when they reflected upon not being able to depend on other professionals to come to meetings. By not consistently attending meetings, the key component of having trust in another professional, who was able to develop aspects of their role and achieve the agreed next steps identified in a meeting, could be diminished. To achieve the effective use of the professional expertise, there must be a level of trust amongst professionals. With trust, professionals may be in a better position to move beyond discussion and enter into dialogue (Bohm, 1985). Trust and high-quality dialogue of this nature can take time to establish, and as Bryk and Schneider's (2002) model of relational trust highlights, stems from a number of elements:

  Respect – professionals show respect for one another by listening to and considering each other's point of view;
  Regard – professionals have regard for one another shown through a willingness to move beyond the basic requirements of a job;
  Competence – professionals have confidence in each other's roles and ability is evident;
  Integrity – professionals have a high ethical stance, demonstrable when agreed outcomes or promises are kept.

Partnership working

Frost (2005) offers a useful model of action regarding the complex dichotomy of relationships within multi-professional meetings. As a strategic SENCO leader, it can be useful to reflect upon Frost's model (2005) to consider the point at which current multi-professional practice is operating. As Soan (2017:94) considers: 'the manner in which professionals and agencies or bodies work together should not be viewed as static'. However, perceiving Frost's (2005) model as a hierarchy may not in some cases be possible or desirable (Stone and Foley, 2014). The situation a SENCO may find themselves in may be more complex than Frost's model (2005) depicts (Barnes *et al.*, 2018). Therefore, aiming to ultimately achieve integration may not ensure improved outcomes for SEN CYP will be delivered. In Table 14.1, Frost's (2005) model is mapped onto examples of SENCO practice.

Table 14.1 Consideration of Frost's (2005) model through the lens of SENCO practice

Frost's level	Identification of the level	Practice example
Level 1: Cooperation	Working together, professionals achieve consistent goals. Although services are independent, they complement each other.	To achieve mutually supportive goals, the SENCO knows the name, contact details and role of other professionals with whom they cooperate.
Level 2: Collaboration	Professionals plan together. They work towards a common outcome. If there is overlap and duplication of services or gaps in services, then these are addressed.	To achieve collaboration, the SENCO and other professionals have access to adequate planning time and resources to understand each other's practice and avoid overlap and duplication. If overlap and duplication is evident, there is sufficient time for these to be addressed. The consistent attendance of professionals at meetings enables professionals to effectively identify issues of duplication, gap or overlap.
Level 3: Co-ordination	There is a systematic and planned course of action. This enables progression towards goals that are shared and agreed.	To enabled shared goals and agreement, the SENCOs and other professionals understand each other's practice well enough to plan actions that go beyond one meeting. There is a co-ordinated approach. The goals have been discussed and understood by all professionals so each understands the progression necessary for them to be achieved. This may include discussion of professional values, finances and expectations.
Level 4: Merger/ integration	Different professionals work as one. Service delivery is enhanced.	The SENCO and other professionals consider that all professional are working as one unified voice. The SENCO can identify why this has occurred in order to influence and enhance future practice. The SENCO has ensured that although the professionals are working as one, a person-centred approach has been achieved.

Table 14.2 Consideration of Frost's (2005) model through the lens of SENCO practice: time, workload, lead professional continuity and efficiency

Frost's term			Action $\longrightarrow$		Frost's term
	Time	*Workload*	*Lead professional and continuity*	*Efficiency*	
Cooperation	*A request to the senior leadership team results in time to talk with the other professionals.*	*The SENCO discusses with other professional where they think their roles duplicate. Each professional understands the pattern of each other's working week. Each professional considers their role within the Local Offer.*	*The SENCO establishes if any other professional has led a meeting before. It is established when each professional would be comfortable being the lead professional. If professionals work as part of a wider team, then the details of the team are discussed to ensure continuity is achieved if another team member needs to attend future meetings. Relevant contact details are shared.*	*The SENCO and the other professionals discuss what they consider a successful meeting to be. The SENCO and the other professionals discuss how the agreed outcomes of a meeting will be monitored.*	**Collaboration**

Having reflected upon Frost's (2005) theory, SENCOs can consider, as strategic leaders, how they will plan to reflect upon existing and past practice to achieve better future multi-professional practice: 'Successful leaders must also learn how to connect the past, the present and the future' (Stoll *et al.*, 2003:105). In Table 14.2, the key challenges identified in this chapter are explored as actions that build towards increased levels of collaboration.

Conclusion

Shared commitment and responsibility

In order to achieve the expected outcomes for SEND CYP, SENCOs will often find themselves working with other professionals, which can be 'confusing and time-consuming on occasions' (Wearmouth, 2016:175). The way that these professionals work together can be largely framed by the relationship developed through meetings involving, for example, the Common Assessment Framework and Education, Health and Care Plan pathways (DfE and DoH, 2014). However, nationally there is great variance between the way these meetings are conducted and the resulting outcomes for SEN CYP and their parent/carers (National Audit Office, 2019). Multi-professional meetings hold the potential for holistic outcomes built upon an integrated approach. They can result in innovative outcomes (Kinder *et al.*, 2001).

With shared responsibility and commitment, each professional holds the potential to reinforce each other's work. Efficient SEND CYP focused dialogue meetings may illuminate the active listening approach required to enable positive outcomes to be realised. The SENCO does not stand alone in ensuring positive outcomes for SEND CYP (Szwed, 2007). Other professionals stand equally accountable to achieve this aim. In order to build levels of trust, the agencies involved in meetings need to have positive working relationships, which requires time and effort (Bank, 1992).

Effective shared commitment and responsibility can not only result in positive outcomes for SEND CYP and their parents/carers, but also foster a positive sense of achievement for professionals as they work alongside others. Multi-professional meetings have the potential to develop a holistic viewpoint as expertise and skills are shared and drawn upon to problem solve and find solutions. By developing trust and accepting the contributions of others, each professional can become open and receptive to differing points of view. For the SENCO this could increase their leadership abilities, as new networks could be developed which could influence procedures and actions taken within the school community in the future.

Supporting the SENCO and developing good practice

The SENCO, along with the headteacher and governing body of the educational setting, should strategically develop SEN policy and provision (DfE and DoH, 2014). The role of the SENCO is varied and cannot be prescribed to a set template. Support for SENCOS from within their settings is essential if they are to meet the aims of developing an effective, strategic multi- professional role.

By reflecting upon models such as AT, headteachers and governing bodies can begin to envisage and understand the complexity of the dialogue that occurs within meetings: 'AT is more than a descriptive tool and can be used for generating data and guiding professional practice' (Greenhouse, 2013:413). Through a joint reflection, SENCOs, headteachers and governing bodies can help to find solutions alongside other professionals. Joint accountability and shared vision amongst professionals can lead to change that is lasting, impactful and beneficial.

SEND CYP and their parents/carers who access multi-professional services need to benefit from a collaborative approach providing a seamless service (DfES, 2004). Reflection upon the SENCOs interviewed focuses attention on the need for there to be clearer and more efficient dialogue among multi-professionals. The interviewed SENCOs highlighted the need for all professionals to be able to devote the required time, effort and resources to meetings to ensure a person-centred approach is achieved. To function effectively and develop the inclusive practices in their schools, SENCOs cannot work in isolation. They need to develop communities of support for themselves and the SEND CYP in their schools/settings.

By doing so, the metaphorical empty chairs at multi-professional meetings can be filled by supported, informed, committed professionals working together to enhance delivery and professional understanding. Such integrated service delivery should improve outcomes for their own communities and therefore for the betterment of SEND CYP.

Reflective questions

- Why might delays in organising multi-professional meetings be detrimental to the process of identification and support?
- How might levels of trust be developed among multi-professionals?
- How could SENCOs use the skill set they develop through involvement in multi-professional meetings to strengthen other aspects of their role?

References

Audit Commission (2002) *Statutory Assessment and Statements of Special Educational Needs*. London: HMSO.

Audit Commission (2007) *Out of Authority Placements for Pupils with Special Educational Needs*. London: HMSO.

Bank, J. (1992) *The Essence of Total Quality Management*. Hemel Hempstead: Prentice Hall.

Barnes, J. with Crociani, S., Daniel, S., Feyer, F., Giudici, C., Guerra, J., Karwowska-Struczyk, M., Leitão, C., Leseman, P., Meijers, C., Melhuish, E., Pastori, G., Petrogiannis, P., Skamnakis, C., Takou, R., Van Rossum, E., Wysłowska, O. and Zaxhrisson, H. (2018) *Comprehensive Review of the Literature on Interagency Working with Young Children, Incorporating Findings From Case Studies of Good Practice in Interagency Working with Young Children and their Families within Europe*. ISOTIS. Available at: http://archive.isotis.org/wp-content/uploads/2018/06/D6.2.-Review-on-inter-agency-working-and-good-practice.pdf [Accessed 11.08.20].

Barnes, P. (2008) Multi agency working: What are the perspectives of SENCOs and parents regarding its development and implementation. *British Journal of Special Education*, 35(4), 230–240.

Bohm, D. (1985) *Unfolding Meaning*. New York: Doubleday.

British Medical Association (2019) *Failing a Generation: Delays in Waiting Times for Referral to Diagnostic Assessment for Autism Spectrum Disorder*. London: BMA.

Bryk, A. and Schneider, B. (2002) *Trust in Schools*. New York: Russell Sage Foundation.

Children and Families Act 2014. London: Her Majesty's Stationery Office.

Children's Act 2004. London: Her Majesty's Stationery Office.

Clough, P. and Corbett, J. (2006) *Theories of Inclusive Education*. London: Paul Chapman.

Curran, H., Moloney, H., Heavey, A. and Boddison, A. (2018) *It's About Time: The Impact of SENCO Workload on the Professional and the School*. Available at: www.bathspa.ac.uk/media/bathspaacuk/education-/research/senco-workload/SENCOWorkloadReport-FINAL2018.pdf [Accessed 11.08.20].

Department for Education (2019) *Special Educational Needs in England: January 2019*. Available at: https://assets.publishing.service.gov.uk/government/uploads/system/uploads/attachment_data/file/814244/SEN_2019_Text.docx.pdf [Accessed 11.08.20].

Department for Education and Department of Health (2014) *Special Educational Needs and Disability Code of Practice: 0 to 25 Years*. London: DfE and DoH.

Department for Education and Skills (2003) *Every Child Matters: Change for Children*. London: DfES.

Department for Education and Skills (2004) *Removing Barriers to Learning*. London: DfES.

Education Act 1981. London: Her Majesty's Stationery Office.

The Education (Special Educational Needs Co-ordinators) (England) (Amendment) Regulations 2009. London: Her Majesty's Stationery Office.

Engestrom, Y. (2011) From design experiments to formative interventions. *Theory of Psychology*, 21(5), 598–628.

Engestrom, Y. and Sannino, A. (2010) Studies of expansive learning: Foundations, findings and future challenges. *Educational Research Review*, 5(1), 1–24.

Frost, N. (2005) *Professionalism, Partnership and Joined Up Thinking: A Research Review of Front Line Working with Children and Families*. Dartington: Research in Practice/Blacklers.

Gaskell, S. and Leadbetter, J. (2009) Educational psychologists and multi-agency working: Exploring professional identity. *Educational Psychology in Practice*, 25(2), 97–111.

Greenhouse, P. (2013) Activity theory: A framework for understanding multi-agency working and engaging service users in change. *Educational Psychology in Practice*, 29(4), 404–415.

Hackman, J. (2012) From causes to conditions in group research. *Journal of Organizational Behavior*, 33(3), 428–444.

Kinder, K., Halsy, K., Kendall, S., Atkinson, M. and Moore, M. (2001) *Working Out Well: Effective Provision for Excluded Pupils*. Slough: National Foundations for Educational Research.

Lamb, B. (2009) *Lamb Inquiry: Special Educational Needs and Parental Confidence*. London: DCSF.

Lamb, N. and All Party Parliamentary Group on Autism (2018) *The Autism Diagnosis Crisis*. London: All Party Parliamentary Group on Autism.

Laming (Lord), H. (2009) *The Protection of Children in England: A Progress Report*. London: The Stationery Office.

Local Government Association (2019) *Local Government Association Briefing House of Commons Debate: Special Educational Needs and Disabilities Funding*. Available at: www.local.gov.uk/sites/default/files/documents/20190212%20LGA%20briefing%20-%20SEND%20Funding.pdf [Accessed 11.08.20].

Milbourne, L., Macrae, S. and Maguire, M. (2010) Collaborative solutions or new policy problems: Exploring multi-agency partnerships in education and health work. *Journal of Education Policy*, 18(1), 19–35.

Morrison, K. (2002) *School Leadership and Complexity Theory*. London: Routledge Falmer.

National Audit Office (2019) *Support for Pupils with Special Educational Needs and Disabilities in England*. London: NAO.

National Health Service Employers (2019) *Improving Staff Retention: A Guide for Employers*. London and Leeds: NHS Employers. Available at: www.nhsemployers.org/-/media/Employers/Documents/Retention-guide.pdf [Accessed 11.08.20].

National Institute for Health and Care Excellence (2015) *Looked-after Children and Young People*. Public health guideline [PH28]. Available at: www.nice.org.uk/guidance/ph28 [Accessed 11.08.20].

Ofsted (2020) *Annual Report of Her Majesty's Chief Inspector of Education, Children's Services and Skills 2018/19*. London: Ofsted.

Parkin, E., Long, R., Powell, A. and Jarrett, T. (2020) *Briefing Paper, Number 7172: Autism – Overview of Policy and Services*. London: House of Commons Library. Available at: https://commonslibrary.parliament.uk/research-briefings/cbp-7172/ [Accessed 11.08.20].

Pearson, S. (2010) The role of Special Educational Needs Coordinators (SENCOs): 'To be or not to be'. *Psychology of Educational Review*, 34(2), 30–38.

Roaf, C. (2002) *Coordinating Services for Included Children*. Maidenhead: Open University Press.

Soan, S. (2017) *The SENCO Essential Manual*. London: Open University Press.

Social Exclusion Unit (2001) *Preventing Social Exclusion: Report by the Social Exclusion Unit*. Wetherby: ODPM.

Stoll, L., Fink, D. and Earl, L. (2003) *It's About Learning (and It's About Time)*. London: Routledge Falmer.

Stone, B. and Foley, P. (2014) Towards integrated working. In Foley, P. and Rixon, A. (eds.), *Changing Children's Services: Working and Learning Together*. Bristol and Milton Keynes: Policy Press and The Open University.

Swed, C. (2007) Managing from the middle? Tension and dilemmas in the role of the primary school Special Educational Needs Coordinator. *School Leadership and Management*, 27(5), 437–451.

Truss, C. (2008) Peter's story: Reconceptualising the UK SEN system. *European Journal of Special Needs Education*, 23(4), 365–377.

United Nations (2006) *United Nations Convention on the Rights of Persons with Disabilities*. New York: United Nations.

United Nations Educational Scientific and Cultural Organisation. (1994) *The Salamanca Statement and Framework for Action on Special Needs Education*. Paris: UNESCO.

Van de Putte, I., De Schauwer, E., Van Hove, G. and Davies, B. (2018) Rethinking agency as an assemblage from change management to collaborative work. *International Journal of Inclusive Education*, 22(8), 885–901.

Warnock, M. (1978) *Special Educational Needs: Report of the Committee of Enquiry into the Education of Handicapped Children and Young People*. London: Her Majesty's Stationery Office.

Wearmouth, J. (2016) *Effective SENCO Meeting the Challenge*. Maidenhead: Open University Press.

15 Working with families

Gianna Knowles

Parents know their child best, and they will know what they and their child need.

(DfE, 2014:13)

The importance of a close working relationship with families

Those that work in educational settings and schools have long known the importance of families in the lives of children and young people. As educationalists we have the most contact with the child or young person, and we support their learning journey, but the child or young person always carries their family with them; they are present in everything a child or young person says, does, thinks and feels. Families shape us, our sense of self, our understanding of the world and the values and attitudes we live by. For those of us who had no family as a child, or have distanced ourselves, as adults, from our family – this too has shaped who we are.

While this chapter is called Working with Families, parents is sometimes used as a shorthand term for those who the child or young person goes home to at the end of the learning day and those who, in the vast majority of cases, nourish and cherish the children and young people we are working with. Parents and families are also the people who see more of the children than we do and see them in a wider range of situations than school provides; they are the people who have the archive of the child's history and know details of the child's likes, interests, fears and experiences.

As Kelly (2016) discusses: parents and families are those that 'know' their children and young people the best. They have spent many hours, days and years observing, monitoring and meeting the child's needs, wants and emotions. As professionals we may not always agree with the way every family chooses to support and 'raise' their child, but that does not detract from the fact the family is putting in the care, time, effort and money and who have a moral and legal need to be listened to and consulted on matters affecting their child or young person. Children and young people, too, feel safe and secure while in the setting or school if they see that their parents are respected and feel comfortable there. Working in partnership with families creates a shared level of expectation, which in turn supports the child.

A partnership is two-way, and this is important for sharing information or any concerns on either side, since sometimes what is happening in the child's home life may impact on what happens in school, and families are more likely to share information if they feel they have a good relationship with the school. Families, too, who feel secure in their relationship with the school are more likely to seek advice, help and support should they need it. A strong working relationship with families will make transitions throughout the setting or school and between schools smoother and, overall, strong partnerships with families improve practice and outcomes for the children, ensuring every child or young person has their full individual needs met (Kelly, 2016).

Good practice – a case study example

At 13, Alex, with an Education, Health and Care Plan (EHCP) for a diagnosis of autism and from a White/Caribbean background, was moved to a Pupil Referral Unit (PRU), having been excluded from his mainstream school due to: 'persistent disruption' and for assaulting a member of staff.

Alex had generally had a supportive experience in his primary school. The school had worked closely with his family to support Alex, as it became apparent, when he was in Year 2, that it was likely he was autistic. Working with the family, a diagnosis of autism and an EHCP was secured when Alex was nine years old. Again, the primary school and the family worked together to try and ensure a smooth transition to secondary school. Initially things seemed fine for Alex, but from Year 8 Alex and his family felt he was not being appropriately supported to cope with school 'systems' and that he was being bullied by a group of other pupils. The family shared their concerns with the school, but they too did not feel their knowledge and understanding about Alex was listened to. Gradually the relationship with the family broke down and Alex dealt with his anxiety and frustration through exhibiting crisis behaviour and eventually assaulting a teacher.

On joining the PRU, it quickly became clear that Alex's family were very distrustful of the staff there. Alex's mother was extremely anxious about her son attending a PRU and had kept him out of school due to her concerns. She had been trying unsuccessfully to gain a place at a setting which she felt was better suited to his needs. A lot of time was taken to share with Alex's mother, in particular, the referral routes of pupils to the PRU, explaining that young people found themselves at a PRU for a very broad range of reasons and that currently only 25% of the pupils at the PRU were there due to permanent exclusion.

It was essential to gain Alex's mother's confidence, and she was given a tour of the site when pupils were in situ; the referral and consultation processes were explained to her, as well as the opportunities for her son to experience a good-quality education, in very small class sizes, plus the opportunities the PRU could offer for reintegration into a non-PRU setting. It was emphasised to her the important role she had in supporting her son's transition out of the PRU, through advocating for Alex with the LA and possible new schools.

Time was spent getting to know Alex – his likes, dislikes and interests and additional assessment showed that Alex saw himself as disruptive, and his self-esteem and self-confidence was low. Strategies for supporting Alex were discussed with Alex and his mother, and initially he was provided with one-to-one support.

After approximately six weeks it was felt that Alex was coping well, and the PRU began to withdraw Alex's one-to-one support. This was discussed with Alex, and his mother was also contacted; it was explained that the support was being moved physically away from him, but that a member of staff would still be in close proximity should he require encouragement or assistance, the next stage being to progress with the transition of Alex to a more appropriate setting.

Initially, the responses from the schools that Alex might move to were all negative. However, the PRU's SENCO made personal contact with the SEN base leader of the school that seemed most suitable. The most significant barrier to securing a place for Alex was the 'negative reports' from his secondary school. However, trusting the reports from their colleagues in the PRU, a teacher from the proposed secondary school agreed to make a visit to the PRU to observe Alex and discuss options. The observation went well and a tentative offer was put in place. However, the PRU were concerned to not raise Alex's expectations and those of his mother, and some work was needed to get his mother to agree to the possible placement; her support was key to ensuring that Alex's anxieties were well managed both at home as well as at school.

The PRU continued to work with Alex's mother, and a learning mentor from the PRU's staff and one from the new setting were set up. The PRU's learning mentor was also given the time to be able to continue mentoring of Alex after he started at his new school, to support Alex and liaise with his mother. The complete transition took about six weeks, and after six months Alex currently remains successful.

The voice of the child and the family

This case study is a good example of how the learning outcomes and general well-being of a child or young person are greatly enhanced by the school and family working together. The case study also underlines how much time and effort, on the part of all parties, is needed to repair the damage done, where the school/family relationship breaks down. Another significant theme throughout the case study is that of the importance of the 'voice' the child and the family have in the situation. Particularly, whether their voice is valued and who is listening to, or failing to listen to, what is being said and then acting upon what they are hearing. As Murray (2019) writes: 'the terms "student voice" and "pupil voice" reflect a hierarchy where "students" or "pupils" are othered as less powerful than teachers' (Murray, 2019:1), and the same is often true in relation to parent voice. Parents and families are 'othered' and less powerful. Murray (2019) goes on to argue that 'if we do not listen actively and attend to each child's voice, we convey to the child and others that we do not value the child's perspective, and ultimately, that we do not value the child' (Murray, 2019:2). It is also the case that if the voice of parents and families are not attended to, what is conveyed is that their views have no value.

In her work, Murray (2019) states, under the United Nations Convention of the Rights of the Child (UNCRC), children have a right to 'freedom of expression' and a 'right to be heard' (Murray, 2019:1). The UK Government 'signed-up' to the UNCRC in 1990. However, as a convention, the UNCRC has no legal force in UK law; it sets only a moral imperative. That is to say, there is no Children's Rights Act in UK law, so when something is claimed as a 'child's right', it is a moral right, not a legal right. This may seem like a fine distinction, but for professionals working with children and families, it is important to be able to distinguish between the two, since the law holds precedence in legal matters around children and families. This point will be returned to later in the chapter, but it is helpful, for clarity, to give an example of what is being discussed here. An example being, a situation where relationships within a family have broken down and parents have separated, and sometimes it is thought that it is a 'child's right' to be able to have access to both parents. This is not so, because in law, it may be that the child is not permitted access to both parents.

The UK Government has been repeatedly criticised by the UN for its failure to uphold the children's rights it agreed to when it signed the UNCRC. In 2016 it was found that:

> Despite some progress from their last report in 2008, the UN Committee on the Rights of the Child warns that the UK is not doing enough to prioritise children and give them the opportunity to fulfil their potential.
>
> (Children's Rights Alliance for England, 2016:[online])

The same committee made 150 recommendations to the UK Government in relation to fulfilling its obligations on children's rights, including that it should develop a comprehensive strategy: to make sure these children's needs are not ignored and they can access vital services (CRAE, 2016). The response of the Government (since it signed the UNCRC in 1990) has been that it is enshrining the UNCRC articles in UK law, through legislation such as the Equality Act 2010 and the Children and Family Act 2014.

The Children and Family Act 2014 contains significant legal articles pertaining to the duty of schools to listen to and act on the views and wishes of children and families – articles which form the underpinning principles of the SEN Code of Practice (SEN CoP) (DfE and DoH, 2015). Indeed, the changes to the previous SEN CoP were felt necessary because research (DfE, 2011) was showing that not all children with SEND were being supported in their learning, and that those working with children with SEND often had expectations too low in relation to the children's actual ability. It was taking too long to identify children's needs and provide appropriate support. The research also found that parents did not have enough information about what help was available and which schools were best for their child (DfE, 2011), and too many parents were having to constantly seek information from schools for the help they were entitled to or needed. The overriding feeling being that 'teachers, health workers and social care workers' (DfE, 2011:3) were not always working together to get the best help for a child and their family; rather, the different professional groups were working separately.

Most practitioners who work with children and families are aware of the SEN CoP (DfE and DoH, 2015), and while it is not of itself a legal document, it is a regulatory tool, for guidance – it explains how the law pertaining to children and families with SEND should be complied with. It also states that where the term 'must' is used within the document, this refers to a legal duty that must be complied with. For example, 'where a setting or school identifies a child as having SEN they **must** work in partnership with parents to establish the support the child needs' (DfE and DoH, 2015:101).

While, clearly, the SEN CoP (DfE and DoH, 2015) is written with specific reference to children and young people with a special educational needs and/or disability, the principles it is built on, with reference to working in partnership with families, provides for examples of good practice across all schools' policies and practices. In particular, the principle that parents and families should (and in some instances must) be part of decisions schools are making about their children, although acknowledging this may not be a straightforward process:

> At times, parents, teachers and others may have differing expectations of how a child's needs are best met. Sometimes these discussions can be challenging but it is in the child's best interests for a positive dialogue between parents, teachers and others to be maintained, to work through points of difference and establish what action is to be taken.
>
> (DfE and DoH, 2015:21)

The Children and Families Act 2014

The Children and Families Act 2014 changed and updated the law regarding a number of issues affecting children and families, for example, the law relating to the UK's adoption procedures and support for children whose parents are separating. In terms of children with special educational needs and/or disability (SEND), the Children and Families Act 2014 also instituted *a new system to help children with special educational needs and disabilities* (DfE et al., 2014), the overall intention of the law being to provide 'greater protection to vulnerable children' (DfE et al., 2014). It should be noted that the Children and Families Act 2014 provides the legal definition of SEND, the definition as it appears in the SEND CoP (DfE and DoH, 2015), derives directly from the Children and Families Act 2014.

As we have already discussed, one of the fundamental principles that underpins the SEN Code of Practice (DfE and DoH, 2015) is the belief that 'parents know their child best, and they will know what they and their child need' (DfE, 2011:12). This statement is supported by the Children and Families Act 2014 and, therefore, as we have seen, legally underpins the current SEN Code of Practice (SEN CoP; DfE and DoH, 2015), the aim of the SEN CoP being to put children and parents at the heart of assessing and supporting where there is SEND and to ensure confusion is avoided and the right decisions made. To ensure this happens, the SEN CoP sets out in detail how parents should be fully informed and involved in all aspects relating to support for their SEND child or young person, from initial assessment though to gaining an EHCP (if appropriate) and including the appeals process available to them – again where appropriate. In this way, the SEN CoP is an example both of good practice and legal duties that pertain to schools developing appropriate, positive working relationships with parents and families, where families are consulted about and involved in the support and education of their children. As stated by the DfE: 'parents should have a real say in decisions that affect their children, should have access to impartial information, advice and support and know how to challenge decisions they disagree with' (DfE, 2014:11).

The legal definition of parent

Throughout this chapter the term parent or family has been frequently used, and it might be helpful here to note the legal definition of parent. This is because relationships between children, young people and adults in families can be complex. They are a mixture of biological and emotional relationships; those adults a child or young person is emotionally closest to and, in return, might provide the most support for the child may in law have no legal position in relation to the child. This means a setting or school needs to know who the legal parent or guardian of a child is, since a setting or school may only contact these persons. However, in actuality, from the child and setting's/school's point of view, the most supportive relationships may not be with the legal parents or guardian – and this can further complicate establishing strong partnerships with parents and families.

The law states that 'all mothers and most fathers have legal rights and responsibilities as a parent – known as "parental responsibility"' (Gov.uk, 2020). It also goes on to state what the role of parenting is, including: provide a home for and protecting and 'maintaining' the child (Gov.uk, 2020). A parent is also responsible for: disciplining the child, the child's education and medical treatment. A failure to meet any of these responsibilities is a safeguarding issue.

Where a child does not have parents, or is not with their parents, there may be those who are appointed as the child's guardian or guardians. Again, this is a legal position, and for an adult to claim guardianship, they must have gone through the appropriate legal process to become a guardian (Gov.uk, n.d.). An adult can apply to be a guardian where: the child lives with them through a child arrangements order; has lived with them for three of the past five years; is a relative or a foster parent (for at least one year); has the agreement of all the people with parental responsibility for the child or the agreement of the local council, if the child is in care (Gov.uk, n.d.).

Having considered the legal duties settings and schools have in relation to the parents of children and young people they work with, it is also helpful to support building strong working partnerships with parents to explore further why parents or families are so important in the lives of children, young people and educationalists.

What do families look like in the first half of the 21st century?

When the UK Government talks or writes about families, the definition they use for a family is 'a family is a married, civil partnered or cohabiting couple with or without children, or a lone parent, with at least one child, who live at the same address' (ONS, 2020:[online]). While in 2019, there were 19.2 million families in the UK, with married or civil partner couples being the most common family type, representing two-thirds of families in the UK, the married, civil-partnered and cohabiting statistics include same- and opposite-sex couples and show an increase of same-sex families by 53.2% from 2015 to 2018 (ONS, 2020). The same statistics show that '4.9% of families in the UK (2.9 million) were lone parent families and that multi-family households (consisting of two or more families) were the fastest growing household type over the last two decades to 2019' (ONS, 2020:[online]), where families in multi-family households may or may not be related. The rise in such households seems to reflect more than one family choosing to live together out of necessity, or 'because of reasons such as housing affordability, childcare responsibilities and caring for older relatives' (ONS, 2020:[online]). In terms of the school population in January 2018, 14.6% of the children and young people attending were children or young people with special educational needs. This means 14.6% of the families schools and settings are working with are families who have a child with SEND (DfE, 2020). It must also be noted that in England in 2019 there were approximately 78,150 children and young people in care, with 56,160 of those children and young people living in 44,450 foster families. This statistic tells us that some of these children and young people will have SEND, and that they are living in care or with foster families will change the dynamic between the educational setting and the 'family', both legally and in terms of personal relationships (The Fostering Network, n.d.). This quick round-up of the statistics most readily available show that there is a rich, varied and diverse range of family groups in the UK at present, and as such this requires schools to be open and responsive to such diversity.

The importance of families

Families are a fundamental part of formative human experience, and the lack of a family, or family support, can have catastrophic and long-term effects on children, often lasting throughout adulthood. Research shows that care leavers (HMPPS, 2019), young people who have spent some or all of their lives as children in care (NSPCC, 2020), are 'less likely to be in education, employment or training . . . [and] more likely to have a criminal conviction' (HMPPS, 2019). While, for children and young people who have SEND, families are their greatest advocates when it comes to working with settings and schools to navigate through the sometimes complex aspects of the SEND educational processes: initial assessment, establishing an Education, Health and Care Plan and subsequent reviews, liaising with multi-agency professionals, possible correspondence with local authorities and supporting transitions between schools.

Not only are families important for the support they provide for their own children, but they also have a much wider societal impact. Families shape the values, attitudes and beliefs society lives by, and they are good places for learning about how to form relationships, deal with conflict and live with others. As Bernardes (1997) stated: 'for most of our lives, "our family" is the most important thing of all' (Bernardes, 1997:1). The service families provide in supporting family members is, quite literally, priceless – it cannot be quantified in financial terms. Whatever the goodwill, professional integrity and intentions of non-family members, family care and support cannot be replicated by the state: it is too time consuming, complex and costly. Families are essential for the well-being of individuals and society as a whole.

The psychology and sociology of the importance of families

Bowlby's attachment theory

Bowlby's attachment theory (Prior, 2006) has had considerable impact on our understanding of how important it is for human beings, from earliest infancy, to have capable, loving and caring persons around them – people with whom they can form mutual supportive attachments (Knowles and Holmstrom, 2013; Mayseless, 2002; Prior, 2006) and relationships with those around them who are providing for their immediate needs of hunger, warmth and comfort. For most infants, these relationships develop into mutually affectionate and rewarding bonds for both the infant and their caregivers. Over time the theory of attachment has developed into an understanding that a biological relationship between the child and caregiver is not as important as the quality of the relationship.

Children and young people who have formed secure attachments and have loving, caring families around them are, perhaps not surprisingly, more likely to thrive in school. And, in families where there are strong attachments of the kinds described, it is also likely that those providing the care for the child want to be involved in helping the child achieve. In this way, settings and schools need to be sensitive to who it is they need to work with in the family to support a child's learning. This theory is helpful as it makes clear that the quality of the attachment relationships within the family is important – it is how those involved, children and others, experience those relationships that leads to well-being. These strong attachments happen across all cultures and in all socio-economic groups, between children and adults who may or may not be biologically related, and between those who may be disabled or non-disabled.

Maslow's hierarchy of needs

As well as having mutually supportive and enriching relationships with others, including family members, Maslow states that humans needs a range of other needs met and opportunities provided, to ensure flourishing and well-being – or, what Maslow calls 'self-actualisation' (Knowles, 2018). Maslow's theory is often visually represented as a layered pyramid. At the bottom of the pyramid is the first level of needs, which include basic physiological needs such as food, water, warmth, shelter and sleep. Once these needs are met there is a next level of need, which includes safety needs, such as personal security and health. The next level of need is love and belonging, then self-esteem, and only when these needs are met can self-actualisation and flourishing be achieved. For Maslow it is important that self-actualisation is achieved, as it is only when this happens that we also develop 'a sense of morality, creativity, spontaneity, problem solving, lack of prejudice and acceptance of facts' (Spohrer, 2008:18).

Bronfenbrenner

Families, however, exist side by side with other families and in a wider social context, and the social context has a considerable impact on families and family members, be that for better or worse. This is a concept explored by Bronfenbrenner in what is known as Bronfenbrenner's ecological environment model (Knowles and Holmstrom, 2013).

Bronfenbrenner's model, often represented as a set of concentric circles, with the child and family in the innermost 'micro' circle, and the widening circles around them representing increasingly wider 'macro' aspects of society – moving out from the 'micro' local neighbourhood, often including schools, to the local region and then the 'macro' national and international environment. However, it is not simply the geographical aspects of the child's expanding environment that the theory considered, but also how the family manages the transition for children through the cultural, political and social complexities of engaging with ever-widening social experiences.

The theory also considers not only the child's experience and understanding of the world from the middle out, but also how children's lives, even from birth, are impacted by what is happening at the macro level in the society into which they are born and grow up. A society that is peaceful and thriving economically will impact on individual families and, therefore, children very differently from a society experiencing economic hardship and conflict.

There are many theories surrounding child development, and the ones briefly outlined here are helpful to consider when we are thinking about how we build partnerships with parents and families. They remind us that the children and young people we work with are integrally bound to and influenced by the family and contexts they live with and in. Therefore, what may seem very straightforward for processes and necessary strategies to support a SEND child or young person may be outside the scope, experience and culture of those we are working with.

It is helpful to think about:

- How will the lack of a significant or appropriate attachment figure impact on a child's capacity to thrive? How might this be exacerbated if the child has SEND?

- How does a parent's attachment relationship with their child impact on the relationship they will seek with settings and schools? For example, they may be overly protective or unable to provide the child with the necessary support, failing to engage appropriately with the school.
- In a situation where a family is struggling to provide for a child's basic needs, how might this impact their capacity to engage with the setting/school?
- If a family feels isolated in the place where they live, or are unsure of how to connect with the services they need, again how might this impact a school's relationship with the family?

In thinking these questions through, very quickly we can see that some families are in a strong position to provide for the basic and higher-order needs of children, including being fully engaged with a child's education, whereas other families – often through events they have no control over – are not so well positioned.

Barriers to positive partnership with families

While we have seen that everyone benefits from the work done by families, historically the importance of families can be overlooked. And sometimes, this lack of recognition has been by settings and schools. As explored by Hornby and Blackwell (2018), all settings and schools know how important strong, working relations are with the families of the children and young people they teach. That said, 'although there is widespread acknowledgement of the potential benefits of PI [parental involvement]' (Hornby and Blackwell, 2018:109), there are in fact clear gaps (Hornby and Blackwell, 2018) between what settings and schools intend in terms of their relationship with families and what families actually experience.

Barriers to positive partnership with families – as seen by families

Hornby and Blackwell (2018) explore how barriers can occur where settings and schools are failing to or are unwilling to work with the real-life, diverse contexts experienced by many families. Instead, families are approached as a homogenous group – all comprised in the same way, having the same experiences and needs. For example, there can be a basic failure in the simple acknowledgement that most 'parents' work (as a matter of financial necessity), including mothers. Therefore, it is not possible for family members to attend meetings or answer phone calls during the school day.

Hornby and Blackwell (2018) also found that schools can be guilty of, often unwittingly, discrimination against 'non-traditional' family units. The statistics show that while two-thirds of families in the UK are composed of married adults, those in civil partnerships or co-habiting adults (this figure includes same-sex couples and adults who may not be the biological parent), a further one-third of families (33%) do not fall into this category. Not all settings and schools reflect the range of ways families are constituted, thus making some parents feel marginalised. This may be remedied through such simple approaches as ensuring the learning environment reflects the diversity of family life through displays, curriculum activities and resources, or can be more thoughtless where parents are addressed by incorrect names and pronouns. Outside of large urban areas of the UK, such as London, many areas are monocultural, and parents from Black and minority ethnic families are still reporting direct and indirect discrimination by settings and schools on the grounds of race (Hornby and Blackwell, 2018).

General good practice in building partnerships with parents and families

As with all successful relationships, they are built up over time and need 'work' by all parties involved. Parents and families need to feel respected by settings and schools and that they can trust that the setting or school has the best interests of their child or young person at heart. Working successfully with specific parents and families will be set against a wider setting or school context where all parents feel welcomed and valued.

For the relationship to be successful, good communication among settings, schools and families is essential. The form of communication will vary, depending on the age of the child or young person and the purpose of the communication. Settings and schools that have good home/

school relationships have achieved this partly through the use of handwritten diaries, emails, blogs and texts. These tools are a useful way of sharing information between home and school about how a child has been during the day or night, any incidents or events (both good and less positive) that might impact on a child's behaviour, and educational information and individual children's successes.

In establishing these forms of communication, it is useful to set out a few ground rules to establish the content and purpose of the communication, for example:

• what method of communication is to be used;
• how often the communication takes place;
• who the communication is between and is there a system for all children, or is it for particular children/young people, for a specific reason;
• what the content of the communication is – social, emotional or educational.

However, for such formal aspects of home/school communication to be successful, it also helps if some aspects of the home/school relationship can be experienced in less formal ways. For example, through social events such as coffee mornings and workshops, which parents and families can attend to meet staff and other families in a more relaxed atmosphere than ones relating specifically to the education of their children. The timing of these events might need careful thought and flexibility, since as noted earlier schools sometimes marginalise parents when they forget that many parents cannot attend events during the traditional school day.

Conclusion

For parents and families to have a strong sense that a setting or school is truly committed to a good working partnership with them, settings and schools need to be:

• welcoming;
• non-judgemental;
• able to offer real support in a timely way;
• able to provide activities that foster a partnership ethos.

This will be achieved through an approach that is consistent and includes activities that are frequent and accessible – both in terms of the times they take place and in terms of embracing the diversity of the parents and families involved.

Reflective questions

• How does a child's educational experience benefit from educational settings having close links with parents and families?
• How can educational settings ensure that parents and families feel welcome?
• How can educational settings demonstrate they listen to and act on the ideas and advice of parents and families?

References

Bernardes, J. (1997) *Family Studies: An Introduction*. London: Routledge.
Children and Families Act 2014. London: Her Majesty's Stationery Office.
Children's Rights Alliance for England (2016) *United Nations Has 'Serious Concerns' About UK Government's Failure to Prioritise Children's Needs*. Available at: www.crae.org.uk/news/united-nations-has-%E2%80%9Cserious-concerns%E2%80%9D-about-uk-government%E2%80%99s-failure-to-prioritise-children%E2%80%99s-needs/ [Accessed 29.04.20].

Department for Education (2011) *Support and Aspiration: A New Approach to Special Educational Needs and Disability*. London: DfE.

Department for Education (2014) *Special Educational Needs and Disability: A Guide for Parents and Carers*. London: DfE.

Department for Education (2020) *Special Educational Needs in England: January 2018*. Available at: https://assets.publishing.service.gov.uk/government/uploads/system/uploads/attachment_data/file/729208/SEN_2018_Text.pdf [Accessed 30.01.20].

Department for Education and Department of Health (2015) *The Special Educational Needs and Disability Code of Practice: 0 to 25 Years*. London: DfE and DoH.

Department for Education, Department for Business, Innovation and Skills, Department for Work and Pensions, Department of Health and Social Care, Ministry of Justice, Timpson, E., Hughes, S. and Willott, J. (2014) *Landmark Children and Families Act 2014 Gains Royal Assent*. Available at: www.gov.uk/government/news/landmark-children-and-families-act-2014-gains-royal-assent [Accessed 18.11.19].

Equality Act 2010. London: Her Majesty's Stationery Office.

The Fostering Network (online). *Fostering Statistics*. Available at: www.thefosteringnetwork.org.uk/advice-information/all-about-fostering/fostering-statistics [Accessed 30.01.20].

Gov.uk (n.d.) *Becoming a Special Guardian*. Available at: www.gov.uk/apply-special-guardian/who-can-apply [Accessed 14.08.20].

Gov.uk (2020) *Parental Rights Responsibilities*. Available at: www.gov.uk/parental-rights-responsibilities [Accessed 18.04.20].

Her Majesty's Prison and Probation Service (2019) *Care Leavers in Prison and Probation. A Summary of Evidence About How People in Prison and on Probation May Be Affected by a History of Being in Care as a Child and How Services can Improve Outcomes for Them*. Available at: www.gov.uk/guidance/care-leavers-in-prison-and-probation [Accessed 30.01.20].

Hornby, G. and Blackwell, I. (2018) Barriers to parental involvement in education: An update. *Educational Review*, 70(1), 109–119.

Kelly (2016) *Why Parent Partnerships Are So Important*. Available at: www.earlyyearscareers.com/eyc/early-years-practice/parent-partnerships-important/ [Accessed 13.01.20].

Knowles, G. (2018) What do we mean by inclusive practice? In Knowles, G. (ed.) *Supporting Inclusive Practice*. 3rd edn. Abingdon: Routledge, 7–21.

Knowles, G. and Holmstrom, R. (2013) *Understanding Family Diversity and Home-school Relations*. Abingdon, Oxon. Routledge.

Mayseless, O. (2002) *Parenting Representations: Theory, Research, and Clinical Implications*. Cambridge: Cambridge University Press.

Murray, J. (2019) Hearing young children's voices. *International Journal of Early Years Education*, 27(1), 1–5.

National Society for the Prevention of Cruelty to Children (2020) *Looked-after Children*. Available at: https://learning.nspcc.org.uk/children-and-families-at-risk/looked-after-children/ [Accessed 30.01.20].

Office for National Statistics (2020) *Families and Households in the UK: 2019. Trends in Living Arrangements Including Families (With and Without Dependent Children), People Living Alone and People in Shared Accommodation, Broken Down by Size and Type of Household*. Available at: www.ons.gov.uk/peoplepopulationandcommunity/birthsdeathsandmarriages/families/bulletins/familiesandhouseholds/2019 [Accessed 30.01.20].

Prior, V. (2006) *Understanding Attachment and Attachment Disorders: Theory, Evidence and Practice*. London: Jessica Kingsley.

Spohrer, K. (2008) *Teaching Assistant's Guide to Emotional and Behavioural Difficulties*. London: Continuum.

16 Working in partnership with parents

Heather Green and Becky Edwards

Introduction

When parents of children with special educational needs and/or disability (SEND) are asked about their relationship with professionals, service providers and the organisations designed to support them and their children, the most common responses are:

> *"It feels as though we are constantly doing battle" (Parent, 2018).*
> *"We have to fight for everything" (Parent, 2018).*
> *"The only person on this earth who truly cares enough about my child to fight for him, is me" (Parent, 2015).*

These are not responses to recent changes in legislation but reflect, rather, parents' cumulative experiences of trying to access appropriate services for their children. As Rix wrote in 2003, 'our experiences wear us down. We have to fight education, social and health systems to make sure that our son is included in the way they claim he will be' (Rix, 2003:78). These are words of confrontation and helplessness, not co-production and partnership. More than 50 years after the publication of the Plowden Report (1967), when the importance of working collaboratively with parents was officially recognised, there are still important questions to answer regarding why some parents are still feeling sidelined, powerless, isolated, angry and exhausted. This chapter will explore the relationship between parents and professionals and look at ways in which Special Educational Needs Co-ordinators (SENCOs) and parents can develop more effective partnerships.

Historical overview

In 1946 the National Association for Parents of Backward Children (later to become MENCAP) was set up by Judy Fryd, the mother of a child with SEND, who, like many other parents, felt anger and sorrow at the lack of services available for her child (Robinson and Staker, 1999). Largely as a result of campaigning by MENCAP and other grassroots parental organisations, the Plowden Report (1967) finally recognised the positive impact that working in close partnership with parents can have on the education of children with SEND. Yet it was not until the publication of the Warnock Report (1978) that the perception of parents as equal partners in their children's learning was officially recognised and embedded into legislation in the 1981 Education Act. Over the next 50 years the crucial importance of joined-up working with parents to ensure effective support for children was formally recognised in SEND legislation and Codes of Practice. However, support remained patchy, and in 2009 the Lamb Inquiry was established to look at ways in which parental confidence in services could be improved:

> We met some of the happiest parents in the country and some of the angriest. Many had children who are well-supported and making good progress. But we also met parents for whom the education system represents a battle to get the needs of their child identified and for these to be met. The crucial issue is that both experiences happen within the same system.
> (Lamb, 2009:2)

One of the key recommendations from the Lamb Inquiry (2009) was strengthening the voice of parents. This was included in the Children and Families Act 2014 and implemented through the SEND Code of Practice: 0–25 years (2015), which put the voice of children, young people and parents at its centre.

There is, however, a difference between having legitimised rights and having the power to exercise those rights (Swann, 1987:23). Just because something is passed as legislation does not mean it is implemented in practice. Although parents are now consulted and invited to meetings, they often feel their views are not listened to and their presence is tokenistic. Until parents and professionals share an understanding of what is meant by partnership, agreed outcomes will be hard to reach.

Working in partnership

The concept of partnership in relation to working with parents of children with SEND is subjective and open to (mis)interpretation. According to Ryan and Runswicke-Cole (2008), the term *partnership* is often loosely understood by professionals as a model of involvement rather than a true partnership which supports the rights of the parents to make decisions about their children. Definitions have changed as the importance of the role of parents has been increasingly acknowledged. In 1983 Mittler and Mittler (1982) defined partnership between parents and professionals as 'a full sharing of knowledge and experience' (Mittler and Mittler, 1982:10–11) while Pugh and De'Ath (1989) emphasised that partnership is a working relationship characterised by 'a shared sense of purpose, mutual responsibility, skills, decision-making and accountability' (Pugh and De'Ath, 1989:68). The findings of the Lamb Inquiry (2009) supported this view, adding that partnership needed to include 'good, honest and open communication' (Lamb, 2009:39).

In order for a partnership based on mutual understanding and trust to be developed, parents must also feel that their role as experts is acknowledged (Cheminais, 2011; Nutbrown et al., 2008; Dyson, 2004) and the challenges of their lived experience recognised. This is often difficult because the relationship between parents and professionals is often polarisation: parents striving constantly to get the best for their child and professionals balancing reduced budgets and increased workloads. Effective partnerships can build bridges, allowing honest discussion and negotiation to take place where professionals and parents are treated as equals. This changing view of the role of the parent in the decision-making process is reflected in legislation and policy and in the following changing models of partnership that have been developed over the last 50 years:

The Expert Model (Cunningham and Davis, 1985): professionals use their specialist knowledge and expert power to make decisions and judgments (professionals have the power).

The Transplant Model (Mittler and Mittler, 1982): expert skills are 'transplanted' to the parents from the professionals in order to help them become more competent, confident and skilled (professionals have the power).

The Consumer Model (Cunningham and Davis, 1985): parents should be considered as consumers with the right to choose appropriate services and interventions from a range of options provided by the 'specialists' and based on information from the specialist (professional power lessened as it can now be challenged by the parents).

The Empowerment Model (Appleton and Minchom, 1991): professionals must take into account the unique situation of each family, tailor services and interventions to meet these needs and provide help to empower parents to become partners (power moving between professionals and families).

The Negotiating Model (Dale, 1995): a working relationship where the partners use negotiation and joint decision-making and resolve differences of opinion and disagreement, in order to reach some kind of shared perspective or jointly agreed decision on issues of mutual concern (parents and professionals share power).

The effectiveness of working in partnership with parents depends, to a large extent, on the views and attitudes of the professionals involved. Partnerships should not be viewed as static but as a responsive and collaborative movement towards shared goals based on mutual respect, complementary expertise and a willingness to learn from each other (Swann, 1987:293).

The challenges of building partnerships

Although the concept of partnership working is not a new one and despite terminology changing from working with parents (Warnock, 1978) to the current idea of co-production, many of the barriers to effective partnerships have remained unchanged. Parents rarely seem to feel they are treated as equals, perceived as experts or informed.

> If they reach conclusions which you know to be wrong, do not take advantage of your presence . . . or pay attention to all presented evidence, you lose trust in their opinions, feel them to be arrogant and worry about the implications of their inaccuracies.
>
> (Wolfendale, 1988:35)

Whilst understanding the critical importance of working collaboratively with parents, even Warnock was clear that she did not perceive them as educational equals:

> In educational matters, parents cannot be equals to teachers if teachers are to be regarded as true professionals. Even though educating a child is a joint enterprise . . . parents should realise that they cannot have the last word.
>
> (Warnock, 1985:12)

With such views endemic to policy makers and the pathway to true partnership working strewn with obstacles, it is not surprising that parents give up or that all they can see is the battle rather than the benefits. Whilst parents believe they are fighting for their child, professionals often perceive the parent as part of the problem:

> Many parents have had to fight long and frustrating battles to have their children accepted. . . . These parents have often been regarded as trouble-makers because of their determination to get what is best for their children.
>
> (Bailey, 1998:177)

This sense of stress anxiety when meeting with professionals is common:

> *"Before meetings, I go into the toilets, stare at my reflection in the mirror and tell myself that this time, I won't cry."*
>
> (Parent, 2019)

For parents, every conversation, phone call or form that needs filling in becomes part of their battle to get what they need for their child. Professionals are often perceived by parents to be both the problem and the solution. Professionals have access to the material resources that are needed, and therefore they are perceived to hold the power: they can provide the resources or refuse to do so (Dyson, 2004). This power imbalance continues to be one of the greatest challenges to effective partnership working.

Parents, on the one hand, cite a range of other obstacles, including lack of information, lack of transparency, lack of equality of status, lack of understanding of their child's case and the use of jargon (Lamb, 2009; Roffey, 2001). Professionals, on the other hand, can often feel that parents are making unreasonable demands from an already stretched service. Responses from parents and their capacity to engage are often shaped by their lived experience (Roffey, 2001). Understanding this will help to form a partnership based on empathy and mutual trust where parents feel valued and listened to.

The lived experience of parents of children with SEND

Chronic sorrow

Chronic sorrow (Olshansky, 1962) is a hidden sorrow experienced specifically by parents of children with SEND. It begins at birth or diagnosis. The genesis of the sadness is the recognition of the loss of the hoped-for child and the reality of the life their child will be living. It is described by Roos (2002) as a living loss and by Busch (2015) as a sorrow that is ongoing and cyclical. It is lifelong and is re-experienced every time a child fails to meet a milestone, e.g. walking, talking, passing a driving test, leaving home. It is estimated that 80% of parents of children with SEND experience chronic sorrow. The fact that chronic sorrow is interwoven with periods of satisfaction and happiness (Teel, 1991) means that it is sometimes unrecognised and overlooked by professionals as a cause of parental anxiety.

Professional response

- Recognise the emotional impact of chronic sorrow on a parent.
- Listen with empathy and understanding.
- Label the feeling and help parents to understand that it is a normal and inherent part of parenting a child with SEND.

I thought I was the only person who felt this way. It helps knowing that it has a name.

(Anonymous Parent, words spoken in 2017)

Personal tragedy theory

The personal tragedy theory (Oliver, 1990) often defines the way in which parents and children with SEND are perceived and treated by professionals, specialists and society. It describes how disability is represented as a tragedy where disabled people (and their parents) are perceived as victims of a tragic happening (Oliver, 1990). This can lead to a loss of their internal locus of control (Rotter, 1966), low self-esteem and an expectation that decisions will be made about, rather than with, them.

Professional response

- Ensure that collaborative decisions are based on the social not the medical model.
- Be person-centred at all times.
- Be open-minded to parental ideas.
- Ensure that parents' views are given high status and value in any discussions.
- Ensure that decisions are not based on a model of compensation but on overcoming societal barriers.
- Recognise that parents are experts on their own children.
- Empower parents to become pro-active co-producers of the support for their child.

Emotional labour

Emotional labour is a term coined by Hochschild (1983) and described by Mastracci as 'the effort within oneself to conjure appropriate feelings or subdue inappropriate ones, and the effort to induce particular feelings in another person or stifle other feelings' (Mastracci *et al.*, 2012:28). Emotional labour is the unpaid emotional work. It is the work parents do to comfort, support and protect their children, helping them to be resilient and positive. For most parents, the main burden of emotional work ends as the children get older. For parents of children with SEND, this is not the case. They must often continue to labour emotionally for their children throughout their lives. This can lead to burnout and emotional exhaustion (Newman *et al.*, 2008). Parents are often unaware of the physical and emotional impact of emotional labour and do not ask for support (Dyson, 2004).

Professional response

- Ask parents if they are feeling tired or overwhelmed.
- Build open and trusting relationships where parents feel that they can talk honestly.
- Do not overburden parents with tasks – be aware of what is possible and feasible for them to do.
- Listen with empathy and unconditional positive regard.

(Rogers, 1957)

Working with parents/carers: SENCO responsibility

In schools and settings, the relationship with the Special Educational Needs Co-ordinator shapes this shared vision. The SENCO is sometimes the first professional that parents have to work with, and the relationship between SENCO and parent can be a crucial stepping stone into successful parent partnerships.

In a school it has been acknowledged that when professionals and parents work together effectively, the outcomes for children are more likely to be favourable, and children thrive, progressing in their learning and social development. This is even more evident when children at the heart of the partnership have a special educational need and/or disability.

Statutory guidance in the form of the SEND Code of Practice: 0–25 (DfE and DoH, 2015) outlines how professionals and parents should be working in partnership and collaboration to meet the needs of children and young adults in their care. Specifically, the roles and responsibilities of the SENCO are underpinned by the principles of the SEND Code of Practice: 0–25 (DfE and DoH, 2015), which states that the SENCO should provide:

> 6.89 Professional guidance to colleagues and will work closely with staff, parents and other agencies. The SENCO should be aware of the provision in the Local Offer and be able to work with professionals providing a support role to families to ensure that pupils with SEN receive appropriate support and high-quality teaching.

> 6.90 The key responsibilities of the SENCO may include: liaising with parents of pupils with SEN.
> (DfE, 2015, section 6.89–90)

An effective SENCO will listen to others, especially parents. This is key if the needs of the child with Special Educational Needs (SEN) are to be met as fully as possible. SENCOs often rely on parents' help and support in order to meet children's needs. However, the reality of budgetary and other constraints can make life hard for both schools and families. It is, therefore, essential that SENCOs consult and liaise with staff, parents and carers, external agencies and appropriate professionals and voluntary bodies in order to ensure that support is co-ordinated and targeted appropriately, and that all are informed and updated about children on the SEN register.

Discussion

The 2009 Lamb Inquiry (2009) highlighted the importance of schools communicating openly, frequently and honestly with parents and carers of learners with SEND, as well as with the learners themselves. It concluded that there was a lack of aspiration and focus on securing good outcomes in the school system for children with SEND. Parents' (and children's and young people's) views were not properly listened to and acted on. Further engagement and confidence in schools was and remains low for families of children with SEND (Lamb, 2018). As stated earlier, it could be argued that this continued lack of confidence is surprising since the reforms of statutory guidance set out in the SEND Code of Practice: 0–25 (DfE and DoH, 2015) make it clear that parents' and carers' views should be at the heart of decisions made about their children.

The role of the family is especially significant for young people with SEND because they rely on support and guidance from parents and carers for longer than their peers do (Dovey-Pearce *et al.*, 2012). Parents are a child's first teachers and the home their first school (Berger, 1995). However, the delegation of this role to other adults once formal education begins may in itself cause difficulties (Crozier, 1999). As previously mentioned, parental involvement in a child's education can have a significant impact on learner outcomes (Desforges and Abouchaar, 2003). Yet it appears there remain some significant challenges in working collaboratively and in partnership with parents and schools. Wedell (2017) suggests that SENCOs are usually regarded by the parents of children with special educational needs and disability as their advocates within the schools' systems. Sometimes, however, circumstances can arise which put the relationship under strain (Wedell, 2017).

Goodhall and Vorhaus (2011) reviewed evidence on successful approaches to parental partnerships and engagement within schools. They found that the following were key to parental involvement:

- Parental engagement strategies need to be part of a whole-school approach.
- There must be clear leadership from senior practitioners to enhance parental engagement within the school.
- Schools need to be proactive in engaging parents.

(Goodhall and Vorhaus, 2011)

Perceived challenges

As the system stands, it often creates 'warrior' parents at odds with the school and feeling they have to fight for what should be their children's by right, engendering conflict in place of trust.

(Lamb, 2009:2)

The notion of parents as warriors has also been identified by SENCOs as being a barrier to developing effective parent partnership. SENCOs have stated that a fight response from some of the parents they work with has become a normalised behaviour from parents who have either expected barriers and conflict or have become conditioned to challenge bureaucracy to secure their child's rights. This links back to the concept of polarisation and the importance of professionals understanding the lived experience of being a parent of a child with SEND, unless they have had the relevant experience. This will be discussed further in this chapter.

One of the main difficulties experienced by SENCOs is the curtailing of available resources in relation to a school's own resources and to the reduced levels of specialist services from the local authority and health and social services. This lack of specialist advice and support means that SENCOs are dealing with problems which may be beyond their own professional competence. As one SENCO stated, 'any good SENCO is probably permanently tormented by what provision they can and cannot provide' (Wedell, 2017:485). This is supported by SENCOs who have stated that managing parent expectations, coupled with meeting statutory requirements, has been one of the most prominent challenges in meeting the needs of children with SEN, whilst working with limited funding and resources. Whilst parents feel that professionals hold the power, professionals feel powerless in the face of these professional and political pressures and limitations.

Trainee SENCOs from the National Award for Special Educational Needs Coordination (NASENC) programme were asked for their thoughts about working with parents. Having gained ethical clearance from the awarding university and in line with guidance from the British Educational Research Association (BERA), their responses were collated and are summarised here in this chapter.

The trainee SENCOs were asked what they perceived to be the challenges of working with parents. Their responses consisted of mainly emotive perceptions from the viewpoints of both the parents and the SENCO:

- Managing parent expectations
- The expert SENCO to fix problems
- The expert SENCO in any aspect of SEND
- Parents engaging too much
- Parents engaging not enough
- Parents' levels of acceptance
- Parents grieving for the child they thought they would have
- Parents being school phobic
- Parents are angry
- Parents have challenges themselves

Actual challenges

SENCOs from the NASENC programme were asked what they find are the main challenges of working with parents and maintaining partnership working with parents. Their responses are as follows and are discussed further:

- Managing parent expectation
- Misunderstanding of SEN entitlement/labelling/categorising
- Finding convenient times to meet
- Parents are reluctant to engage
- Parents requesting an EHCP

- Children arrive/go home on school transport – maintaining lines of communication
- Understanding of school/setting giving different levels of support
- Jargon and paperwork too much and too confusing
- Fight response now the norm as have been fighting for so long

One key challenge of collaborative working with parents is to ensure SEND systems can accommodate those who want to be active participants in their child's education, but not marginalise those who do not have the time or resources to do the same (Harris, 2019). SENCOs have stated that finding mutually convenient times to meet with parents is a real challenge to working in partnership. They also stated that parents and professionals alike can find the jargon and paperwork too confusing. Reports from professionals can be saturated with technical language and acronyms. These terms are often specific to each group of professionals within either education, health or the social care sectors. It could be suggested that deciphering and understanding what is meant by such specific technical language can often contribute to a resistance of collaborative working. This may then result in a time delay of the child's or young person's needs being met. Fox *et al.* (2017) take this point further in considering not just technical terminology in isolation, but the challenge of considering specific diagnosis and labels of conditions. They suggest that community attitudes towards mental illness, challenging behaviours and disability, combined with the lack of vocabulary to describe and explain certain conditions, i.e. autism, can make acceptance by parents extremely challenging. It can therefore be difficult for parents to recognise that their child's disability may be characteristic to certain conditions, for example, autism. These attitudes can also prevent parents from sharing their concerns about their child, meaning that assessment and diagnosis can sometimes be delayed (Fox *et al.*, 2017).

Accessing health and education services may be challenging for any family in the period after their child's diagnosis. This may be intensified for those to whom the system is unfamiliar and for whom English is not their first language. Even parents who are proficient English speakers report that terms or words used can be incomprehensible to them (Fox *et al.*, 2017). The technical language, the complexities of assessment criteria and deciphering professional reports can lead to misunderstandings and confusion. Also consider parents who have experienced a continuous fight response (as discussed earlier), which can contribute to the misunderstanding of what the entitlements of access to resources may be for a child with SEN. These challenges can be real for both parents and professionals and may contribute to unrealistic expectations. The outcome will result in either parents and professionals working together cohesively or dissonance.

It is fundamental that parents and professionals work in partnership to decide whether the needs of a child can be met best in either a mainstream setting or a specialist setting, to ensure the best outcomes for the child. The challenge here can be that both groups, parents and professionals, can have perceptions and expectations of what each type of setting can provide in terms of resources. This reinforces the importance of the Model of Negotiation, where views from both parties are listened to and acknowledged and agreed actions are implemented.

Case Study

A parent describes here her lived experience of being a parent of a child with SEN and working collaboratively and in partnership with schools. Her story illustrates and represents many of the challenges and issues that have been discussed in this chapter.

At state school, his difficulties weren't seen as 'bad enough' to warrant a statement (as it was then), and as a parent I was made to feel like I was expecting too much from him. The SENCO even told me outright that I shouldn't be comparing him to his big sister. As a parent, this negation of concerns is really damaging.

The most positive parent collaboration I experienced was at a small independent school for primary-aged children with specific learning difficulties. My son was about seven and a half, and it was the first time that his differences were properly acknowledged and understood. We were listened to and, because of their vast experience, they recognised exactly what was going on and reassured us that they could help. It was his most positive schooling experience. Unfortunately, in the state schools he'd been to, when his difficulties were recognised, the appropriate support simply wasn't there. But it's not necessarily a state vs independent school problem. At the independent private secondary school he attended in year 7, the support was not nearly as good.

> *Given that specific learning difficulties, such as dyslexia, dyspraxia and dyscalculia are 'hidden' and sometimes costly to 'prove', I think that the most positive collaborations must start with teachers listening carefully to parents' concerns and not assuming that they are being overly concerned or 'pushy'.*
>
> *He is now (at the age of 20) still experiencing difficulties in terms of his confidence as a result of poor understanding of his needs at school* (Parent, 2019).

Strategies: a focus on good practice

Fox *et al.* (2017) identify that good communication is a key to effective partnerships between parents and educational staff. This factor lies at the heart of an approach that has been adopted by Maggie MacDonnell, who is a Global Teacher prize winner. MacDonnell (2018) suggests that taking a deliberate approach of asking for permission and an invitation to become involved in their child's life is a key starting point in connecting with parents, guardians and family members. There is no assumption of a position of authority. MacDonnell (2018) goes on to explain that she asks for their permission to visit the family at home. She asks them to share insights about their children, their likes, hobbies, interests and stressors. She shares expectations and asks for their advice and input. She also starts off each year with several deliberate positive interactions with the parent, trying to find informal ways to come together and build connections. MacDonnell (2018) also believes that keeping herself visible and participating in community events is a useful way to connect informally with parents.

Gladman (2018) also suggests adopting an approach that ensures he is visible within the school community. He suggests that in addition to regular reviews for learners with SEND, parents are invited to termly SENCO 'drop-ins'. At parent evenings the SEND team are available to provide updates on how learners are progressing as well as provide information and strategies that enable parents to support their children at home. Gladman (2018) also states that while parents are the experts on their child and how their child's special educational needs affect them, they may be unaware of the number of families in similar situations or of local organisations which aim to support young people and their families. The school organises parent workshops that often feature a specialist speaker. An example of one such workshop focused on children on the autism spectrum and led to the school becoming increasingly involved with the National Autistic Society and learner-led National Autism Awareness Week activities. Another example was when an independent advisory service was invited to discuss with parents the issues around SEND law, EHCPs and the application process (Gladman, 2018).

It has been stated that home-school partnership is not considered as a one-way street. Parents' views are regularly sought in order to do even better in identifying and addressing any concerns that may arise. Feedback from parents regarding their views on SEND provision and practice enable the school to work effectively to ensure that learners and parents feel positively about the support they are receiving. Gladman (2018) goes on to state that the school hosts SEND parent forums throughout the year, providing opportunities for families to meet with the SEND Governor to share their experiences. They believe that transparency leads to trust, which in turn leads to greater success (Gladman, 2018).

Another concept that supports home-school partnerships are learner profiles. The learner profiles are created in collaboration with parents and staff and are routinely reviewed and updated whenever new reports or recommendations are published. Learners contribute to their individual targets and meet with SEND staff every term to review and identify how and what they can do to achieve these targets. Parents are informed on a regular basis with updates on what the school is doing to support their child and include strategies and suggestions on what the parents can do to support them at home. Working together breaks down home-school barriers and provides consistent collaboration, always aiming to place the child at the centre of any decision-making processes (Gladman, 2018).

Wedell (2017) suggests it is crucial that SENCOs view parents as partners in making decisions about meeting their child's needs. This principle is underpinned in the SEND Code of Practice: 0–25 (DfE and DoH, 2015) and clearly emerges as a crucial basis for SENCOs' relationships with parents. Also implicit in this is the recognition that parents are experts in understanding their children and can contribute essential information about their lives at home. SENCOs must remember that in their interactions, although they are focusing on one child out of many, for the parent, their child is a very 'special' individual. One SENCO affirmed that 'if we are genuinely respectful, listen to them and show we care passionately about their child's progress and well-being, the walls come down and the plans that emerge are unfailingly successful' (Wedell, 2017:486). It could also be very helpful to invite parents to be silent observers to lessons. For one thing, there can be different behaviour in different settings (Wedell, 2017).

Making time for regular meetings with parents and listening to their views can be a real challenge when the SENCO has many responsibilities to fulfil in their working week. It is possible, however, that this can save time in the long term. As one SENCO we spoke with said:

> Although listening to parents is time-consuming . . . it saves me a lot of time and a great deal of potential unpleasantness later!

Some SENCOs in larger schools have set up regular discussion groups for parents whose children are receiving support. Parents have an opportunity to share their concerns and satisfaction, and the SENCO can also arrange for any available outside specialist professionals to explain their approaches to working with the SENCO and school staff in supporting pupils (Wedell, 2017).

The importance and justification for consulting parents is exemplified here by one SENCO: 'if there are any concerns from parents, we don't dismiss them and say it's not important. It is important to them because it is their child, and they need an answer to whatever the problem is' (Maher, 2016:8). This comment identified the importance of parents being a part of the mechanism through which SEN information flows so that they can ask relevant questions relating to their children (Maher, 2016). Another SENCO suggested that consultation allows parents to take a more active than reactive role because the parents are the people who know the child best (Maher, 2016). SENCOs from the NASENCO programme were asked what strategies they use to support parent partnership and work in collaboration with parents. Their responses are as follows:

- Being visible
- Keeping regularly in touch
- Time to listen
- Being honest
- Being on the school gate am and pm
- Quick responses
- Invite to meetings
- Make conversations about their child
- Be mindful that the parent is the expert
- Consistent approaches across the whole school and staff team
- Structured conversations
- Time and space to vent
- Have colleague join difficult conversations
- Keep calm
- Open-door policy – opportunity to observe teaching approaches

Whilst recognition of the role of parents has grown inexorably over the last 50 years, the sense that parents are in a constant state of war with the system and the professionals who represent it remains strong. Effective co-production depends on a clear understanding of the lived experience of parents and acknowledgement, from both sides, of the true meaning of partnership. Building true partnership takes time and emotional effort. Trusting relationships must be developed, mutual expertise acknowledged and a shared vision created. But the time invested in creating partnerships based on equality and mutual respect is an investment in a better future and in raising aspirations for each child with SEND.

Conclusion

In Chapter 2 of this book, Rix (2021:7) refers to 'the while' *which* involves underpinning tensions around power, support and voice. These topics have been explored in this chapter and continue to be a dynamic challenge to effective partnership working. The *while* is both a physical and personal experience, socially created from the collective resources, understandings and interactions. In its widest sense, the *while* is an ongoing process (Rix, 2021), emphasised in this chapter as co-production, collaboration and partnership working. Drawing together key ideas from both this chapter and Chapter 2, it is important that professionals are mindful of tensions involved in 'the while' (Rix, 2021:7) and reflect upon the ways they invest time and effort into building true partnerships and establishing effective co-production. For as Rix (2021) points out:

> It is possible to find ways to open up our working. We can create situations which support people to work with a variety of others. And by attempting to do these kinds of things, we will create moments, new opportunities which will lead us . . . somewhere . . . together.
>
> (Rix, 2021:7)

Reflective questions

- How might SENCOs and other professionals optimise opportunities for parent voice?
- How might awareness of power dynamics impact upon the efficacy of co-production?
- How far does legislation and SEND systems support or reduce effective co-production between professionals and parents?

References

Appleton, P. and Minchom, P. (1991) Models of parent partnership and child development centres. *Child: Care, Health and Development*, 17, 27–38.

Bailey, J. (1998) Australia: Inclusion through categorisation. In Booth, T. and Ainscow, M. (eds) *From Them to US: An International Study of Inclusion in Education*. London: Routledge, 171–185.

Berger, E. (1995) *Parents as Partners in Education: Families and Schools Working Together*. (4th edn). Columbus: Merrill.

Busch, S. (2015) *Chronic Sorrow in Parenting a Child with a Disability*. Available at: https://susanellison-busch.com/chronic-sorrow-in-parenting-a-child-with-a-disability/ [Accessed 9.1.19].

Cheminais, R. (2011) *Family Partnership Working*. London: Sage.

Crozier, G. (1999) Is it a case of 'We know when we're not wanted'? The parents' perspective on parent/teacher roles and relationships. *Educational Research*, 41(3), 315–328.

Cunningham, C. and Davis, H. (1985) *Working with Parents: Frameworks for Collaboration*. Maidenhead: Open University Press.

Dale, N. (1995) *Working with Families of Children with Special Needs: Partnership and Practice*. East Sussex: Routledge.

Department for Education and Department of Health (2015) *Special Educational Needs and Disability Code of Practice: 0–25 Years*. London: DfE.

Desforges, C. and Abouchaar, A. (2003) *The Impact of Parental Involvement, Parental Support and Family Education on Pupil Achievement and Adjustment: A Literature Review*. Research Report 433. London: DfE.

Dovey-Pearce, G., Price, C., Wood, H., Scott, T., Cookson, J. and Corbett, S. (2012) Young people (13–21) with disabilities in transition from childhood to adulthood: An exploratory, qualitative study of their developmental experiences and health care needs. *Educational and Child Psychology*, 29(1), 86–100.

Dyson, S. (2004) *Mental Handicap Dilemmas of Parent-Professional Relations*. New York: Croom Helm.

Fox, F., Aabe, N., Turner, K., Redwood, S. and Rai, D. (2017) 'It was like walking without knowing where I was going': A qualitative study of autism in a UK Somali migrant community. Journal of *Autism* and Developmental Disorders, 47, 305–315.

Gladman, J. (2018) Part 4: Working with learners, parents and carers. Jake gladman, SENCO Lilian Baylis Technology school. In Bartram, D. (ed.) *Great Expectation: Leading an Effective SEND Strategy in School*. Woodbridge: John Catt, 60–62.

Goodhall, J. and Vorhaus, J. (2011) *Review of Best Practice in Parental Engagement*. London: DfE.

Harris, J. (2019) *Treacle of Bureaucracy: Report on Special Educational Needs Is a Huge Relief for Parents Like Me*. Available at: www.theguardian.com/education/2019/nov/05/treacle-bureaucracy-report-special-educational-needs-huge-relief-parents-john-harris?CMP=Share_AndroidApp_Gmail [Accessed 05.11.19].

Hochschild, A. (1983) *The Managed Heart: Commercialization of Human Feeling*. Berkeley: University of California Press.

Lamb, B. (2009) *Lamb Inquiry, Special Educational Needs and Parental Confidence*. London: DCFS.

Lamb, B. (2018) Part four: Working with learners, parents and carers. Professor Brian Lamb OBE, Education Consultant. In Bartram, D. (ed.) *Great Expectations: Leading an Effective SEND Strategy in School*. Woodbridge: John Catt, 52–55.

MacDonnell, M. (2018) Part four: Working with learners, parents and carers. Maggie MacDonnell, Global Teacher Prize winner. In Bartram, D. (ed.) *Great Expectations: Leading an Effective SEND Strategy in School*. Woodbridge: John Catt, 56–59.

Maher, A. (2016) Consultation, negotiation and compromise: The relationship between SENCOs, parents and pupils with SEN. *Support for Learning*, 31(1), 4–12.

Mastracci, S., Guy, M. and Newman, M. (2012) *Emotional Labor and Crisis Response: Working on Razor's Edge*. Abingdon: Routledge.

Mittler, P. and Mittler, H. (1982) *Partnership with Parents*. Stratford-upon-Avon: National Council for Special Education.

Newman, M., Guy, M. and Mastracci, S. (2008) Beyond cognition: Affective leadership and emotional labor. *Public Administration Review*, 69(1), 6–20.

Oliver, M. (1990) *The Politics of Disablement*. London: Macmillan

Olshansky, S. (1962) Chronic Sorrow. A response to having a mentally defective child. *Social Casework*, 43(4), 190–193.

Plowden, B. (1967) *Children and Their Primary Schools: A Report of the Central Advisory Council for Education (England)*. Vol. 1. London: HMSO.

Pugh, G. and De'Ath, E. (1989) *Working Towards Partnership in the Early Years*. London: National Children's Bureau.

Rix, J. (2003) A parent's wish list. In Nind, M., Rix, J. and Sheehy, K. (eds.) *Inclusive Education: Diverse Perspectives*. London: John Fulton, 74–86.

Rix, J. (2021) Inclusive relationships: Creating the space for each other. In Beaton, M., Codina. G. and Wharton, J. (eds.) *Leading on Inclusion: The Role of the SENCO*. Abingdon: Routledge, XX–XX.

Robinson, C. and Staker, K. (1999) *Growing Up with Disability*. London: Jessica Kingsley.

Roffey, S. (2001) *Special Needs in the Early Years: Collaboration, Communication and Coordination*. London: David Fulton.

Rogers, C. (1957) The necessary and sufficient conditions of therapeutic personality change. *Journal of Consulting Psychology*, 21(2), 95–103.

Roos, S. (2002) *Chronic Sorrow. A Living Loss*. London: Routledge.

Rotter, J. (1966) Generalized expectancies for internal versus external control of reinforcement. *Psychological Monographs*, 80(Whole No. 609).

Ryan, S. and Runswicke-Cole, K. (2008) Repositioning mothers: Mothers, disabled children and disability. *Disability and Society*, 23(3), 199–210.

Swann, W. (1984) *Conflict and Control: Some Observations on Parents and the Integration of Children with Special Needs*. Paper presented to the Annual Conference of the British Psychological Society, Education Section (1987) Statements of intent: An assessment of reality. In Booth, T and Swann, W. (eds.) *Including Children with Disabilities: Curricular for all*. Milton Keynes: Open University Press.

Teel, C. (1991) Chronic sorrow: Analysis of the concept. *Journal of Advanced Nursing*, 16(11), 1311–1319.

Warnock, M. (1978) *Special Educational Needs: Report of the Committee of Enquiry into the Education of Handicapped Children and Young People*. London: Her Majesty's Stationery Office.

Warnock, M. (1985) Teacher teach thyself (The 1985 Dimbleby lecture). *The Listener*, 28th March, pp. 10–14.

Wedell, K. (2017) Points from the SENCo-Forum: SENCos supporting parents. *British Journal of Special Education*, 44(4), 484–487.

Wolfendale, S. (1988) *Working with Parents of SEN After the Code of Practice*. London: David Fulton.

17   SENCOs and social workers

Working together

Julie C. Wharton

Special Educational Needs Co-ordinators (SENCOs) often find themselves working in an inter-agency way with a range of professionals from different disciplines. This chapter considers the SENCO's role and responsibilities alongside those of the social worker when working in this important partnership.

Social care and education are often in a position to work together to support the needs of an individual and their family. Professionals use a range of terminology to describe this way of working. The Children's Workforce Development Council (2007) outlines three broad models of multi-agency working:

- *The multi-agency panel:* in which professionals gather to jointly plan to meet the needs of the child being discussed. Each professional is employed by their own agency.
- *The multi-agency team:* where a team leader co-ordinates the work of the team supporting the child.
- *An integrated service:* where representatives from different services are co-located and work together to address the plan for the child.

SENCOs are more likely to be involved in multi-agency panels and teams. Lloyd *et al.* (2001:[online]) offer an alternative set of definitions to clarify the ways in which different professionals might find themselves working together:

- *Interagency working* – when more than one agency works together in a *planned and formal* way.
- *Joint working* – professionals from more than one agency working directly together on a project, for example, teachers and social work staff offering joint group work. School-based interagency meetings may involve *joint* planning, which reflects *joined-up* thinking.
- *Multi-agency working* – more than one agency working with a young person, with a family or on a project (but not *necessarily jointly*). It may be *concurrent*, sometimes as a result of *joint planning* or it may be *sequential*.

As a professional working in partnership, it is important to consider how each member of a team is working: in a joint manner (interagency) or in parallel (multi-agency). Ultimately, the purpose in joint working for all team members is to work for the best possible outcomes for a child or young person, who should be at the centre of the process. Tomlinson (2003:iii) identifies these factors as good practice when working in a multi-agency way:

- full strategic and operational-level commitment;
- shared aims and values;
- involving relevant people;
- role and responsibilities;
- team commitment;
- communication.

These aspects of good practice allow for professionals to work well to assess and agree on the optimum provision to empower a child or young person to achieve the best outcomes. Keeping the child or young person at the centre of the process, coupled with developing good working professional relationships, is paramount for the success of any interagency working (Devaney *et al.*, 2017).

The role of the social worker

Forrester (2017) outlines the ways in which the broad range of support required by society poses a challenge for children's social workers in the United Kingdom. They explain that social workers' remit is to ensure that children come to no serious harm and have their needs met. Social workers in Children's Services fulfil a range of roles: some are concerned with safeguarding (social workers who undertake the statutory assessment of children in need (section 17, Children Act, 1989) and others who lead child protection enquiries (section 47, Children Act, 1989)). Section 17 of the Children Act also defines 'children in need' as children and young people with a disability; some social workers choose to specialise in children and young people's disability social care. Some social workers also oversee the care of children and young people who are in foster care (section 22, Children Act, 1989), and other social workers may be primarily concerned with adoption (Adoption and Children Act, 2002, section 3). Where children and young people are in care or going through the adoption process, an Independent Reviewing Officer (IRO) (section 25B, Children Act, 1989) oversees their case and the support that is provided by the local authority. As Beckett *et al.* (2016:148) explain, 'IROs are specialist social workers whose function is to review the cases of children in public care and ensure that they have appropriate plans and that these plans are being implemented in a timely manner'. Therefore, SENCOs may come into contact with a whole range of social workers with different roles and responsibilities, as well as social workers working across a range of local authorities which may have different procedures and practices. All social workers are trained to approach individual cases with a 'theory' to allow them to explain a situation (Teater, 2014). Social workers will employ a solution-focused 'method' (sometimes referred to as an 'intervention') to plan for improved outcomes for the client. Social workers are expected to understand and employ a range of theoretical frameworks, and Erik Erikson's psychosocial theory underpins much social work practice (Teater, 2014). A psychosocial approach takes into account a child's psychological needs as well as the impact of their social environment. As Cross and Cross (2017) explain, children are influenced by the people around them: their relations, their peer group and the wider society. A parallel may be drawn with the school setting, where teachers are working to the social model of special educational needs and disability – a model in which the context in which a learner is situated will be examined in order that any barriers to learning and participation are removed (Alderson, 2018). This may involve a consideration of the impact of a variety of relationships, peer-to-peer, learner/teacher or teaching assistant and how this may help or hinder inclusive practice (Shady and Larson, 2010).

The medical model of special educational needs and disability in school manifests itself in 'diagnosis' and labelling, whereby the child or young person is seen as having a 'deficit'. Alderson (2018:178) elucidates, 'the medical model identifies disabling problems within individuals and aims to diagnose, relieve and possibly cure these problems'. Social workers may sometimes be viewed as the professional who might 'fix' a child or young person's problems. However, Forrester (2017:148) is clear that many Children's Social Care evaluative approaches are based on a 'broadly medical metaphor in which a professional provides help for a specified problem'. As outlined previously, social workers may be involved with a child or young person and their family in a variety of ways: through child protection, the care system or a disability team. SENCOs work with social workers from all of these teams, and it is helpful to consider the parallel with the role of the SENCO, who also has a responsibility to identify and assess an individual's needs whilst considering the changes to provision and the environment (DfE and DoH, 2015).

The role of the social worker and SENCO working together

The Special Educational Needs and Disability (SEND) Regulations (2014) are very clear about the role that a SENCO has in relation to assessing the needs of children and young people with SEND. The Regulations (2014) are the statutory framework which educational settings are expected to follow. The Regulations (2014) outline how SENCOs are expected to identify the pupil's special educational needs (SEN) and ensure that provision is in place to meet these needs. In the same way, social workers are also expected to undertake an assessment and an initial task, once a referral has been made, and to assess whether an intervention should take place or not.

The Health and Care Professionals Council currently oversee the standards for social workers, and social workers are expected to fulfil a range of criteria outlined in the *Standards of Proficiency: Social Workers in England* (HCPC, 2017) document. One direct parallel to the SENCO's requirement to assess, identify and respond to need is outlined in Standard 1.3, 'Registrant social workers in England must be able to undertake assessments of risk, need and capacity and respond appropriately'. In assessing need, either as an educational or social care professional, two aspects need to be considered: whether the assessment of need is coming from a deficit approach concerned with measuring and categorising or from environmental and social factors that have an impact on the individual.

The Department of Health and Social Care (2019:24) are very clear about the implications of this dilemma for social workers:

> Over time, we have seen how care management approaches have predominantly focused on a deficit model, for example with questioning such as what are the problems and Issues the individual is experiencing? What are they unable to do and how can we solve this?

In their *Strengths-based approach: practice framework and practice handbook* (DHSC, 2019), the Department seeks to address this dilemma in order to avoid a relationship where an individual becomes dependent on the social worker, with the solution being to 'fix' the problems being experienced. SENCOs are also faced with this quandary; Lindqvist (2013) outlines the tension between being in the role of the 'special educator' addressing the deficits whilst also being a professional who leads on inclusive practices. The DHSC (2019:24) outlines how 'a strengths-based approach explores, in a collaborative way the entire individual's abilities and their circumstances rather than making the deficit the focus of the intervention'. Educators can learn much from this approach. As a SENCO, leading on inclusion, it is important to consider the SEND Regulations (2014) that state the SENCO has the responsibility to promote 'the pupil's inclusion in the school community and access to the school's curriculum, facilities and extra-curricular activities'.

Ways of working together

By adopting a social model approach to SEND, professionals consider how to remove barriers to learning and participation rather than focusing on the difficulties associated with the body (Algraigray and Boyle, 2017). Therefore, when working in an interagency way, it will be important to consider whether all professionals are adopting a consistent approach. When working in this way, it is possible to identify which members of the team are coming from a medical/deficit approach while others are focused on a social model approach. However, it is possible to draw on both models in an interactive way so that a balance of approaches can be agreed on (Shakespeare, 2006). Daniels (2011a:49) highlights that the most effective interagency working occurs when 'meaningful cross agency sense can be made of the young person's life circumstances and a sustained pattern of responsive, rather than rule bounded formulaic intervention can be offered'. This coupled with collective accountability for the young person's outcomes leads to a more individualised approach to enabling a child's or young person's inclusion. Forrester (2017:150) believes that the social worker should also look to address not only the needs of the child and their family, but that they should also consider the wider context in which the family is situated: 'social workers can and should critique and challenge unfair or discriminatory policies'. An example of this might be where a child in care has been excluded from school, and the social worker can see that this might be considered discriminatory as reasonable adjustments have not been made to take the child's disability into account prior to the incident that led to an exclusion. The Professional Capabilities Framework is very clear that social workers must 'recognise discriminatory practices and inequality and develop a range of approaches to appropriately challenge service users, colleagues and senior staff' (BASW, 2019:[online]). *The National Award for Special Educational Co-ordination: Learning outcomes* are clear that SENCOs are also required to 'lead, develop and, where necessary, challenge senior leaders, colleagues and governors to understand and meet their statutory responsibilities towards children and young people with SEN and/or disabilities' (NCTL, 2014:7). Statutory responsibilities would encompass the requirements of the Equality Act 2010.

Ways of working collaboratively with others

Apart from the requirement for both SENCOs and social workers to challenge discrimination, both professions are expected to work collaboratively with other agencies. SENCOs are expected to 'promote, facilitate and support effective multi-agency working for all children and young people with SEN, through, e.g. person-centred planning, "team around a child or family", the Common Assessment Framework and the Education, Health and Care Plan' (NCTL, 2014:8). In comparison, social workers should 'be able to engage in inter-professional and interagency communication' (HCPC, 2017:9), as well as 'be able to contribute effectively to work undertaken as part of a multi-disciplinary team' (HCPC, 2017:10).

In 2003, The Laming Inquiry into the death of Victoria Climbié underlined many important recommendations for improving interagency working, including the establishment of a

> 'common language' for use across all agencies to help those agencies to identify who they are concerned about, why they are concerned, who is best placed to respond to those concerns, and what outcome is being sought from any planned response.
>
> (Laming, 2003:366)

In 2009, Laming's *The Protection of Children in England: A Progress Report* outlined the progress that had been made with interagency working. The report found that professionals were committed to interagency working, and it worked well when information, expertise and resources were shared. It also highlighted the way in which interagency working failed when services were under pressure; for example, where key professionals were unable to attend meetings. The House of Commons Education Committee's (2019:57) enquiry into SEND has found that this often remains the case 'with health and social care staff often not in attendance at meetings and reviews'.

Overcoming barriers to working together

For both SENCOs and social workers, finding mutually convenient times is a constant barrier. SENCOs often have teaching responsibilities during the day and social workers are often in court or involved in other meetings that mean their attendance at meetings may be problematic. The House of Commons Education Committee (2019:57) found that the success of this joint working often rests on the 'personalities' of the professionals involved. Ahmad *et al.* (2004:35) interviewed a range of professionals to examine multi-agency and partnership working. One respondent stated:

> If one person traditionally has not got on with someone else just for a clash of personality or an incident that happened ten years ago, you know . . . are they going to come around the same table and share information with each other?

McKean *et al.* (2017) highlighted another aspect of collaborative working which may be problematic is the area of 'border disputes' over who ultimately has the responsibility for funding provision. These situations are usually resolved by considering the *Belonging Regulations* (The Education Regulations, 1996). However, a lack of shared 'common language' (McKean *et al.*, 2017:516) might also create barriers to effective joint working. With careful planning, positive interagency working is crucial to support children and their families (McKean *et al.*, 2017). Leadbetter (2008) described a study, *The Learning in and for Interagency Work Project*, which explored interagency working following the establishment of Children's Services in England. This study provides some suggestions for successful interagency working that might overcome the barriers mentioned here. The study found that it was important to maintain a whole-child focus that took the child's context into consideration. Where professionals considered the child's needs across a range of services (rather than just focusing on their own particular area, e.g. education or health), the outcomes were much improved. The importance of being 'responsive' to others (both the child and the other professionals around the child) was stressed, along with ensuring that everyone in the team around the child knew what outcomes the team were collectively working towards. A particularly helpful finding of the study was 'the need to understand oneself and one's professional values' (Leadbetter, 2008:207). The study highlighted that when practitioners were able to articulate their values and describe their expertise, it enabled them to understand their role much better (Leadbetter, 2008). Patsios and Carpenter (2010) found that where training was delivered in an interagency way, professionals gained a greater understanding of each other's roles, and misconceptions and prejudices were lessened. Daniels (2011b) describes how professionals might develop their working practices:

> Standard notions of professional expertise imply a vertical model, in which practitioners develop in competence over time as they acquire new levels of professional knowledge, graduating 'upwards' level by level in their own specialism. By contrast, boundary-crossing suggests that expertise is also developed when practitioners collaborate *horizontally* across sectors.
>
> (Daniels, 2011b:40)

This hopeful model suggests that a greater understanding of others' professional practice might be developed and that ultimately this might result in 'the emergence of hybrid professional types' (Daniels, 2011b:41).

The Munro Review of Child Protection (Munro, 2011) highlighted concerns from headteachers who felt that the thresholds for referral to access support from social care were too high. This left schools unsure about the optimum way to support children and young people that they felt were vulnerable. The Review found that there was a paucity of feedback about referrals so that schools were not always sure whether or not a case warranted a referral. The Review also recommended that the statutory document *Working Together to Safeguard Children* (DfE, 2018a) be revised to strengthen interagency working. Each local authority will have its own protocol for assessment (DfE, 2018a), and *Working Together* is clear that a multi-agency approach to assessment should be taken. An assessment model suggested in *Working Together* examines three domains:

- the child's developmental needs, including whether they are suffering or likely to suffer significant harm;
- the capacity of parents or carers (resident and non-resident) and any other adults living in the household to respond to those needs;
- the impact and influence of wider family and any other adults living in the household as well as community and environmental circumstances.

(DfE, 2018a:26)

Educational advice is an important part of the assessment of a child's development needs. This should be child-centred and take the child's views into account. Harris and Allen (2011:411) explored young people's views of multi-agency support and found that the young people in the study felt more self-confident when an interagency approach is taken: 'they reported considerable effects on their ability to articulate their opinions and to share their needs'. Building on this child-centred approach, the SENCO is in an ideal position to lead on the co-ordination of a graduated approach to assessment, provision and review of the child's educational needs. Working in partnership with social care will provide the opportunity to facilitate a discussion regarding the approach towards an individual's needs and to consider how joint working will provide a greater level of support than a single-agency response. Where a child or young person is in public care ('looked after'), there is a statutory requirement for education and social care to work together, in particular around the Personal Education Plan (DfE, 2018c).

The SENCO and the designated teacher

In addition to the statutory requirement that each maintained school has a qualified teacher who is appointed to the role of the SENCO (The Special Educational Needs and Disability Regulations, 2014), schools must appoint a Designated Teacher for children who are looked after (DfE, 2018b). The role of the Designated Teacher is to ensure that each child in care makes good educational progress (DfE, 2018d). The Regulations (DfE, 2018d) also state that 'in some cases, the governing body may consider that it is appropriate for the SENCO to also take on the role of the designated teacher for looked-after and previously looked-after children' (DfE, 2018d:48). However, not all children and young people in care have special educational needs and/or disability, and therefore some educational settings separate the role. There is the expectation that the SENCO and the Designated Teacher work closely when this is appropriate (NCTL, 2014). It is important that the roles and responsibilities of the SENCO and the Designated Teacher are made very clear to any other agencies, such as social workers, who are working to support a child who is looked after or previously looked after. Whilst some commonalities exist, there are two distinct sets of responsibilities which may not always be clear to professionals outside of education – thus it is with the role of the SENCO and the role of the social worker.

SENCOs and social workers working in similar ways

The SENCO and the social worker share many tasks in common. Examining the overlaps in the two roles allows for a better understanding of the ways in which professionals can cross boundaries and work with a common purpose. When the following list of tasks is explored, it is clear that this could be a list that applies to the activities that a SENCO or social worker might undertake:

- Meetings with children and their families/carers
- Meetings with professionals
- Staff meetings
- Supervision
- Telephone calls
- E-mails and recording
- Liaising with families
- Interacting with colleagues
- Maintaining assessment records
- Monitoring the effectiveness of provision
- Liaising with other agencies to secure support

Holt *et al.* (2018) identify that, due to financial constraints and pressures on local authority services, social workers spend an increasing amount of time on administration of their caseloads and less time working with children, young people and their families. The British Association of Social Workers (2018) are attempting to reverse this situation with the *80–20 Campaign*, which has identified that social workers are spending 80% of time on administration and 20% working with children and their families. Curran *et al.* (2018) found that SENCOs are faced with similar time constraints where paperwork and 'fire-fighting' take them away from their strategic role. The administrative work created by the Education, Health and Care Plan process is highlighted as a pressure on SENCO workload (Curran *et al.*, 2018). When the SEND Reforms were instigated, the idea of Education, Health and Social Care working together was ambitious and hopeful, with the goal that joint working would enable children and young people to reach a wide range of outcomes. However, the House of Commons Education Committee (2019) enquiry into SEND found that social care and health were not fully prepared for their new roles and responsibilities in this process: 'in reality health and social care are still not equal partners in the process' (House of Commons Education Committee, 2019:37).

   Holt and Kelly (2018) highlight that for social workers, relationship-based work with families and strong partnership working ensure the best outcomes. Holt and Kelly (2018) also outline the power relationship that might occur when parents are working with social workers. It is important to be mindful of the tensions that this might bring when working in partnership; parents may perceive power being used as a form of control and, at times, a form of support. Therefore, the relational leadership role 'concerned with productive social and socializing relationships where the approach is not so much about controlling relationships through job descriptions or team processes but is about how the agent is connected with others in their own and other's learning' (Gunter, 2006:263) is vital to effective interagency working.

The SENCO's position

Struyve *et al.* (2018) look at the role of the SENCO in relation to positioning theory, which enables an examination of how the SENCO positions themselves in relation to others in school. This could be considered further by SENCOs to explore how they position themselves in relation to the professionals with whom they work. Harr and Langenhove (1998) describe how people might choose to position themselves and others when working together. SENCOs may self-position deliberately to present a certain persona, or this might be done by outlining a personal biography or giving a point of view. SENCOs might be forced into a self-position; for example, when being asked to give an account of their behaviour. SENCOs may deliberately position another professional by giving their views of the other's personality. Harr and Langenhove (1998) state when this happens without the presence of the other person, this would be seen as gossiping. Where there is forced positioning of another, this may also happen when the person is present and when they are absent. In school, a forced positioning might be a disciplinary proceeding. These discursive practices are important to take into account when SENCOs and social workers work together. As leaders, SENCOs should be consciously aware of any form of positioning that might interfere with the best possible outcomes for a child. In this way, interagency working can become a dynamic process that puts the child or young person at the centre of the collaboration between professionals.

Conclusion

Leading on a strengths-based model supports strong collaborations between professionals and families, resulting in a positive impact on the outcomes for a child or young person (Devaney *et al.*, 2017). When leading on inclusion, SENCOs work in a person-centred way with a range of professionals, including social workers (NCTL, 2014). All professionals working to co-ordinate provision for children and young people with SEND need to understand that they have shared ways of working governed by each profession's frameworks (NCTL, 2014; HCPC, 2017). The importance of developing this understanding of the different ways of working improves children's and young people's confidence in the professionals supporting them (Harris and Allen, 2011). SENCOs as leaders have a key role to develop this understanding in their settings and to ensure that they are aware of their self-positioning and the influence that this might have on school staff (Harr and Langenhove, 1998). With positive attitudes towards collaboration, SENCOs and social workers are able to contribute towards a highly positive way of working. This will ultimately lead to improvements in the well-being and learning of children and young people (Cheminais, 2009). As a leader on inclusion, SENCOs can make a difference and, by working together with social workers, they can enact change.

Reflective questions

- How might SENCOs and social workers optimise their joint working opportunities?
- What might professionals expect to see when joint working is successful?
- What conditions might support collaborative working?

References

Adoption and Children Act 2002. London: Her Majesty's Stationery Office.

Ahmad, Y., Broussine, M., Davies, J., Hoggett, P., Kimberlee, R., Kushner, S., Miller, C., Santos, C. and Sirota, J. (2004) *A Review of Partnership and Multi-agency Working*. Bristol: University of the West of England.

Alderson, P. (2018) How the rights of all school students and teachers are affected by special educational needs or disability (SEND) services: Teaching, psychology, policy. *London Review of Education*, 16(2), 175–190.

Algraigray, H. and Boyle, C. (2017) The SEN label and its effect on special Education. *Educational and Child Psychology*, 34(4), 70–79.

Beckett, C., Dickens, J., Schofield, G., Philip, G. and Young, J. (2016) Independence and effectiveness: Messages from the role of Independent Reviewing Officers in England. *Children and Youth Services Review*, 71, 148–156.

British Association of Social Workers (2018) *BASW England 80–20 Campaign's Latest News and Resources: Improving Working Conditions for Social Workers to Drive Better Outcomes for Children*. Available at: www.basw.co.uk/media/news/2018/may/basw-england-80-20-campaigns-latest-news-and-resources [Accessed 20.11.19].

British Association of Social Workers (2019) *Professional Capabilities Framework*. Available at: www.basw.co.uk/professional-development/professional-capabilities-framework-pcf/the-pcf [Accessed 28.08.19].

Cheminais, R. (2009) *Effective Multi-Agency Partnerships: Putting Every Child Matters into Practice*. London: Sage.

Children Act 1989. London: Her Majesty's Stationery Office.

The Children's Workforce Development Council (2007) *Multi-agency Working: Fact Sheet*. Available at: https://webarchive.nationalarchives.gov.uk/20130104031048/http://media.education.gov.uk/assets/files/pdf/m/multi-agency%20working%20factsheet.pdf [Accessed 20.10.19].

Cross, T. and Cross, J. (2017) Maximising potential: A school-based conception of psychosocial development. *High Ability Studies*, 28(1), 43–58.

Curran, H., Moloney, H., Heavey, A. and Boddison, A. (2018) *It's About Time: The Impact of SENCO Workload on the Professional and the School*. Bath: Bath Spa University.

Daniels, H. (2011a) Exclusion from school and its consequences. *Psychological Science and Education*, 1, 38–50.

Daniels, H. (2011b) The shaping of communication across boundaries. *International Journal of Educational Research*, 50(1), 40–47.

Department for Education (2018a) *Working Together to Safeguard Children: A Guide to Inter-agency Working to Safeguard and Promote the Welfare of Children*. London: DfE.

Department for Education (2018b) *Keeping Children Safe in Education*: Statutory Guidance for Schools and Colleges. London: DfE.

Department for Education (2018c) *Promoting the Education of Looked-after Children and Previously Looked-after Children: Statutory Guidance for Local Authorities*. London: DfE.

Department for Education (2018d) *The Designated Teacher for Looked-after and Previously Looked-after Children: Statutory Guidance on Their Roles and Responsibilities*. London: DfE.

Department for Education and Department of Health (2015) *The Special Educational Needs and Disability Code of Practice: 0 to 25 Years*. London: DfE and DoH.

Department of Health and Social Care (2019) *Strengths-based Approach: Practice Framework and Practice Handbook*. London: DHSC.

Devaney, C., McGregor, C. and Cassidy, A. (2017) Early implementation of a family-centred practice model in child welfare: Findings for an Irish case study. *Practice*, 29(5), 331–345.

The Education (Areas to which Pupils and Students Belong) Regulations 1996. London: Her Majesty's Stationery Office.

Equality Act 2010. London: Her Majesty's Stationery Office.

Forrester, D. (2017) Outcomes in children's social care. *Journal of Children's Services*, 12(2–3), 144–157.

Gunter, H. (2006) Educational leadership and the challenge of diversity. *Educational Management Administration and Leadership*, 34(2), 257–268.

Harr, R. and Van Langenhove, L. (1998) *Positioning Theory: Moral Contexts of International Action*. London: Wiley and Sons.

Harris, A. and Allen, T. (2011) Young people's views of multi-agency working. *British Educational Research Journal*, 37(3), 405–419.

Health and Care Professions Council (2017) *Standards of Proficiency: Social Workers in England*. London: HCPC.

Holt, K. and Kelly, N. (2018) Limits to partnership working: Developing relationship-based approaches with children and their families. *Journal of Social Welfare and Family Law*, 40(2), 147–163.

House of Commons Education Committee (2019) *Special Educational Needs and Disabilities. First Report of Session 2019*. Available at: Special educational needs and disabilities (parliament.uk) [Accessed 26.10.19].

Laming, W. (2003) *The Victoria Climbié Inquiry*. London: The Stationery Office.

Laming, W. (2009) *The Protection of Children in England: A Progress Report*. London: The Stationery Office.

Leadbetter, J. (2008) Learning in and for interagency working: Making links between practice development and structured reflection. *Learning in Health and Social Care*, 7(4), 198–208.

Lindqvist, G. (2013) SENCOs: Vanguards or in vain? *Journal of Research in Special Educational Needs*, 13(3), 198–207.

Lloyd, G., Stead, J. and Kendrick, A. (2001) *Interagency Work to Prevent School Exclusion*. London: National Children's Bureau/Joseph Rowntree Foundation. Available at: www.jrf.org.uk/report/inter-agency-working-prevent-school-exclusion [Accessed 20.10.19].

McKean, C., Law, J., Laing, K., Cockerill, M., Allon, S. J., McCartney, E. and Forbes, J. (2017) A qualitative case study in the social capital of co-professional collaborative co-practice for children with speech, language and communication needs. *International Journal of Language and Communication Disorders*, 52(4), 514–527.

Munro, E. (2011) *The Munro Review of Child Protection*. London: DfE.

National College of Teaching and Leadership (2014) *National Award for SEN Learning Outcomes*. Nottingham: NCTL.

Patsios, D. and Carpenter, J. (2010) The organisation of interagency training to safeguard children in England: A case study using realistic evaluation. *International Journal of Integrated Care*, 10, 1–12.

Shady, S. and Larson, M. (2010) Tolerance, empathy or inclusion? Insights from Martin Buber. *Educational Theory*, 60(1), 81–96.

Shakespeare, T. (2006) *Disability Rights and Wrongs*. London: Routledge.

The Special Educational Needs and Disability (SEND) Regulations 2014. London: Her Majesty's Stationery Office.

Struyve, C., Hannes, K., Meredith, C., Vandecandelaere, M., Gielen, S. and De Fraine, B. (2018) Teacher leadership in practice: Mapping the negotiation of the position of the Special Educational Needs Coordinator in schools. *Scandinavian Journal of Educational Research*, 62(5), 701–718.

Teater, B. (2014) *An Introduction to Applying Social Work Theories and Methods*. 2nd edn. Milton Keynes: Open University Press.

Tomlinson, K. (2003) *Effective Interagency Working: A Review of the Literature and Examples of Good Practice*. Slough: National Foundation for Educational Research.

18 Hearing their voices

The role of SENCOs in facilitating the participation of all learners

Mhairi C. Beaton

Background

Although some academic literature can be found which examines how the voices of children and young people are heard prior to 1989, since the publication of the United Nations Convention on the Rights of the Child (UNCRC) (1989), there has been a widespread upsurge in focus on the role of children and young people within society, whether their opinions and perspectives are listened to and whether they have agency to influence decisions being made about their lives (Flutter and Rudduck, 2004; Rudduck and McIntyre, 2007; Tisdall *et al.*, 2009).

Since its publication, the UNCRC has been ratified in every country in the world, with the exception of the United States of America. For the purposes of this chapter, which will focus specifically on the English context, the UNCRC was ratified by the United Kingdom government, which holds responsibility for education provision within England, in 1991. The ratification of the UNCRC principles within England would seem to guarantee all children and young people the rights and freedoms outlined within the document. Indeed, the Children's Commissioner Review in 2010 stated there was a 'commitment that the government will give due consideration to the CRC articles when making new policy and legislation' (Teather, 2010:[online]).

Robinson *et al.* (2020) highlight that the first part of Article 12 is potentially the most influential part of the UNCRC when considering education legislation, policy and practice:

> State Parties shall assure to the child who is capable of forming his or her own views the right to express those views freely in all matters affecting the child, the views of the child being given due weight in accordance with the age and maturity of the child.
>
> (UNCRC, 1989:5)

It is easy now to underestimate the ground-breaking nature of the UNCRC and the implications that this document had for the lives of children and young people across the globe (Smith, 2011). Historically and culturally, in many countries, children and young people had not enjoyed many of the rights and freedoms that the UNCRC advocated (Aries, 1962; Corsaro, 1997; James *et al.*, 1998; Postman, 1982). Historical attitudes towards children and young people contributed to long-held beliefs within Western societies that position children and young people as requiring protection due to their status as minors (Aries, 1962). Wyness (2006) notes that children and young people are not physically as mature as adults, and therefore were historically treated as different to adults; viewed as 'becomings' rather than 'beings' and requiring to be protected until they had reached maturity. Historically, children and young people were not viewed as capable of making informed decisions about their lives; it was considered essential that those decisions should be made by adults in positions of power – their parents, teachers and other professionals.

In the latter part of the 20th century, this historical viewpoint was challenged by an international group of sociologists known collectively as the 'new sociologists of childhood' (Corsaro, 1997; James *et al.*, 1998; Wyness, 2006; Heath *et al.*, 2009). These writers claimed that childhood as a concept was socially constructed, and instead of thinking of children and young people as requiring to be only protected, children and young people should be seen as 'active in the construction and determination of their own social lives, the lives of those around them and of their societies in which they live' (James and Prout, 1990:7).

The 'new sociologists of childhood' group were influential in changing perspectives of children as active social agents within their own lives, proposing that children had the ability to contribute to decisions about their own lives, as outlined within the UNCRC. This original document and subsequent national policy documents obviously have implications for the children's and young people's participation in educational processes and the relationships with adults in school settings, leading to disruption of the traditional power relationships between staff and pupils.

For the purposes of this chapter, adoption of these ideas of children's place in society and specifically in schools has clear implications for Special Educational Needs Co-ordinators (SEN-COs), who must consider how all young people, including those with special educational needs, might have the opportunity to contribute their perspectives on decisions being made about their educational experience.

The Special Educational Needs and Disability (SEND) Code of Practice

The role and remit of the SENCO in educational provision in England is set out in the SEND Code of Practice (DfE and DoH, 2015). There is clear evidence within the Code of Practice (DfE and DoH, 2015) of the translation of Article 12 of the UNCRC into educational legislation. The Code of Practice (DfE and DoH, 2015) states that there is a clear focus on the participation of children and young people – and their parents – in decision-making at both individual and strategic levels.

At the beginning of the Code of Practice (DfE and DoH, 2015), it is stated that the principles of the document are designed to support the participation of children, their parents and young people in decision-making, greater choice and control for young people and their parents over support offered and provided, and successful preparation for adulthood, including independent living and employment (2015:18–19).

This stated aim to support children, young people and their parents to take an active part in decision-making and planning for educational provision aligns with the Children and Families Act (DfE, 2014). This legislation states that in relation to disabled children and young people and those with special educational needs (SEN), it must have regard to:

- the views, wishes and feelings of the child or young person, and the child's parents;
- the importance of the child or young person, and the child's parents, participating as fully as possible in decisions, and being provided with the information and support necessary to enable participation in those decisions;
- the need to support the child or young person, and the child's parents, in order to facilitate the development of the child or young person and to help them achieve the best possible educational and other outcomes, preparing them effectively for adulthood.

Both the Children and Families Act (DfE, 2014) and the Code of Practice (DfE and DoH, 2015) as legislation and policy guidance have clear implications for the role and remit of the SENCO to take a leadership role in demonstrating the importance of involving children, young people and their parents in all element of educational provision. For example, in relation to Education, Health and Care Plans (EHCPs) and on behalf of governing bodies, all SENCOs must ensure that young people and their parents are actively supported in contributing to needs assessments, and in developing and reviewing EHCPs.

Examples given within the Code of Practice of how this must be achieved are that SENCOs must:

- ensure the child's parents or the young person are fully included in the EHCP needs assessment process from the start, are fully aware of their opportunities to offer views and information, and are consulted about the content of the plan (Chapter 9);
- consult children with SEN or disabilities, and their parents and young people with SEN or disabilities when reviewing local SEN and social care provision (Chapter 4);
- consult them in developing and reviewing their Local Offer (Chapter 4);
- make arrangements for providing children with SEN or disabilities, and their parents, and young people with SEN or disabilities with advice and information about matters relating to SEN and disability (Chapter 2),

(2015:20)

The Code of Practice (DfE and DoH, 2015) also outlines the responsibility of the SENCO in relation to children and young people with SEN but no EHCP. It is envisioned that pupils with SEN will normally be educated with their peers in mainstream settings, and it is expected that the SENCO will provide a leadership role in advising classroom practitioners on the most advantageous manner in which to include these pupils in classroom learning – be it with a focus on pedagogy, curriculum or ongoing assessment.

Beaton (2020) has noted that many current classroom practices are underpinned by theories that in their turn are underpinned by understandings of children and young people as active agents in their own lives in line with the writing of the new sociologists of childhood. The traditional view of children and young people as *tabula rasa* into which teachers poured knowledge with transmission pedagogies are viewed as inappropriate in modern classrooms. In contrast, new classroom practices such as formative assessment (Black and Wiliam, 1998; Reay and Wiliam, 1999; Pryor and Crossouard, 2008, 2010) are based on the idea that pupils can and should take an active participatory role in their learning, discussing their progress and next steps in learning with each other and with their teachers. Black and Wiliam (1998) outline the following elements which they consider essential to the effective use of formative assessment in schools:

- finding out where pupils are in their learning through dialogue;
- agreeing on clear learning intentions with pupils and providing feedback that helps them to achieve these goals;
- sharing success criteria with pupils based on agreed learning intentions;
- developing meta-cognitive skills to enable peer and self-assessment as key components of learning;
- enabling young people to take greater ownership of their learning.

Although not all pedagogical innovations have been proved to be successful in the classroom, there is significant evidence that many of the innovations that include pupils being involved in dialogue and decisions about various aspects of their education result in improved educational outcomes for pupils in classrooms. The leadership role of the SENCO must include guiding other staff in how these pedagogies might be implemented for those pupils with SEN within their classrooms alongside their peers. This leadership role will contribute to the aspiration of the Code of Practice that 'children and young people with SEN engage in the activities of the school alongside pupils who do not have SEN' (DfE and DoH, 2015:92), and children and young people with SEN 'achieve their best, become confident individuals living fulfilling lives and make a successful transition into adulthood, whether into employment, further or higher education or training' (DfE and DoH, 2015:92), as outlined in the next section.

Benefits

During the last 20 years, academic literature has outlined the benefits to educational processes that can accrue if student voice is implemented correctly with pupils both with and without SEN. For example, Flutter and Rudduck (2004) outline a list of benefits based on extensive research over a period of ten years in a wide variety of schools. These are helpfully listed under the following headings: benefits for pupils, benefits for teachers and benefits for schools more widely.

Benefits for pupils

Flutter and Rudduck (2004) suggest that involving pupils in self-assessment and decisions about their learning can lead to the promotion of higher-order thinking skills such as meta-cognition. As the pupils discuss their learning with teachers and their peers, this permits them to develop a more informed understanding of their learning, take a more serious attitude toward their education and potentially enhance their self-confidence. Through this process of entering into dialogue with their teachers about their learning, they will no longer act as merely recipients of learning but begin to make judgements about how they learn best.

Benefits for teachers

The benefits for the teachers of involving the pupils in dialogue described by Flutter and Rudduck (2004) about their learning are significant. As pupils begin to view themselves as in collaboration with the teachers in their learning, this can lead to improved pupil-teacher relationships.

Pupils can offer feedback to the teachers on the approaches to teaching, learning and assessment used in their classrooms. Pupils also can provide key information about their progress in learning and can identify barriers they are experiencing as individuals, which can assist teachers to collaboratively identify appropriate next steps.

Of course, the teacher remains the professional with knowledge and experience of curriculum and pedagogy, but the information provided by the pupils can be invaluable to inform the professional decisions the teachers make (Beaton, 2020).

Benefits for schools

Finally, Flutter and Rudduck (2004) suggest that there are potential benefits for the schools when pupil voice is implemented effectively. In addition to a more positive learning culture throughout the school, involving pupils in discussion about teaching and learning may suggest new directions for school improvement planning (Fielding, 2001, 2004).

As leaders in learning, SENCOs' promotion of student voice activity within classrooms will have wide benefits for all pupils, but it might be argued that the benefits for pupils, teachers and the school are even greater when implemented with pupils with SEN. For example, though at times challenging to enact, facilitating the voices of pupils with SEN can provide invaluable information for teachers about the pedagogies that pupils with SEN find most helpful in progress in their learning. As pupils with SEN can experience atypical ways of learning, engaging them in dialogue about their experiences as to what is working for them and what might be a barrier to their learning can inform future pedagogical decision-making (Ravet, 2007; Rudduck and McIntyre, 2007).

More widely, Ravet (2007) and Rudduck and McIntyre (2007) identify additional benefits to those identified by Flutter and Rudduck (2004). They suggest that enacting pupil voice may promote inclusion and foster tolerance of diversity. These benefits speak closely to the role of the SENCO, as they are closely linked to the enhancement of social skills and emotional literacy, which is often developed in alignment with the implementation of pupil voice.

Challenges

Implementation of pupil voice within schools in not without its challenges. The Welsh government implemented the UNCRC directly into their national legislation in 2011 (Lundy *et al.*, 2013), followed by the Scottish government enacting the same process in 2018 (Scottish Government, 2018). In contrast, the UK government, who have responsibility for the English education system, stated that they did not intend to include the UNCRC directly into legislation (DCSF, 2010), instead committing to only 'consider' the implication of the Articles of the UNCRC when making new policy and legislation. This results in the UK government having no legal obligation to ensure that the UNCRC is effectively implemented within English educational policies or processes.

I'Anson *et al.* (2017) highlight that the translation of the UNCRC either directly into national legislation or indirectly into policy and practice such as the Code of Practice (DfE and DoH, 2015) has been fraught with difficulties. I'Anson *et al.* (2017) and Robinson *et al.* (2020) discuss that when the UNCRC is translated into legislation, and from there into policy discourse, professional expectations and practice, the aspirational principles underpinning the UNCRC are often diluted. Robinson *et al.* (2020), through their analysis of the translation process of the UNCRC to the English educational system, identify a number of instances where the principles have been diluted in such a way that they are less effective than might be expected.

This is particularly true for those pupils with SEN. For example, Robinson *et al.* (2020) point out that the proposal that 'there will be recognition by those listening to children that views may be expressed in non-verbal, as well as verbal ways' (UNCRC, Principle 5) is not translated practically into English educational policy. Thus, those children who may be able to express their viewpoints about the assessment and implementation of EHCPs through non-verbal ways do not have this option supported within the UK government policy documentation

Beaton (2020) also highlights an ongoing challenge to the effective implementation of pupil voice in schools. Beaton (2020) highlights that teachers' professional identity is predicated on their professional knowledge and desire to protect the children and young people in their care, believing that an essential element of their remit is to make professionally informed decisions about pupils' educational progress. The teachers in Beaton's study (2020) demonstrated a view of their pupils as innocents who required protection and who were not sufficiently ready to participate in such an 'adult' activity as dialogue about their education. These findings are similar to those of Gallagher (2009) and Rudduck and McIntyre (2007). This assumption that children and young people do not possess the ability to participate in dialogue about their learning can be particularly acute when the children are very young (Wall, 2017) or have SEN (Franklin and Sloper, 2009).

However, for those adopting the SENCO role, a key element of their leadership role is to ensure that the voices of all children and young people are listened to in authentic and meaningful ways. Franklin and Sloper (2009), in their study of how social workers view participatory practice with children and young people with disability, identified that social workers worked with a concept of 'ideal participation', considering anything less than 'a child taking part fully in a review meeting or contributing to complex decision-making was not valid' (Franklin and Sloper, 2009:7). In contrast, Hajdukova, Hornby and Cushman state that students with SEN can provide 'knowledge, and unique insights into the educational system' (2016:207). It is within the remit of the SENCO to consider and lead on the implementation of pupil voice in innovative and creative ways that suit the abilities of children and young people with SEN and permit them to contribute.

Many teachers may consider that inclusion of children and young people in dialogue about their learning is time consuming (Rudduck and McIntyre, 2007). It is acknowledged that classroom practitioners in the English education system are over-burdened by workload, much of it administrative and externally imposed. A key message which might be communicated by an informed SENCO within the school is that pupil voice and enactment of participatory approaches that include all children and young people in decision-making about their learning is not an additional task but one that will inform more effective teaching and learning. In contrast to viewing it as an additional task that must be carried out, as it is assessed by external bodies such as Ofsted, SENCOs can advocate that the practice become intrinsic to classroom life, with many benefits for both staff and pupils.

It should be noted that pupils may not initially be keen to participate in this type of consultation and dialogue and set up barriers to its effective implementation (Pollard *et al.*, 1997). The pupils may not be aware of the potential benefits which may accrue through their participation and initially may lack confidence in their ability to contribute meaningfully. However, Gallagher (2009) and Flutter and Rudduck (2004) note that if the process is fully explained to the pupils and it proves not to be tokenistic, then their interest and willingness to be involved will increase.

In summary, teachers and pupils need to have the benefits of authentic pupil voice explained to them, and the SENCO can lead with this role – being informed of the benefits that will accrue to all.

Role of SENCO in leading student voice

The question remains as to how children and young people might be included in this type of dialogue and agency about their educational experience. It has already been noted that the processes which are effective when seeking to engage children without SEN may not necessarily be those that are effective with children who do have identified SEN (Wall, 2017; Franklin and Sloper, 2009). Lundy (2007) states that if Article 12 of the UNCRC is to be effectively implemented, then adults must provide children with the space and opportunity to express their views, facilitate their ability to express those views, listen to what they have to say and, when appropriate, act on what they have heard.

For many children and young people with SEN, how their views are facilitated may be different to traditional means that may have been effective with other pupils. In line with Malaguzzi's suggestion that all children are born with 'hundred languages', the term used within the Reggio Emilia approach to describe the diverse ways children have of expressing themselves and relating to the world (Moss, 2016), it might be suggested that these 'hundred languages' must be utilised to facilitate young people with SEN in their participation in dialogue and decision-making about their learning. Wall *et al.* (2019) note that in most cases verbal language is privileged. Additionally, as pupils progress through their schooling, it might be argued that the written word comes to be privileged over verbal language. Challenging this, Wall *et al.* (2019:268) suggest that when facilitating the voices of young children, although this is true also of those children and young people with SEN,

> any definition of voice will be, by necessity, broader and more inclusive of a greater range of communication strategies beyond words and cannot exclude behaviour, actions, pauses in action, silences, body language, glances, movement, and artistic expression.

To enable this facilitation of voice, Wall *et al.* (2019) elucidate a set of principles or factors which can be adapted to the specific context of the SENCO, which can be utilised as lenses to examine the current practice of pupil voice and consider how it might be enhanced: definition, power, inclusivity, listening, time and space, approaches, processes. It is argued within their work that each of these factors must be considered by practitioners if pupil voice is to be implemented effectively for all children and young people in educational settings.

To aid the practitioner, resources have been provided which can be used either by a teacher reflectively considering his/her practice on his/her own or within staff groups as they collaboratively enhance the provision of their school (www.voicebirthtoseven.co.uk/talking-point-posters/). These resources have been developed and trialled with practitioners in a range of educational settings, including with practitioners who work with pupils with SEN.

Included in the resources are colourful posters which can aid the reflections of the practitioner/s, allowing practitioners to recognise the work they are already engaged in and challenging them to consider how this might be enhanced.

To further challenge the practitioners in how they are implementing each of the principles outlined in the posters, Wall *et al.* (2019) provide additional reflective questions which can be used for individual reflection or staff discussion. For example, the questions aligning with the poster on democracy focus on issues of inclusion:

- Do I marginalise some voices?
- Does everyone have an equal voice?
- Is there a time or space for minority voice?
- What does that look like?
- How is it mediated?
- Do I value some voices more than others?
- Is opting out a key part of inclusion?
- How are differing opinions and views included?
- How is disagreement mediated?

The resources can allow the SENCO to take a leadership role in fostering an inclusive approach where diversity is celebrated and dignity and respect are key to how children and young people participate in making decisions about their learning based on the notion of inclusivity, which allows for everyone to be seen as a competent actor and holder of rights.

Conclusion

This chapter has focused on the legislative and ethical issues surrounding listening to all children and young people, including those with SEN, and the leadership role that a SENCO can adopt in promoting this practice within their educational context. The chapter is based on the proposal that decisions about educational processes need to represent the experiences and viewpoints of all pupils (Walmsley and Johnson, 2003) and that, as Mitra (2009) states, those students who are not succeeding in our educational provision may be the most important voices to be heard.

As such, it is essential that schools and their staff take time to consider current understandings of pupils and how their voices are heard within educational processes. Only by subsequently reframing those understandings can the traditional power relationships be disrupted within our educational provision. This disruption will permit pupils, including those with SEN, to share the unique knowledge and understanding they hold about their experiences of their educational provision and how it might be enhanced. This is a key role for SENCOs to model in their own practice and to take a strategic lead through the promotion of creative, courageous and innovative approaches to allow all pupils to have their voices heard.

References

Aries, P. (1962) *Centuries of Childhood*. London: Penguin.

Beaton, M. C. (2020) Old Learning, New Learning: The Need for Teacher Educator Critical Reflection. In Swennen, A. and White, E. (eds.) (2019), *Being a Teacher Educator*. Abingdon, Oxon: Taylor and Francis.

Black, P. and Wiliam, D. (1998) *Inside the Black Box: Raising Standards Through Classroom Assessment*. London: King's College.

Corsaro, W. A. (1997) *The Sociology of Childhood*. Thousand Oaks, CA: Pine Forge Press.

Department for Children, Schools and Families (DCSF) (2010) *The United Nations Convention on the Rights of the Child: How Legislation Underpins Implementation in England: Further Information for the Joint Committee on Human Rights* (London, DCSF). Available at: https://assets.publishing.service.gov.uk/government/uploads/system/uploads/attachment_data/file/296368/uncrc_how_legislation_underpins_implementation_in_england_march_2010.pdf [accessed 5 January 2020].

Department for Education (DfE) (2014) *Listening to and Involving Children and Young People*. London: DfE. Available at: https://dera.ioe.ac.uk//19522/ [accessed 11 January 2020].

DfE (Department for Education) and Department of Health (DoH) (2015) *Special Educational Needs and Disability Code of Practice 0–25 Years*. London: DfE and DoH.

Fielding, M. (2001) Students as Radical Agents of Change. *Journal of Educational Change*, 2, 123–141.

Fielding, M. (2004) Transformative Approaches to Student Voice: Theoretical Underpinnings, Recalcitrant Realities. *British Educational Research Journal*, 30(2), 295–311.

Flutter, J. and Rudduck, J. (2004) *Consulting Pupils What's in It for Schools?* Abingdon, Oxon: Routledge.

Franklin, A. and Sloper, P. (2009) Supporting the Participation of Disabled Children and Young People in Decision-making. *Children and Society*, 23, 3–15.

Gallagher, M. (2009) Data Collection and Analysis. In Tisdall, E. K. M., Davis, J. M. and Gallagher, M. (eds.), *Researching with Children and Young People Research Design, Methods and Analysis*. London: Sage, 65–88.

Hajdukova, E. B., Hornby, G. and Cushman, P. (2016) Bully Experiences of Students with Social, Emotional and Behavioural Difficulties (SEBD). *Educational Review*, 68(2), 207–221.

Heath, S., Brooks, R., Cleaver, E. and Ireland, E. (2009) *Researching Young People's Lives*. London: Sage.

I'Anson, J., Quennerstedt, A. and Robinson, C. (2017) The International Economy of Children's Rights: Issues in Translation. *The International Journal of Children's Rights*, 25(1), 50–67.

James, A., Jenks, C. and Prout, A. (1998) *Theorizing Childhood*. Cambridge: Polity Press.

James, A. and Prout, A. (1990) *Constructing and Reconstructing Childhood: Contemporary Issues in the Sociological Study of Childhood*. London: Falmer Press.

Lundy, L. (2007) 'Voice' is not enough: Conceptualising article 12 of the United Nations convention on the rights of the child. *British Educational Research Journal*, 33(6), 927–942.

Lundy, L., Kilkelly, U. and Byrne, B. (2013) Incorporation of the United Nations convention on the rights of the child in law: A comparative review. *International Journal of Children's Rights*, 21(3), 442–463.

Mitra, D. (2009) Increasing student voice and moving towards youth leadership. *The Prevention Researcher*, 13(1), 7–10.

Moss, P. (2016) Loris Malaguzzi and the schools of Reggio Emilia: Provocation and hope for a renewed public education. *Improving Schools*, 19(2), 167–176.

Pollard, A., Thiessen, D. and Filer, A. (1997) *Children and Their Curriculum: The Perspectives of Primary and Elementary School Children*. London: Routledge Falmer.

Postman, N. (1982) *The Disappearance of Childhood*. London: Comet.

Pryor, J. and Crossouard, B. (2008) A socio-cultural theorisation of formative assessment. *Oxford Review of Education*, 34(1), 1–20.

Pryor, J. and Crossouard, B. (2010) Challenging formative assessment: Disciplinary spaces and identities. *Assessment and Evaluation in Higher Education*, 35(3), 265–276.

Ravet, J. (2007) Enabling pupil participation in a study of perceptions of disengagement: Methodological matters. *British Journal of Special Education*, 34(4), 234–242.

Reay, D. and Wiliam, D. (1999) 'I'll be a nothing': Structure, agency and the construction of identity through assessment. *British Educational Research Journal*, 25(3), 343–354.

Robinson, C., Quennerstedt, A. and I'Anson, J. (2020) The translation of articles from the United Nations convention on the rights of the child into education legislation: The narrowing of article 12 as a consequence of translation. *The Curriculum*, 31(3), 517–538.

Rudduck, J. and McIntyre, D. (2007) *Improving Learning Through Consulting Pupils*. Abington, Oxon: Routledge.

Scottish Government (2018) *Delivering for Today, Investing for Tomorrow: The Government's Programme for Scotland, 2018–19* (Edinburgh, Scottish Government). Available at: https://www.gov. scot/publications/delivering-today -investing-tomorrow-governments-programme-scotland2018-19/ [accessed 5 January 2020].

Smith, A. B. (2011) Respecting children's rights and agency: Theoretical insights into ethical research procedures. In Harcourt, D., Perry, B. and Waller, T. (eds.), *Researching Young Children's Perspectives Debating the Ethics and Dilemmas of Educational Research with Children*. London: Routledge, 11–25.

Teather, S. (2010) *Children's Commissioner Review*, in written Ministerial Statement on 6 December 2010. Available at: https://www.theyworkforyou.com/wms/?id=2010-12-06a.5WS.1 [accessed 5 January 2020].

Tisdall, E. K. M., Davis, J. M. and Gallagher, M. (eds.) (2009) *Researching with Children and Young People Research Design, Methods and Analysis*. London: Sage.

United Nations (1989) *Convention on the Rights of the Child*. Available at: www.unhchr.ch/html/menu3/b/k2crc.htm [accessed 20 September 2019].

Wall, K. (2017) Exploring the ethical issues related to visual methodology when including young children's voice in wider research samples. *International Journal of Inclusive Education*, 21(3), 316–331.

Wall, K., Cassidy, C., Robinson, C., Hall, E., Beaton, M. C., Kanyal, M. and Mitra, D. (2019) Look who's talking: Factors for considering the facilitation of very young children's voices. *Journal of Early Childhood Research*, 17(4), 263–278.

Walmsley, J. and Johnson, K. (2003) *Inclusive Research with People with Learning Disabilities: Past, Present and Futures*. London: Jessica Kingsley.

Wyness, M. (2006) Children, young people and civic participation: Regulation and local diversity. *Educational Review*, 58(2), 209–218.

19 Developing SENCO resilience

Understanding and meeting the challenge of the role

Helen Curran

Introduction

The role of the Special Educational Needs Co-ordinator (SENCO) holds a unique position in schools. Tasked with overseeing provision for children with special educational needs (SEN) in their setting (DfE and DoH, 2015), the SENCO is required to be both strategic and operational in their approach (Rosen-Webb, 2011; Morewood, 2012). This mandatory role, with the requirement to be suitably qualified, is typically considered to be a senior role (DfE and DoH, 2015), with the recognition that it has the potential to influence whole-school practices (Griffiths and Dubsky, 2012). Yet this role is normally undertaken by one person (Szwed, 2007; Curran *et al.*, 2018).

It could be argued that the SENCO holds a role which is particularly unique in schools, in part due to the breadth and complexity of the role (Qureshi, 2014). However, it could also be argued that this uniqueness may be exacerbated by a lack of clarity in policy and literature (Pearson, 2010; Rosen-Webb, 2011; Robertson, 2012; Cole, 2005; Tissot, 2013), the variation in approaches to role facilitation (Tissot, 2013) and the qualification requirements of the role (SENCO Regulations, 2008, 2009). Such variation is predominantly evident when considered in relation to other middle and senior leadership roles. As a consequence, the experience of each SENCO differs in each context (Hallett and Hallett, 2017), which leads to further variation of the role (Cowne, 2005). Whilst the unique nature of the role can present challenges for its effective facilitation (Hallett and Hallett, 2017), this equally can provide opportunities for the SENCO to determine and shape policy in relation to their role, as well as shape the development of SEN and inclusive policy within their setting (Curran, 2019a).

This chapter seeks to explore some of the specific challenges a SENCO may experience, particularly in relation to the nuances of the role and how others perceive their function. Facilitation of SENCO responsibilities, and variances within this, will be considered alongside the relationship between role fulfilment and ethical considerations. Finally, the chapter will explore potential opportunities for the role, in terms of its facilitation and development, with consideration given as to the notion of developing resilience within the role and the factors that can positively influence growth in this area.

The SENCO role: a uniquely perceived role in schools

The Special Educational Needs and Disability (SEND) Code of Practice (DfE and DoH, 2015) provides the statutory guidance for schools and organisations relating to how Part 3 of the Children and Families Act 2014 should be implemented. Specifically, the SEND Code of Practice outlines the duties, policies and procedures for schools and other organisations in relation to the provision for children with SEN. Central to the implementation of these duties is the SENCO (Ekins, 2012). The statutory guidance includes 11 'key responsibilities', which may form part of the SENCO role, with an acknowledgement that the SENCO 'has an important role to play with the head teacher and governing body, in determining the strategic development of SEN policy and provision in the school' and with a further explanation that 'the SENCO has day to day responsibility for the operation of SEN policy and coordination of specific provision made to support individual pupils with SEN, including those who have Education, Health and Care Plans' (DfE and DoH, 2015: 108).

A key challenge associated with the role is the way in which the responsibilities, as outlined by the SEND Code of Practice (DfE and DoH, 2015), are interpreted and applied in different settings (Pearson, 2010). Ekins (2012) argues that the role has historically experienced significant change and development since its inception, which has contributed to the variance in interpretation.

Dobson and Douglas suggest that the use of the terminology 'may include' within the SEND Code of Practice in relation to their responsibilities further lends to the legal uncertainty as to the expectations of the SENCO role (2020a:300). In turn, this has led to disparity, which Smith and Broomhead argue has created a role which is 'wide and complex' (2019:54).

However, a further challenge relates to how the SENCO role is perceived by others. The SENCO is in a position where they will be expected to work with various individuals, concurrently. This typically includes families, multi-agencies, teachers, other schools and the local authority (Edwards, 2016). Such collaboration is essential to ensure that the needs of the child or young person are met effectively (Ekins, 2012). Yet, different groups may hold varying understandings regarding the enactment of the SENCO role, leading to different expectations.

The National SENCO Workload Survey suggested that SENCOs felt their role was not widely understood by staff, with only 27% of respondents agreeing or strongly agreeing that they felt their role was understood in school (Curran *et al.*, 2018). Smith and Broomhead (2019) suggest that parents and staff often view the SENCO as the expert, supporting Mackenzie (2007), who suggested that parents would often go directly to the SENCO for advice and support, viewing them as the expert, perhaps circumnavigating the teacher. This contrasts with how SENCOs often view themselves, with Layton (2005) suggesting that SENCOs did not see themselves as a leader. Such a dichotomy in role perception could lead to high expectations and an increased pressure on the role (Smith and Broomhead, 2019).

Whilst the varied interpretations may be due to the way the role has evolved over time (Ekins, 2012), it could also be suggested that there is a current vacuum of knowledge and information in relation to the role. Certainly, Allan and Youdell (2015) would agree, suggesting that whilst the SEND Code of Practice (DfE and DoH, 2015) contains a number of mandatory activities, the document lacks substance. Lehane supports this notion, describing the content as, 'a grey area in terms of statutory guidance' (2016:61). Whilst this vagueness presents challenges, it can equally present an opportunity to shape the role specifically to the setting, within the parameters of the guidance (Curran, 2019b). Ball and colleagues, when considering the various roles individuals assume during the implementation of policy, may refer to this as a *policy narrator*, a crucial role for policy implementation, describing its function as 'explaining policy, deciding and then announcing what must be done, what can be done and what cannot' (2011:626). Yet, from the perspective of the SENCO, perhaps the opportunity lies within the role of the policy entrepreneur. Entrepreneurs are 'charismatic people and "persuasive personalities" and forceful agents of change, who are personally invested in and identified with policy ideas and their enactment' (Ball *et al.*, 2011:628). Given the breadth of the role, and the varied interpretations of policy (Dobson and Douglas, 2020a), this suggests that the SENCO has scope to interpret policy as a tool to not only facilitate change in their setting but also to shape their role due to the 'clout' that statutory guidance can provide (Curran, 2019a:19).

Furthermore, it could be argued that the emphasis should be placed on the teachers' understanding of their role and duties in relation to supporting children with additional needs, as this then, by default, makes the coordination aspect of the SENCO role more apparent. The SEND Code of Practice stresses that 'teachers are responsible and accountable for the progress and development of the pupils in their class' (DfE and DoH, 2015 99). However, internationally it is recognised that there is a lack of competency within the teaching profession in relation to teaching pupils with SEN (Cooc, 2019). This suggests a requirement for teachers' continuing professional development (CPD), with the SEND Code of Practice indicating that part of the SENCO role is to provide 'professional guidance to colleagues' (DfE and DoH, 2015: 108). The majority of SEN-focused CPD within schools is determined by the senior leadership team alongside the SENCO, with the SENCO being the key deliverer of such activities (Wall *et al.*, 2019). There is scope here for the SENCO to strategically determine the focus of such activities, with suggestions that the teachers with the highest need, in terms of cohort but also their own CPD requirements, should be the focus for school CPD activities (Cooc, 2019). Yet this also suggests that initial CPD focused on outlining the role and duties of the teacher would be beneficial in supporting the wider understanding of all roles within school (Curran, 2019b).

The SENCO role: facilitating the role in school

A further distinctive feature of the SENCO role, in comparison to others within school, is the disparate way in which time is allocated to the role, which consequently impacts on how the role is facilitated – a perennial issue since the role was introduced (Garner, 1996; Cowne, 2005; Curran *et al.*, 2018). Dobson and Douglas highlight the inconsistency of the SENCO role in varying school contexts, attributing this in part to the 'significant local autonomy', which has led to differences in interpretation at a senior leader level (2020a: 300), with research suggesting that there is also inconsistency among schools with similar demographics (Smith and Broomhead, 2019).

However, whilst Soan (2017) argues that as the SENCO role has developed over time, so has the need for more time to execute the role, particularly due to the requirement to demonstrate leadership skills, it could also be argued that, since its inception, the role has been burdened with bureaucratic demands (Bowers *et al.*, 1998; Curran *et al.*, 2018). As a result, SENCOs typically do not consider that sufficient time is allocated to the role (Smith and Broomhead, 2019). The National SENCO Workload Survey (Curran *et al.*, 2018) illustrated this point, with 70% of SENCO respondents stating that they did not feel they had enough time allocated to the role, with 71% citing administration tasks as the primary function of their role.

With a disparate system, the challenge is compounded due to the limited statutory guidance regarding time allocation for the role, with the SEND Code of Practice stating: 'The school should ensure that the SENCO has sufficient time and resources to carry out these functions' (DfE and DoH, 2015: 109). Dobson and Douglas (2020a) suggest that the issue of role facilitation is exacerbated because SENCOs are influenced by their own experiences of the SENCO role throughout their teaching career, and as a consequence this impacts on how they interpret and facilitate their role once they are in post. Certainly, time for the SENCO role varies significantly, with the recent National SENCO Workload Survey (Curran *et al.*, 2018) illustrating that nearly half of all primary SENCOs were allocated two days or less to the role on a weekly basis. The work of Smith and Broomhead (2019) suggested that SENCOs who had been in post for longer periods of time tended to be able to negotiate increased non-contact time, tentatively concluding that this may be related to an increased understanding of their role over time. This further highlights the importance of understanding the duties, as well as the parameters, of the role.

Whilst to date there is no specific statutory guidance regarding SENCO time allocation, a recent publication by the Whole School SEND consortium (Whole School SEND, 2020), which is funded by the Department for Education, made reference to the time allocation guidance devised as part of the National SENCO Workload Survey (Curran *et al.*, 2018), including the suggestion that a SENCO in an average-sized primary school, with their percentage of children with SEN in line with the national average, should have between three and four days non-contact time to fulfil the functions of the role. This suggests that guidance is emerging in response to the issue of how a SENCO can meet the statutory functions of their role.

Perhaps one of the key developments, which has further impacted on the facilitation of the role, has been the introduction of the requirement for a SENCO to be a qualified teacher and to gain 60 credits at Masters Level, as part of the National Award for SEN Coordination (NA SENCO) within three years of taking up their post (The Education [SENCO] regulation 2008, 2009). Mandatory training to fulfil a specific role within school only applies to the SENCO, since the requirement for headteachers to have the National Professional Qualification for Headship (NPQH) was made non-mandatory (Soan, 2017). It is undeniable that undertaking a Masters-level qualification whilst beginning a new role will temporarily impact on the facilitation of the SENCO role. Therefore, it is important to consider its purpose and potential.

The NA SENCO 'represents an important stage in developing the credibility and preparedness of individuals fulfilling the SENCO role' (Brown and Doveston, 2014:506), developed with the specific aim of raising the status of the role, particularly strategically (Ekins, 2012). However, whilst the qualification may provide opportunities for learning about the role and related theory, there are further benefits to undertaking the qualification. Mackenzie (2012) suggests that the academic challenge associated with the role is linked with maintaining motivation for the role. In addition to this, although pre-NA SENCO, Barnes (2008) highlighted that a SENCO's knowledge can impact on the process of identification, in particular how pupils' needs are perceived by the SENCO, suggesting a positive impact on operational practice. From a strategic perspective, the work of Griffiths and Dubksy (2012) suggests that undertaking the NA SENCO enables practitioners to develop a theoretical understanding with regards to inclusive education, therefore providing a basis from which they can develop into strategic leaders. A final consideration relates to after the NA SENCO is completed and how the positive aspects of undertaking the training as described by SENCOs may be continued (Dobson and Douglas, 2020a), indicating that sustaining the learning and networks developed during the award may be a positive factor for the SENCO (Curran, 2019b).

The SENCO role: the potential to influence inclusive policy

It is unequivocal that the SENCO is expected to lead the school strategically (DfE and DoH, 2015). Furthermore, the notion of leading strategically links directly to the development of an inclusive ethos within settings, with the SEND Code of Practice stating that the 'UK Government is committed to inclusive education of disabled children and young people and the progressive removal of barriers to learning and participation in mainstream education' (DfE and DoH, 2015:25). The NA SENCO learning outcomes state that the award should:

> enable SENCOs to develop and demonstrate the personal and professional qualities and leadership they need to shape an ethos and culture based upon person-centred, inclusive, practice in which the interests and needs of children and young people pupils with SEN and/ or disabilities are at the heart of all that takes place.
>
> (NCTL, 2014:8)

Yet, it could be argued that one of the key challenges a SENCO may face is that the SEND Code of Practice does not state a definition of inclusion and no longer makes reference to the Centre for Studies on Inclusive Education's Index for Inclusion (CSIE, 2014; DfE and DoH, 2015). The idea of inclusion remains tenuous and open to debate; the concept of inclusion will mean different things to different people at different times and in different contexts (Glazzard *et al* ., 2015). Whilst this does pose a challenge for the SENCO, it also presents a unique opportunity to explore and define inclusion within their own settings (Curran, 2019b). Hodkinson suggests that 'a school or college's approach to inclusion depends upon its teachers' attitudes and professional competencies' (2019:115). Equally, Lehane (2016) argues that teaching assistants, often a key element of provision for SEN, in part form their interpretation of inclusion based on their relationship with the teachers with whom they work. This further supports the earlier discussion regarding the importance of developing teacher understanding in relation to their roles and responsibilities regarding not only provision for children with SEN, but also inclusion in general.

It is evident that developing a whole-school ethos towards inclusion is a collective approach among all stakeholders. However, both Pearson (2008) and Morewood (2012) draw attention to the conflict of having an individual responsible for a group of learners, which by definition is separatist. Smith and Broomhead (2019) echo this sentiment with their research suggesting that a common issue relates to how responsibility for SEN is perceived in schools, with 'the assumption from staff that the responsibility for children with SEN was that solely of the SENCO' (Smith and Broomhead, 2019:63), further stating that the development of a whole-school ethos towards inclusion is a collective responsibility. This perhaps further exemplifies Tissot's (2013) suggestion that leadership is central to affecting cultural change – leadership to support the development of collective responsibility.

Certainly, the idea of a SENCO as leading on inclusive policy is intrinsic when considering that the construction of inclusive policy is co-dependent on various stakeholders (Simplican *et al* ., 2015). The SENCO has the potential to influence inclusive educational practices, with Hallett and Hallett (2017) suggesting that 'it is clear that best practice has the role of the SENCO at the heart of the education processes occurring within a setting' (Hallett and Hallett, 2017:2). Through their activities it could be argued that a key part of the SENCO role is 'recruit[ing] others to the possibilities of policy' (Ball *et al.*, 2012:60), a policy actor role Ball would refer to as *policy enthusiasts*. This is defined as someone who advocates for particular policies, in a similar way to an entrepreneur, yet enthusiasts do not simply advocate for a particular policy, but rather they lead by example, ensuring the policy is embedded in their practice (Ball *et al.*, 2012). The embodiment is not only necessarily through work practices, but also wider events and processes, which enable the policy enthusiasts to share and translate for others, thus making it a practical, productive process (Ball *et al.*, 2012). This reflects the view of Alisauskas and colleagues (2011), who suggest that a focus on inclusion in a school is capacity building, therefore highlighting the potential impact of SENCO activities on the wider school.

Yet SENCOs are not merely implementing SEN policy within their settings, they are constructing it (Hellawell, 2019), which indicates that the SENCO role, whilst broad, is equally emphatic regarding the importance it has regarding the development of inclusive policy. The construction of SEN policy does not take place in isolation. A further tension relates to the positioning of the SEN and inclusion policy agenda against other educational priorities. Norwich (2014) suggests that the SEND system is 'interdependent' on the general educational system, which encompasses 'the National Curriculum and assessment, school inspection, the governance of schools and equality legislation' (Norwich, 2014:404). Yet there are also tensions between the inclusion agenda and the standards agenda (Norwich, 2014). As a result, teachers may, in practice, experience conflicting and uncomfortable emotions about the daily practice of inclusion (Norwich, 2008). This further positions the SENCO within the advocacy role, for pupils and families, in relation to school and national educational policy. Certainly, with the sharper focus on the importance of pupil and family voice, and specifically the importance of developing a collaborative approach to support (Pearson *et al.*, 2015; DfE and DoH, 2015), the development of the voice of the SENCO within the wider educational agenda is imperative.

The SENCO role: developing resilience within the role

It is evident that the SENCO role has the potential to enact multiple policy actor roles concurrently (Curran, 2019a), indicating the potential to effect change and influence school practices, but equally demonstrating the need to have a continual drive to do so despite the aforementioned challenges. Robertson might argue that the SENCOs' ability to establish and execute the role despite these issues illustrates their 'resilience and capacity' (2012:82). In addition, it could be argued that such resilience is connected to the reasons why teachers move into the SENCO role initially, which Dobson and Douglas (2020b) suggest include a drive to improve inclusion through developing high-quality provision, new skills through professional development and abilities as a school leader. Certainly, it could be argued that to be an effective SENCO there needs to be a commitment to securing positive outcomes for children, with the view that this may encompass challenging and changing school structures (Mackenzie, 2012). Reid and Soan's (2019) work concurred, citing positive outcomes for children at the heart of a SENCO's commitment and motivation. The work of Mackenzie (2012) equally found that 'situated factors, professional factors and personal factors, as well as the "urge to serve", all interact to enable people to be resilient across a teaching lifetime' (2012:159).

Despite the resilience displayed by SENCOs (Mackenzie, 2012), it is important to consider the potential impact that the role can have on a SENCO, both professionally and personally, with Szwed (2007) suggesting that the role has the potential for being overburdened. The National SENCO Workload Survey suggested that approximately one-third of SENCOs do not see themselves in the role in five years' time, citing reasons related to workload (Curran *et al.*, 2018). Dobson and Douglas (2020b) highlight the financial impact that this has on schools in terms of training, indicating a need to consider how to retain SENCOs in post. As a result, it is important to consider SENCO resilience and the interplay between workload and the impact of 'ethical dilemmas' and 'moral conflicts' (Hellawell, 2019:74), which SENCOs may experience whilst implementing the SEND Code of Practice (DfE and DoH, 2015) within their setting.

Bodenheimer and Shuster highlight that teaching 'does not occur in a social vacuum' and further note the impact of 'emotional labour' on the teacher (2019:72). Whilst their work refers to teachers in a generic sense, it could be hypothesised that the SENCO experiences a specific type and amount of emotional labour, due to the requirements of their role, which consequently may impact on their resilience. Stith and Roth (2010) draw our attention to the socially dynamic classroom and the actors within this environment, specifically the students and the teachers, all of these elements related to emotional impact, the complexity of decision-making and yet the SENCO role is further set apart from teaching colleagues due to the breadth of interactions with other parties, including parents, multi-agencies and local authority colleagues.

Part of the SENCO role, perhaps not explicitly articulated in the statutory guidance (DfE and DoH, 2015), is the ability to sensitively manage and respond to diverse situations, something Sipman and colleagues would describe as 'pedagogical tact', which 'concerns a teacher's ability to adequately handle complex classroom situations that require immediate action' (2019:1186). Certainly, as argued by Edwards (2016), the SENCO role requires good interpersonal skills. This builds on Kearns' (2005) view of the SENCO as someone who rescues and collaborates, as well as concurrently being viewed by others as an expert (Smith and Broomhead, 2019). However, it could be argued that the emotional labour referred to by Bodenheimer and Shuster (2019) equally refers to the moral and ethical responsibility associated with the role.

As Hellawell (2019:74) states, 'the field of SEND is riddled with ethical dilemmas'. It could be argued that measures of accountability for children have gained prominence through SEN legislation (Children and Families Act, 2014; DfE and DoH, 2015). Hodkinson states that 'inclusion has become defined and controlled by the government's agents of accountability, performativity and standards' (2019:109), with Hellawell (2019) suggesting that SEN leaders experience multiple accountabilities, including both professional and moral.

Therefore, due to the potential impact on the SENCO, both personally and professionally, consideration should be given to the way in which the SENCO is supported. SENCOs are frequently engaged in decision-making and prioritising. They concurrently work with, and advocate for, individuals in complex situations. Kennedy and Laverick, when discussing the role of inclusion leaders, specifically headteachers, highlight the multi-faceted role which requires leaders to make complex decisions, with 'flexibility, focused effort and advocacy' (2019:446). It has been argued that SENCOs should be able to access supervision 'to enable them to reflect on decision making . . . to support SENCOs with the complex and challenging situations they are frequently working with' (Curran et al., 2019b:6).

Supervision is an activity which has the potential to help support and maintain SENCO resilience. Recent work by Kennedy and Laverick (2019) explored the potential for supervision for headteachers, in relation to supporting children with SEN, noting that supervision offers time and space to articulate issues and emotions, explore and consider solutions; the product of such an activity has the potential to lead to a more inclusive environment. It would therefore seem appropriate to apply this to those who are 'responsible for the day to day operation of the SEN policy' (DfE and DoH, 2015: 108). Research undertaken by Reid and Soan (2019) also discuss the potential for clinical supervision for SENCOs, where the purpose was to provide 'opportunity to reflect on, air and discuss professional practice issues in a confidential setting' (2019:61). Reid and Soan's work further suggested that access to formal supervision enabled individuals to feel that they could maintain a balance between work and home, whilst feeling that they were remaining an effective practitioner; they claim that 'clinical supervision could be a valuable tool to help build professional resilience' (2019:71).

Whilst supervision is not currently standard practice, there are emerging models (Morewood, 2018) which broadly draw upon the skills of senior leaders within the setting to provide such opportunities. It could be argued that the ability to share concerns and reflect upon decision-making, whether this is through formal supervision or not, has advantages. Howard and Johnson's research indicates that a 'strong support group (including a competent and caring leadership team)' is a feature of helping develop, and maintain, teacher resilience (2004:415). Yet, the SENCO is in a unique position in school, in that it is typically a solitary role (Curran et al., 2018). Therefore, in terms of developing support, and the potential impact this can have on resilience, it may be prudent for SENCOs to consider how they develop their networks of support outside of their settings.

SENCO networks are facilitated through various channels, including local authorities, the NA SENCO and, more recently, the changing structure of the educational system, specifically Multi-Academy Trusts. This infers that there is opportunity for SENCOs to develop networks, an area Pearson and colleagues (2015) suggested would increase following SEND reform. Whilst the previous focus may have been using such networks to share good practice and resources (DfE, 2016), as well as collaboratively delivering CPD (Greenwood and Kelly, 2017), it is a possibility that SENCOs could offer informal supervision-type support (Curran, 2019b).

Conclusion

The SENCO holds a unique role in schools. The SEND Code of Practice (DfE and DoH, 2015) stipulates the potential responsibilities of the role, including both operational and strategic aspects, stating that the 'SENCO has day to day responsibility for the operation of SEN policy' and 'has an important role to play . . . in determining the strategic development of SEN policy and provision in the school' (DfE and DoH, 2015: 108). It is also notable that the SENCO holds a key position within the school with regards to leading the development of inclusive policy in schools (Hallett and Hallett, 2017; Tissot, 2013) and has the potential to be a powerful agent of change (Robertson, 2012; Qureshi, 2014).

However, research has indicated that the interpretation, and the facilitation, of the role is varied in different settings (Hallett and Hallett, 2017; Curran et al., 2018; Smith and Broomhead, 2019), which in turn has led to a role which is considered broad and complex (Qureshi, 2014; Smith and Broomhead, 2019). Several factors have impacted on this variance, but most specifically it has been the local interpretation of national guidance (Dobson and Douglas, 2020a), which does not detail how to specifically facilitate the role (DfE and DoH, 2015; Lehane, 2016). This has led to concerns that the SENCO does not have sufficient time or status to fulfil the demands of the role (Curran *et al.*, 2018).

Yet, despite these reported challenges, it is evident that the SENCO has the potential to be an agent of change and to have a positive impact on developing and furthering inclusive practice in their school settings. Whilst acknowledging that the development of an inclusive environment is a collective enterprise (Hokinson, 2019), the SENCO is able to assume varying policy actor roles (Ball *et al.*, 2012), including that of policy narrator and enthusiast, using policy to create 'clout', and therefore change, in relation to their role and their setting (Curran, 2019a, p. 19). The benefit of such an approach is that capacity is built within the school, and therefore increases the collective inclusive ethos (Alisauskas *et al.*, 2011).

However, to ensure that the SENCO is able to develop and maintain resilience within their role, it is imperative that they have access to appropriate support (Howard and Johnson, 2004). This is particularly important due to the impact the role can have on the individual, both professionally and personally (Hellawell, 2019), but also because of the financial cost to schools in terms of ensuring there is an appropriately qualified SENCO (Dobson and Douglas, 2020b). Effective support mechanisms include access to supervision and increased access to networks (Greenwood and Kelly, 2017; Morewood, 2018). This, alongside policy, has the potential to develop SENCO resilience.

In conclusion, it is worth reflecting on the reasons why SENCOs come into the profession. SENCOs demonstrate themselves to be resilient (Mackenzie, 2012) and committed professionals (Reid and Soan, 2019), who whilst undertaking the role for reasons related to professional development, primarily do so due to their commitment and motivation with regards to securing positive outcomes for children with additional needs (Reid and Soan, 2019; Dobson and Douglas, 2020b). As a consequence, the effective facilitation and support of this unique role in school has the capacity to secure positive change for all involved with inclusive education.

References

Ališauskas, A., Ališauskiene, S., Kairiene, D. and Jones, S. (2011) 'Meeting of Pupils' Special Needs in the Context of Inclusive Education: UK Experience', *Special Education*, 1, pp. 91–104.

Allan, J. and Youdell, D. (2015) 'Ghostings, Materialisations and Flows in Britain's Special Educational Needs and Disability Assemblage', *Discourse: Students in the Cultural Politics of Education*, 30(1), pp. 70–82.

Ball, S., Maguire, M. and Braun, A. (2012) *How Schools Do Policy: Policy Enactments in Secondary Schools*. Abingdon: Routledge.

Ball, S., Maguire, M., Braun, A. and Hoskins, K. (2011) 'Policy Actors: Doing Policy Work in Schools: Some Necessary But Insufficient Analyses', *Discourse: Studies in the Cultural Politics of Education*, 32(4), pp. 625–639.

Barnes, P. (2008) 'Multi-agency Working: What Are the Perspectives of SENCos and Parents Regarding Its Development and Implementation?', *British Journal of Special Education*, 35(4), pp. 230–240.

Bodenheimer, G. and Shuster, S. M. (2020) 'Emotional Labour, Teaching and Burnout: Investigating Complex Relationships', *Educational Research*, 62(1), pp. 63–76.

Bowers, T., Dee, L. and West, M. (1998) 'The Code in Action: Some School Perceptions of Its User-friendliness', *Support for Learning*, 13(3), pp. 99–104.

Brown, J. and Doveston, M. (2014) 'Short Sprint or an Endurance Test: The Perceived Impact of the National Award for Special Educational Needs Coordination', *Teacher Development*, 18(4), pp. 495–510.

Centre of Studies for Inclusive Education (2014) *What Is Inclusion?* www.csie.org.uk/ Available at: www.csie.org.uk/inclusion/what.shtml [Accessed 8th March 2015].

Children and Families Act 2014, c. 6. Available at: www.legislation.gov.uk/ukpga/2014/6/pdfs/ukpga_20140006_en.pdf [Accessed 1st August 2014].

Cole, B. A. (2005) 'Mission Impossible? Special Educational Needs, Inclusion and the Re-conceptualisation of the Role of the SENCo in England and Wales', *European Journal of Special Needs Education*, 20(3), pp. 287–307.

Cooc, N. (2019) 'Teaching Students with Special Needs: International Trends in School Capacity and the Need for Teacher Professional Development', *Teaching and Teacher Education*, 83, pp. 27–41.

Cowne, E. (2005) *The SENCO Handbook: Working within a Whole-school Approach*. 5th edn. Abingdon: David Fulton.

Curran, H. (2019a) '"The SEND Code of Practice Has Given Me Clout": A phenomenological Study Illustrating How SENCos Managed the Introduction of the SEND Reforms', *British Journal of Special Education*, 1, p. 76.

Curran, H. (2019b) *How to Be a Brilliant SENCO: Practical Strategies for Developing and Leading Inclusion Provision*. Abingdon: Routledge.

Curran, H., Moloney, H., Heavey, A. and Boddison, A. (2018) *It's about Time: The Impact of SENCO Workload on the Professional and the School Bath Spa University*. Available at: www.bathspa.ac.uk/schools/education/research/senco-workload/ [Accessed 30th October 2019].

Department for Education (DfE) (2016) *Educational Excellence Everywhere* (Cm 9230). Available at: www.gov.uk/government/uploads/system/uploads/attachment_data/file/508447/Educational_Excellence_Everywhere.pdf [Accessed 13th April 2016].

Department for Education (DfE) and Department of Health (DoH) (2015) *Special Educational Needs and Disability Code of Practice: 0–25 Years*. Available at: www.gov.uk/government/uploads/system/uploads/attachment_data/file/398815/SEND_Code_of_Practice_January_2015.pdf [Accessed 1st February 2015].

Dobson, G. J. and Douglas, G. (2020a) 'Who Would Do that Role? Understanding Why Teachers Become SENCos Through an Ecological Systems Theory', *Educational Review*, 72(3), pp. 298–318.

Dobson, G. J. and Douglas, G. (2020b) *Factors Influencing the Career Interest of SENCOs in English Schools*. Available at: https://onlinelibrary.wiley.com/action/showCitFormats?doi=10.1002%2Fberj.3631 [Accessed 10th May 2020].

The Education (Special Educational Needs Co-ordinators) (England) Regulations 2008 (SI 2008/ 2945). Available at: http://dera.ioe.ac.uk/10702/4/SI%202008%201945.pdf [Accessed 14th September 2013].

The Education (Special Educational Needs Co-ordinators) (England) (Amendment) Regulations 2009 (SI 2009/ 1387). Available at: http://dera.ioe.ac.uk/10702/5/uksi_20091387_en.pdf [Accessed 14th September 2013].

Edwards, S. (2016) *The SENCO Survival Guide: The Nuts and Bolts of Everything You Need to Know*. 2nd edn. Abingdon: Routledge.

Ekins, A. (2012) *The Changing Face of Special Educational Needs: Impact and Implications for SENCos and Their Schools*. Abingdon: Routledge.

Garner, P. (1996) 'Go Forth and Coordinate!' What Special Needs Coordinators Think about the Code of Practice', *School Organisation*, 16(2), pp. 179–186.

Glazzard, J., Stokoe, J., Hughes, A., Netherwood, A. and Neve, L. (2015) *Teaching and Supporting Children with Special Educational Needs and Disabilities in Primary Schools*. London: Learning Matters.

Greenwood, J. and Kelly, C. (2017) 'Implementing Cycles of Assess, Plan, Do, Review: A Literature Review of Practitioner Perspectives', *British Journal of Special Education*, 44(4), pp. 394–410.

Griffiths, D. and Dubsky, R. (2012) 'Evaluating the Impact of the New National Award for SENCos: Transforming Landscapes or Gardening in a Gale?', *British Journal of Special Education*, 39(4), pp. 164–172.

Hallett, F. and Hallett, G. (eds.) (2017) *Transforming the Role of the SENCo: Achieving the National Award for SEN Coordination*. 2nd edn. London: Oxford University Press.

Hellawell, B. (2019) *Understanding and Challenging the SEND Code of Practice*. London: Sage.

Hokinson, A. (2019) *Key Issues in Special Educational Needs and Inclusion*. 2nd edn. London: Sage.

Howard, S. and Johnson, B. (2004) 'Resilient Teachers: Resisting Stress and Burnout', *Social Psychology of Education: An International Journal*, 7(4), pp. 399–420.

Kearns, H. (2005) 'Exploring the Experiential Learning of Special Educational Needs Coordinators', *Journal of In-Service Education*, 31(1), pp. 131–150.

Kennedy, E.-K. and Laverick, L. (2019) 'Leading Inclusion in Complex Systems: Experiences of Relational Supervision for Headteachers', *Support for Learning*, 4, pp. 443–459.

Layton, L. (2005) 'Special Educational Needs Coordinators and Leadership: A Role Too Far?', *Support for Learning*, 20(2), pp. 53–59.

Lehane, T. (2016) '"SEN's Completely Different Now": Critical Discourse Analysis of Three "Codes of Practice for Special Educational Needs" (1994, 2001, 2015)', *Educational Review*, 69(1), pp. 51–67.

Mackenzie, S. (2007) 'A Review of Recent Developments in the Role of the SENCo in the UK', *British Journal of Special Education*, 34(4), pp. 212–218.

Mackenzie, S. (2012) 'I Can't Imagine Doing Anything Else': Why Do Teachers of Children with SEN Remain in the Profession? Resilience, Rewards and Realism Over Time', *Journal of Research in Special Educational Needs*, 12(3), pp. 151–161.

Morewood, G. (2012) 'Is the "Inclusive SENCo" Still a Possibility? A Personal Perspective', *Support for Learning*, 27(2), pp. 73–76.

Morewood, G. (2018) *Establishing a Model for SENCO Supervision*. Available at: https://blog.optimus-education.com/establishing-model-senco-supervision [Accessed 10th May 2020].

National College of Teaching and Learning (2014) *National Award for Special Educational Needs Co-ordination: Learning Outcomes*. Available at: www.gov.uk/government/uploads/system/uploads/attachment_data/file/354172/nasc-learning-outcomes-final.pdf [Accessed 1st September 2014].

Norwich, B. (2008) *Dilemmas of Difference, Inclusion and Disability: International Perspectives and Future Directions*. London: Routledge.

Norwich, B. (2014) 'Changing Policy and Legislation and Its Effects on Inclusive and Special Education: A Perspective from England', *British Journal of Special Education*, 41(4), p. 40.

Pearson, S. (2008) 'Deafened by Silence or by the Sound of Footsteps? An Investigation of the Recruitment, Induction and Retention of Special Educational Needs Coordinators (SENCOs) in England', *Journal of Research in Special Educational Needs*, 8(2), pp. 96–110.

Pearson, S. (2010) 'The Role of Special Educational Needs Co-coordinators (SENCOs): "To Be or Not to Be"', *Psychology of Education Review*, 34(2), pp. 30–38.

Pearson, S., Mitchell, R. and Rapti, M. (2015) 'I Will Be "Fighting" Even More for Pupils with SEN: SENCOs' Role Predictions in the Changing English Policy Context', *Journal of Research in Special Educational Needs*, 15(1), pp. 48–56.

Qureshi, S. (2014) 'Herding Cats or Getting Heard: The SENCo-teacher Dynamic and Its Impact on Teachers' Classroom Practice', *Support for Learning*, 29(3), pp. 217–229.

Reid, H. and Soan, S. (2019) 'Providing Support to Senior Managers in Schools via "Clinical" Supervision: A Purposeful, Restorative Professional and Personal Developmental Space', *Professional Development in Education*, 45(1), pp. 59–72.

Robertson, C. (2012) 'Special Educational Needs and Disability Co-ordination in a Changing Policy Landscape: Making Sense of Policy from a SENCo's Perspective', *Support for Learning*, 27(2), pp. 77–83.

Rosen-Webb, S. (2011) 'Nobody Tells You How to Be a SENCo', *British Journal of Special Education*, 38(4), pp. 159–168.

Simplican, S., Leader, G., Kosciulek, J. and Leahy, M. (2015) 'Review Article: Defining Social Inclusion of People with Intellectual and Developmental Disabilities: An Ecological Model of Social Networks and Community Participation', *Research in Developmental Disabilities*, 38, pp. 18–29.

Sipman, G., Tholke, J., Martens, R. and McKenny, S. (2019) 'The Role of Intuition in Pedagogical Tact: Educator Views', *British Educational Research Journal*, 45(6), pp. 1186–1202.

Smith, M. D. and Broomhead, K. E. (2019) 'Time, Expertise and Status: Barriers Faced by Mainstream Primary School SENCos in the Pursuit of Providing Effective Provision for Children with SEND', *Support for Learning*, 34(1), pp. 54–70.

Soan, S. (2017) *The SENCO Essential Manual*. London: Oxford University Press.

Stith, I. and Roth, W.-M. (2010) 'Teaching as Mediation: The Cogenerative Dialogue and Ethical Understandings', *Teaching & Teacher Education*, 26(2), pp. 363–370.

Szwed, C. (2007) 'Reconsidering the Role of the Primary Special Educational Needs Co-ordinator: Policy, Practice and Future Priorities', *British Journal of Special Education*, 34(2), pp. 96–104.

Tissot, C. (2013) 'The Role of SENCos as Leaders', *British Journal of Special Education*, 40(1), pp. 33–40.

Wall, K., Van Herwegen, J., Shaw, A., Russell, A. and Roberts, A. (2019) *A Study of the Drivers, Demand and Supply for Special Educational Needs and/or Disabilities (SEND)- Related Continuing Professional Development (CPD) for School Staff*. Available at: file:///C:/Users/785376/Downloads/drivers_demand_supply_report.2019.pdf [Accessed 10th May 2020].

Whole School SEND (2020) *Effective SENCO Deployment: A Guide for the SENCOs and Their Line Managers*. Available at: effective_senco_deployment_web.pdf [Accessed 10th May 2020].

Index

Page numbers in *italics* indicate a figure and page numbers in **bold** indicate a table on the corresponding page.

Printed in Great Britain
by Amazon

28867811R00112